The Most Dangerous Branch

The Judicial Assault on American Culture

Edited by

Edward B. McLean

University Press of America,® Inc.
Lanham · Boulder · New York · Toronto · Plymouth, UK

Copyright © 2008 by
University Press of America,® Inc.
4501 Forbes Boulevard
Suite 200
Lanham, Maryland 20706
UPA Acquisitions Department (301) 459-3366

Estover Road
Plymouth PL6 7PY
United Kingdom

All rights reserved
Printed in the United States of America
British Library Cataloging in Publication Information Available

Library of Congress Control Number: 2008930940
ISBN-13: 978-0-7618-4150-0 (paperback : alk. paper)
ISBN-10: 0-7618-4150-4 (paperback : alk. paper)
eISBN-13: 978-0-7618-4271-2
eISBN-10: 0-7618-4271-3

∞™ The paper used in this publication meets the minimum
requirements of American National Standard for Information
Sciences—Permanence of Paper for Printed Library Materials,
ANSI Z39.48—1984

Table of Contents

Edward B. McLean, Preface ... v

Acknowledgements ... xiii

Chapter One: George W. Carey, The Judicial Assault on the Constitution ... 1

Chapter Two: Jack Wade Nowlin, The Judicial Assault on Human Dignity ... 23

Chapter Three: Allan W. Carlson, The Judicial Assault on the Family ... 55

Chapter Four: Charles E. Rice, The Judicial Assault on Religion ... 71

Chapter Five: Ronald J. Rychlak, The Judicial Assault on Criminal Law ... 89

Chapter Six: Joseph F. Johnston Jr., The Judicial Assault on Business ... 127

Chapter Seven: Hans L. Eicholz, The Judicial Assault on Secondary Education ... 153

Chapter Eight: Dane Starbuck, The Judicial Assault on Higher Education ... 173

Chapter Nine: E. Robert Statham, Jr., The Judicial Assault on Public Philosophy ... 193

Biographies ... 213

Preface

Having concluded a long war with their parent government, which it was argued was tyrannical, the creators of the United States Constitution purposefully constructed the national government to prevent the development of tyranny. James Madison in Federalist 47 explains of what tyranny is composed:

> No political truth is certainly of greater intrinsic value, or is stamped with the authority of more enlightened patrons of liberty, than that on which the objection is founded. The accumulation of all powers, legislative, executive, and judiciary, in the same hands, whether of one, a few, or many, and whether hereditary, self-appointed, or elective, may justly be pronounced the very definition of tyranny.

Having clearly enunciated how tyrannical government could occur, he goes on to explain that the formula for dividing powers at the national level, in order to allow one power to balance out the other, and the further division of power between the states and the national government, would be provided in the proposed constitution. He says in Federalist 51:

> ...In a single republic, all the power surrendered by the people is submitted to the administration of a single government; and the usurpations are guarded against by a division of the government into distinct and separate departments. In the compound republic of America, the power surrendered by the people is first divided between two distinct governments, and then the portion allotted to each subdivided among distinct and separate departments. Hence a double security arises to the rights of the people. The different governments will control each other, at the same time that each will be controlled by itself.

Thus he argues that the proposed division of powers among the three branches, and between the national and state governments was necessary to guard against tyranny. At the national, level by distributing the powers of government among the three branches, respect of the sovereignty of the states, this balance would protect the rule of law, and would serve to prevent or at least deter the emergence of tyranny. He elaborates further on the matter of the states in Federalist 45 where he writes:

> The powers delegated by the proposed Constitution to the federal government are few and defined. Those which are to remain in the State governments are numerous and indefinite. The former will be exercised principally on external objects, as war, peace, negotiation, and foreign commerce; with which last the

power of taxation will, for the most part, be connected. The powers reserved to the several States will extend to all the objects which, in the ordinary course of affairs, concern the lives, liberties, and properties of the people, and the internal order, improvement, and prosperity of the State.

It was further assumed that the separation of powers at the national level would assure the rule of law. The idea of the rule of law was to be achieved by the balance of power at this level by dividing power among the three branches. As a result, the legislature would refrain from exercising powers not delegated to it by the constitution, and the executive and judicial branches would operate as checks on any attempt by the legislature to do so. It was further assumed that these two branches also would not exceed their proper functions in this separation of powers, and each would be checked by the other two. In this design the judiciary role was to disallow legislation that would violate the specific provisions of the constitution, and prohibit actions by the other two branches that were contrary to the manifest tenor of the constitution. Illustrative of this intended balance Federalist 78 states:

> Whoever attentively considers the different departments of power must perceive, that, in a government in which they are separated from each other, the judiciary, from the nature of its functions, will always be the least dangerous to the political rights of the Constitution; because it will be least in a capacity to annoy or injure them. The Executive not only dispenses the honors, but holds the sword of the community. The legislature not only commands the purse, but prescribes the rules by which the duties and rights of every citizen are to be regulated. The judiciary, on the contrary, has no influence over either the sword or the purse; no direction either of the strength or of the wealth of the society; and can take no active resolution whatever. It may truly be said to have neither FORCE nor WILL, but merely judgment; and must ultimately depend upon the aid of the executive arm even for the efficacy of its judgments.

Over the years this design seemed to work reasonably well and the balance of powers at the national level remained largely intact. In relatively recent decades, however, the Supreme Court has usurped legislative powers at the national and state levels. This fact coupled with the prevailing view that the Court is the authoritative interpreter of the Constitution has allowed it to operate in ways contrary to the intent of the Constitution's separation of powers doctrine and the federal scheme, and thus disrupted, perhaps irreparably, the balance required for the effectiveness of these doctrines. This development, however, has not been unique only to the Supreme Court of the United States, but has pervaded the entire judicial system, with the consequence that structures of government throughout the nation have been redesigned by judicial action.

The Supreme Court has transformed itself into a center of power that is able to operate as it chooses, without any effective limitation being placed on it by the other branches of government, or the states. In effect this has destroyed the balance to the system intended in the constitutional design. Implicit also in the doctrine of the separation of powers was that such a design would allow the three branches of government and the independent states to operate as "makeweights" against each other. Bertrand de Jouvenal describes "makeweights" as follows:

> Clearly [a makeweight] must be a social authority, an established sectional interest; such were in Montesquieu's day the higher ranks of the English aristocracy, which he so much admired, and the Parliamentary class in France, to which he himself belonged. In our own time syndicates of workmen and employers answer to the description. So do in all time the various conglomerations of interests and loyalties which rise spontaneously in society and which Power seeks instinctively to dissolve. (*On Power*, Liberty Fund Inc., 2000. pp. 317–319).[1]

As he suggests the interests and the loyalties of the legislative and executive branches of government were seen as part of the elements of the balance system in the separation of powers. The success the judiciary has achieved in assuming both legislative and executive powers, has clearly weakened their role as "makeweights." As de Jouvenal argues, "makeweights" provide one of the major elements needed to combat the expansion of power. Such authorities will protect their own interests and purposes, and strive to check the each other's power as well as that of the state. He is aware, however, that state power will instinctively seek to dissolve such oppositional centers of authority, as has been the case in the United States by the actions of the courts. We hasten to note that not only has this almost irreparable damage been done to the institutional design in government, but that judicial power has, devastated the "makeweights" existing in the civic culture and reduced them to relative impotence in their capacity to hedge in and limit the powers of government. This melancholy fact is presented dramatically in the essays in this book.

On various occasions most Americans express surprise regarding this or that decision by a court. They ask themselves how and why such decisions could be made in light of their own common sense understanding of the world in which they live. They represent those who Alasdair MacIntyre calls "plain persons" who have abdicated their own judgment in the face of legal decisions about most matters that affect them individually, their families, their various organizations, and their communities. They seem to have accepted the notion that "plain persons" do not have the capacity to understand and appreciate the fundamental content of the "rule of law." Clearly, MacIntyre's observations, illuminate why people puzzle over "why and how" courts can make decisions that seem to defy common sense and common notions of rightness and wrongness.[2]

It is both a good and a curse that Americans have long respected the rule of law in society. On one hand such respect has served to establish a largely law

---

1 Bertrand de Jouvenal, *On Power: The Natural History of Its Growth* (Indianapolis, Liberty Fund Inc., 1993), pp. 317–319.

2 Alisdair MacIntyre, "Theories of Natural Law in the Culture of Advanced Modernity," in *Common Truths: New Perspectives on Natural Law,"* Edward B. McLean (ed.), (Wilimington, ISI Books, 2000) p. 92.

abiding society, i.e., men's common sense judgment that tells them that their adherence to the norms of just conduct is not only necessary and desirable, but that acceptance of these norms serve their individual interests well and justly. On the other hand, however, in the development of American law, those "plain persons," have abandoned any notion that their common sense notions are satisfactory solutions to the vexing ethical and political problems produced in the society. Instead they have succumbed to the absurd notion that only when the courts speak is truth identified, and justice done. Such acceptance is underscored by Americans almost unquestioning acceptance of the rightness of the courts and their decisions. The courts have stripped away the rights of individuals to life itself. They have assailed and emasculated the other institutions needed for a virtuous public including families, religion, criminal law, the economy, the public philosophy, and education. Americans are denied of the opportunity to fashion their lives and their aspirations according to the dictates of their consciences and will, because it is the will of the courts to redesign their lives in conformance with these various judicial functionaries' notions of propriety and desirability

We can ask how a people who theoretically live in a country or state that has a constitution which delimits the scope and substance of the power of government, must abide by decisions emanating from courts that seem to have lost all connection with the enshrined values and morals that its citizens hold most dear, and which they would choose to preserve, or why their organizations must change in terms of composition, purpose, and action.

It is also important to ask how it has come to pass that our courts are so out of touch with the culture of which they are a part. We would need to look at a whole chain of causes that would account for this development which is not within the scope of this volume. Briefly, however, we can mention the incredibly ineffective and vacuous education from grade school through college and the professional schools that do not convey sufficient information regarding the historical development and design of our nation and its government. Also, law professors, in large measure, are person of no practical experience in the handling of legal cases and who have received highly theoretical and fantasized notions of law at the hands of other law professors. One needs only to read or attempt to read law journals to see the minutiae with which they deal and the conclusions they reach and recognize the audience for whom they are written.

It appears that Americans seem to have lost their vigor and ability to insist upon their right to pursue appropriate goals they choose for themselves and the common principles around which they choose to orient their lives. Most of the founders understood clearly that a "paper parchment" would not protect or sustain a republic in which the citizens would be able to do so. Such a republic could only be sustained, with a virtuous, active, and informed population. A major explanation of why we no longer seem to have such a population is evidenced by the fact that those institutions, manners, mores, and values needed to sustain such a population have been shattered under the hammer blows of judicial power—most of which is centralized in the nation's capital but is present as well in the various states of the union.

Preface

The intent and focus of this volume is to present in topical fashion how the courts have savaged other institutions in our society as well as directing the lives of individuals. This result requires that we all accept and treasure the pronouncements that are issued from the adyta in which these courts function—removed from and disdainful of the "common folk" who they presume must be guided by the wisdom and insights which apparently are only available from these relatively undistinguished folk. Judicial office holders and law professors pay obeisance to transient political sentiments and intellectual fads and have been elevated to positions of power that are contradictory of a constitutional system. The functionaries in them are not gifted with any particular talent or ability, and usually are in their positions, after following the prescribed rules of success in American society which demonstrates clearly how mediocrity shall prevail. The most that can be said in defense of these functionaries is that their ineptitude is equaled by those in the legislative and executive branches. We need not argue that all of these current folk are somehow less able than those in similar positions held by their predecessors, but that they do differ in their obvious belief that they can exercise the powers of government far in excess of what was intended in a constitutional system. They have convinced themselves that they are informed, responsible, and correct; and that limits that should inhere in the law may be casually ignored and rejected if their whims so dictate. Unfortunately the restrictions supposedly found in constitutions to control governmental power are nothing other than pious expressions set forth in documents. It must not be forgotten that ability of a constitution to restrain power can only result from the structural arrangements of jurisdictional authority that properly allocates authority to the various states of the union, the various branches of government, and an active, virtuous, and informed population.

George W. Carey's opening essay provides an examination of the distortion of the court's function that has so dramatically departed from what we can best ascertain as the expectation that the founders had about the nature of the courts and their proper role in the design of the American Republic.

The second essay—The Assault on the Family—by Allan Carlson portrays dramatically and forcefully what injury has been inflicted by the courts on this fundamental institution of our society, and the projection of where this pattern of destruction will lead. As Carlson correctly points out in his essay ". . .marriage, and the autonomous family were the true bulwarks of liberty, for they were the principle rivals to the state." One can readily see that such a role would only be considered as a threat by those infatuated with power.

Charles Rice points clearly to the unimaginable scope of power the courts have assumed in responding to religion and its guaranteed protection by the Constitution of the United States of America and the various state constitutions. As he pointedly observes: "No one can convincingly claim that the Supreme Court's Establishment Clause jurisprudence reflects a rule of law rather than the arbitrary rule of unelected oligarchs." The great tragedy examined in this essay underscores and confirms the willingness of the electorate, state and local officials, and the legislatures to submit to the irrational and unjustifiable decisions emanating from the courts.

Jack Wade Nowlin reviews the devastation the courts have wreaked on human life in his essay on The Judicial Assault on Human Dignity. He observes: "Our nation is dedicated to the proposition, and our constitutional system is designed to safeguard these natural rights from private violence and from governmental invasion. The right to life, of course, is the most basic of these natural rights, and it is the most basic purpose of government to protect it." With great conviction Nowlin examines how the courts, led by the Supreme Court of the United States, have not only ignored this truth, but have divorced it from consideration.

Ronald Rychlak's essay takes on the task of examining what has happened to criminal law which, as all understand, is the first line of defense in the protection and sustaining of a civilized order. Common sense understanding and an enlightened population are the major safeguards in assuring proper police action in pursuit of establishing a civilized order. Judicial action when taken should only be in response to clear violations of the rights of accused and/or convicted persons specified by the constitutions involved. The fashioning of detailed prescriptions for the operation of the criminal law is a purely legislative function that, as Rychlak clearly shows, has been usurped by judicial action that is in excess of the proper functions of the judiciary.

Joseph E. Johnston reviews the imposition of control by the courts on the operations of the economic institutions of this country which should serve both as makeweights to excessive government power, and as rational arrangements for the provision of the goods and services needed to sustain a civilized order. Really bizarre and peculiar decisions of the courts have placed excessive burdens on these economic institutions, and the courts also have blindly and unthinkingly supported the excessive role of bureaucratic control of the economic order, and made the very existence of a flourishing economic order more difficult and extremely costly. The courts using common law principles in evaluating litigation could, with little effort and intelligent action, reign in the excessive bureaucratic control of these economic institutions.

Hans Eicholz points to the confusion surrounding public education that has not been diminished or ameliorated with the judiciary's intimate involvement in this area. He maintains the desirability of private educational establishments, and presents a cogent argument in defense of this solution. However, it is clear that the courts, even though they of necessity get involved in the variety of disputes created by varying beliefs and opinions regarding education, could act with greater restraint and common sense. Again, however this points to the difficulties that have been created by the assumption that the Supreme Court of the United States has the authority to make final solutions about what are purely local issues and problems. If an enlightened citizenry insisted that public schools were to be purely locally controlled and directed, many of the difficulties stemming from judicial involvement could be corrected.

Dane Starbuck's careful examination of the involvement of the courts, particularly federal courts, in supervising the operations, programs, and purposes of institutions of higher education, clearly reveals the mischief that has been done as well as the innervating effect of such judicial involvement. For example he points out that "...the notion of 'academic freedom' has been elevated to a preeminence and given protections that were never envisioned by the Founders..." and concludes that the courts "...have only been too willing to impress upon colleges and universities this viewpoint [tenure] and to adopt...[their]... own social agenda regarding the operations of higher education." The diversity of purposes and programs is a highly desirable condition for a culture of creativity and dynamism, and the courts have been intrusive to the degree that they are stifling the possibility of this being the environment of higher education.

E. Robert Statham, in his essay, provides the final chapter to this book. His focus is on the role of the "public philosophy" in shaping, defining, and guiding the operation of this republic. The public philosophy is composed of those "discoverable in the permanent elements of human nature" a "durable justice which transcends expediency." He identifies two dimensions of the role of the courts. One is procedural and seldom engenders difficulties in sustaining the constitution and the public philosophy. The other he points out is "The *substantive* role of the Judiciary [evidenced in judicial review] in the American political order [and] is the interpretation of the laws in reference to the public philosophy." Thus, he maintains judges should have the knowledge "...of a lawyer and the character of a political philosopher." Judges must have knowledge of the law in combination with the virtue of "right reason in agreement with nature." Therefore, Judges must combine knowledge of the laws with knowledge and fidelity to the public philosophy. He continues that the ... neglect of the public philosophy in the name of democracy has challenged the basic meaning and purpose of the American political order. Democratization places overemphasis on the values of individualism and equality at the expense of liberty and law."

The damage surveyed in the preceding essays demonstrates how the courts have attacked the constitution, the criminal law, the economy, the educational institutions, the federal system, the family, religion and human life itself. As a result, this judicial action has destroyed the balance of power in government institutionally at the national level, and the makeweights designed to operate at the national level. In addition they have effectively destroyed the environment that would be conducive to the developments of "makeweights" in the civic culture that would be able to counter state power. Additionally they have compelled people to abandon their values, aspirations, and opportunities.

A healthy civic culture requires several things. First and foremost it requires that it exist under a rule of law, which means rules of conduct that are general in their content, universal in their application within the proper jurisdiction, and indeterminate in terms of to whom they will apply. Second, since government is only a part of the civic culture, it must not engage in the exercise of power to displace and control the other equally important institutions of the civic culture, such as the family, the churches, the businesses, and the voluntary associations which men form to further their particular aims which are of importance to their members. Third, it must value all human life and assure that each individual's dignity and value are respected and protected. Fourth, limitations that may be properly imposed must be tailored in conformance with the doctrine of subsidiarity, i.e., no matter should be referred to a higher level of government than is necessary in order to assure the maximization of human liberty and responsibility. The courts behavior in regard to all of these elements have greatly weakened or often destroyed them.

This book is intended to help the public understand how seriously the judiciary has damaged the balance of institutions and the national level, diminished the authority of the states, and eviscerated the various voluntary associations men form to aid them in living their lives as they wish in conformance with the values they hold. We hope it may serve to move the public into action to restore the proper institutional balance in our government; sustain constitutional government; revitalize our civic culture; and protect human life, liberty and property.

Acknowledgements

The editor wishes to express his thanks to the Earhart Foundation, Ann Arbor, Michigan for its generous support of this project, and to Ms. Judith Oswalt for her professional help in preparing the manuscript.

One
The Judicial Assault on the Constitution
by George W. Carey

The modern Supreme Court has reached a pinnacle of power that our Founding Fathers never envisioned.[1] As I will endeavor to show the avenues for this growth of judicial power were evident in the controversies surrounding the role of the judiciary during the ratification period. Perhaps because the questions and concerns about the powers of the Court that arose during this period were never satisfactorily answered, they have persisted throughout our history. But there can be little doubt that, given the growth of judicial power over the course of the last century, they are more pertinent today than at any other period in our history. Today, in light of powers asserted by modern courts, these concerns are often expressed in a wider context related to the fundamental principles of the Constitution, republicanism and the separation of powers. Is, for instance, an activist judiciary compatible with the conception of separation of powers embraced by the founding generation? What problems does the modern judiciary pose for republican government? Is it possible to reconcile the claims of modern courts with the original understanding of these principles or can it be that we are, in effect, living under a new, though unwritten, Constitution marked by new, though undefined, distribution of power and lines of accountability?

These are among the questions that will explore by way of pointing up in some detail how the Court has moved well beyond its intended role and then examining major concerns arising from this expansion of judicial authority.

Original understanding of powers and functions

We can best proceed to a consideration of these questions, I believe, by first looking at the Framers' understanding of the extent of the Court's powers in order that we may have some benchmark against which to measure their growth. We can, for our purposes, skirt the issue of whether the Framers intended the Court to possess the authority to declare an act of Congress unconstitutional since this is now a part of our constitutional morality that today is relatively uncontroversial.[2] We can more profitably turn instead to the reasoning of those who initially justified this power with the end of determining its intended purpose and scope.

John Marshall's reasoning in *Marbury v. Madison* has long been regarded as providing the theoretical foundations for judicial review.[3] Without going into the details of his reasoning at this point, certain aspects of it are noteworthy for our purposes. To begin with, it is interesting to observe the approaches Marshall does not use in staking out his claim. For instance, he does not maintain that it was well understood by those who drafted and ratified the Constitution that the Court would possess this authority, the approach he used in *Barron v. Baltimore* in denying the applicability of the provision of the Bill of Rights to the states.[4] Nor does he argue, as some modern scholars have, that the Supreme Law of the Land clause necessitates judicial review; that, in other words, one can reason solely from a specific provision in the Constitution to the conclusion that judicial review must have been intended by the Founders. Instead he employs a reasoning or a logic based on an understanding of the Constitution as *fundamental law*, which is, so to speak, an "imported" doctrine in the sense that it is not to be discerned from reading the Constitution with an innocent eye.

This line of reasoning was hardly novel. It was previously employed by Alexander Hamilton in *Federalist* essay no.78 and, prior to this, in state cases pre-dating the Constitution.[5] By general consensus, the clearest and most extensive elaborations of the case for judicial review prior to the Constitution were those set forth by James Varnum in *Trevett v. Weeden* (1786) and James Iredale in *Bayard v. Singleton* (1787).[6] Their arguments are founded upon and reflect two developments in the American experience summarized by Gerald Stourzh:[7] "The *disassociation* of sovereign and legislative power" in the colonial era and "the institutionalization of the constituent power of the people in the era of constitution building 1776 to 1788."[8] While it is true, as Stourzh points out, that the colonial legislatures were in fact subordinate to Parliament, a state of affairs that may have contributed to the disassociation of sovereign and legislative power in the colonial mind, the second development, that relating the role of the people in instituting government, was by far the more important for the justification of judicial review. Consider Varnum's argument: "The powers of the legislation . . . are derived from the people at large, are altogether fiduciary and subordinate to the association by which they are formed." From this he reasons the judges "are bound . . . by the principles of the constitution in preference to any acts of the General Assembly, because they were ordained by the people anterior to and created the powers of the General Assembly."[8] Similarly, Iredale points out the Assembly "is a creature of the Constitution. . . . The people have chosen to be governed under such and such principles. They have not chosen to be governed, nor promised to submit upon any other; and the Assembly have no more right to obedience on other terms than any different power on earth had a right to govern us."[9] From their perspective, then, the conclusion that the written constitution is fundamental law, superior to simple legislative law, seems inescapable.

The positions of Iredale and Varnum were supported by changes that had taken place in American constitutional practice and theory as a result of the procedures followed in the drafting and ratification of the Massachusetts Constitution of 1780. Prior to this time, state constitutions were written by the state legislatures without any popular participation or consent, a manner of proceeding that placed the resulting constitutions on no higher status or firmer footing than ordinary laws.[10] In Massachusetts, by contrast, citizens participated not only in the selection of delegates to the convention which drafted the Constitution but also in the ratification of the finished document. For the first time, then, constitutions were readily seen as distinct from, and superior to, statutes enacted by legislative assemblies; they now enjoyed, as Iredale and Varnum insisted, the elevated status of a higher or supreme law because they sprang not from the legislature but from the people. That this understanding prevailed by the time of the Philadelphia Convention is attested to by the terms of Article VII which calls for ratification by special conventions within the states; a provision that, in effect, insured the national constitution would rest on the consent of the people within the states and not ratification by the state legislatures.

A Comprehensive View: Hamilton's Justification

With this understanding of the status of constitutions as fundamental law, we can more readily comprehend the entire line of reasoning used to justify vesting the Court with the power of judicial review. To the extent that *The Federalist*, as many contend, is the authoritative source of that constitutional morality necessary for understanding the proper relationships between the branches, their prerogatives, as well as rules and principles necessary for the system to operate as intended, we can profitably examine in some detail Hamilton's justification of judicial review set forth in essay no. 78, the first of six essays dealing with the judicial branch. Two other reasons justify turning to Hamilton's account rather than, say, Marshall's decision in *Marbury v. Madison*. First, Hamilton necessarily had to place the Court and its role in a wider institutional context, presenting us with some idea of its powers and functions relative to those of the legislature and executive. And second, though he is quick to dismiss them, Hamilton possessed an awareness of the potential problems associated with his case for judicial review; problems that have, in fact, emerged in the course of our history.

Having said this much, however, it is also a fact that Hamilton's defense of judicial review needs to be understood in light of basic constitutional principles that were, by all evidences, widely shared by both those who drafted and ratified the Constitution. We must briefly deal with one of the most crucial and, in light of our purpose, relevant of these principles, namely, the separation of powers. In a brace of essays, nos. 47 through 51, Madison stresses the need to preserve the separation of powers as laid down in the Constitution. Why so? Because, as he informs us in essay no. 47—and here he is simply echoing what all sides in the ratification controversy accepted as a given—a concentration of all three powers (legislative, executive, and judicial) in the same hands constituted "the very definition of tyranny."[11] In fact, as he is to note, a concentration of any two powers in the same hands would constitute tyranny. The reasons why such a concentration is so dangerous, which are also alluded to in this essay, relate principally to maintaining liberty and the rule of law by preventing arbitrary and capricious rule. We also see from this brace of essays, particularly from essay no. 48, that the greatest fear is legislature encroachment on both the executive and judicial departments.[12] Madison sees the solution to the problem of preserving the necessary separation to be a strategy of weakening the strong and strengthening the weak; a strategy that was consciously followed in drafting the Constitution. Following this strategy, as he notes in essay no. 51, the Congress is divided into two branches, rendering it less dangerous to the other branches, and the executive is equipped with a qualified veto that might in practice become almost absolute if an affinity between the Senate and president were to develop.

What is the protection accorded the judiciary is this scheme? It is, as intimated in essay no. 51 and clearly stressed at the outset of essay no. 78, that "the judges . . . are to hold their offices *during good behaviour.*"[13] As we might expect, the matter of the judges' tenure is the starting point for Hamilton's discussion of the compelling need for the independence of the judiciary, lest the system degenerate into a tyranny. He begins by noting that beyond any question "the judiciary is . . . the weakest of the three departments of power." Unlike either the executive or the legislature, it "has no influence over either the sword or the purse; no direction either of the strength or wealth of the society; and can take no active resolution whatever." It possesses "neither FORCE or WILL, but merely judgment; and must ultimately depend upon the aid of the executive arm even for the efficacy of its judgments." Because of its weakness he contends that the judiciary "will always be the least dangerous to the political rights of the constitution"; that it can never pose a danger to "the general liberty of the people"; and that "it can never attack with success either" the legislative or executive branches. In keeping with his views on the need for the separation of powers, he takes pains to interject a qualification and warning; namely, while "liberty can have nothing to fear from the judiciary alone," it "would have everything to fear from its union with either of the other departments."[14] The danger he envisions, we should emphasize, is clearly not the judiciary aggrandizing at the expense of the other departments, but rather other department encroaching upon the judiciary.

Having established this much, Hamilton proceeds to provide still another reason for an independent judiciary, namely, it is essential for the preservation of a "limited constitution," i.e., a constitution "which contains certain specified exceptions to the legislative authority." Constitutional prohibitions on congressional power, "that it pass no bills of attainder, no *ex post facto* laws, and the like," he writes, "can be preserved practice no other way than through the medium of the courts of justice; whose duty it must be to declare all acts contrary to the manifest tenor of the constitution void."[15] This imperative follows from the same fundamental law doctrine set forth by Varnum and Iredale, though it can be best understood as resting upon a distinction between "*political* will" and "*constitutive* will." The political will is that which is expressed through the institutions created by the constitutive will of the people, i.e., that which finds expression in the Constitution. The constitutive will is obviously anterior to any political will, but it is also superior to the political will since without it there could be no political will, certainly none that could bear the stamp of legitimacy. In this vein he concludes, "where the will of the legislature declared in its statutes [the political will], stands in opposition to that of the people declared in the constitution [the constitutive will], the judges ought to be governed by the latter, rather than the former."[16] This prescription would apply even when popular majorities back legislation that contravenes the fundamental law. "Until the people have, by some solemn and authoritative act [an amendment to the Constitution], annulled or changed the established form," he writes, "it is binding upon themselves collectively, as well as individually."[17]

Hamilton answers in a straightforward fashion the question of why judges should be the final arbiters of whether a legislative act contravenes the Constitution: "The interpretation of the laws is the proper and peculiar province of the courts," and thus it falls to judges "to ascertain . . . the meaning" of both the fundamental law and "any particular act proceeding from the legislative body." Additionally, he points to the commonsense of the matter: It "cannot be the natural presumption, where it is not collected from any particular provisions in the constitution" that "the legislative body are themselves the constitutional judges of their own powers" for this would defeat the very purpose of a limited constitution. "It is far more rational," he reasons, "to suppose that the courts were designed to be an intermediate body between the people and the legislature, in order, among other things, to keep the latter within the limits assigned to their authority."[18] In sum, the judges, who are independent of the legislature, are in a position to view the contested legislation impartially and they bear a responsibility to the people to uphold their constitutive will.[19]

Problems and the root of modern controversies

Hamilton says a good deal more about the courts and their role in the system that is best understood as answering critics of his position. To appreciate his answers, as well as the nature of the criticisms, it is necessary to return briefly to the theoretical framework from which the concept of fundamental law is derived. As we have seen, the justification for judicial review results from looking at the legislature as created and bound by the fundamental law or constitutive will of the people. Ideally, any laws which it passes that violate this fundamental law, that which created it and gave it authority in the first place, should be rendered null and void by the courts. What is not frequently emphasized is that the theoretical principles which dictate this conclusion also apply to the courts; the courts are also creatures of the fundamental law, bound to its terms as much as the legislature or the executive. Theoretically speaking, this is to say, just as the legislature can exceed its authority under the Constitution, so, too, can the courts. The question arises, then, what would constitute an unconstitutional act on the part of the courts including, of course, the Supreme Court?[20]

Hamilton offers us answers to this question; answers that actually take the form of responses to the trenchant criticisms of Brutus, perhaps the most coherent and profound Anti-Federalist, whose views on the potential abuses of judicial power are still relevant today. To be sure, Brutus was principally concerned with the Supreme Court and how it would rule in cases involving state/national relations, but much of what he has to say about the difficulties surrounding judicial review transcend this specific concern. To begin with, he believes the courts, including the Supreme Court, will render decisions not according to "fixed or established rules" but rather according to what they deem to be "the reason and spirit of the constitution."[21] Moreover, by his lights, "To discover the spirit of the constitution, it is of the first importance to attend to the principal ends and designs it has in view." This, as he sees it, brings into the judicial orbit the Preamble of the Constitution and the ends it sets forth—"a more perfect union," "justice," "domestic tranquility," "common defense," "the general welfare," and "the blessings of liberty." "If the end of government," he points out, "is to be learned from these words, which are clearly designed to declare it, it is obvious it has in view every object which is embraced by any government."[22] From Brutus's perspective, then, the courts—fully in accord with the fundamental law teachings—would clearly have enormous discretion in exercising their authority to invalidate legislation since any contravention of the spirit or purposes would suffice. What is more, Brutus argues that the courts would use their enormous discretionary powers to bring the legislature around to their way of thinking on fundamental constitutional principles. They would do this, not "by direct and positive decrees" since they could not directly force their views on the legislature, but by using their powers to nullify legislation to indicate what is and what is not permissible legislation.[23] "For as on the one hand," as he describes this process, "they [legislators] will not readily pass laws which they know the courts will not execute, so on the other, we may be sure they will not scruple to pass such as they know they will give effect, as often as they may judge it proper." In this way, he concludes, "the judgment of the judicial, on the constitution, will become the rule to guide the legislature in the construction of their powers."[24] On Brutus's showing, the judiciary, far from being the weakest branch of government, could lay claim to being the most powerful, the more so, as he takes care to emphasize, their decisions could only be overturned by constitutional amendment.

A good deal of what Hamilton writes about the judiciary in *The Federalist*, particularly in essays no. 78, is clearly intended to answer these contentions. As we have already seen, for instance, Hamilton would narrowly confine the scope of judicial review to more or less specific provisions of the Constitution. He specifically cites those relating to *ex post facto* laws and bills of attainder that limit legislative authority; limitations which, it should be remarked, are relatively easy to define. Moreover, he limits the courts' discretion in still other ways. They should nullify only measures which violate the "manifest tenor" of the Constitution; an injunction which, given the legal sense of the word "tenor," limits judicial nullification to measures clearly and indisputably contrary to the letter or written provisions of the Constitution . At another place, in keeping with this, he remarks that the courts must find an "irreconcilable variance" between the legislative act and the Constitution, a stringent test that obliges the courts to explore all reasonable interpretations of both the law and Constitution with an eye to finding compatibility between them. Finally, and perhaps the most direct answer to these concerns, Hamilton stresses that the courts should "exercise" "JUDGMENT," not "WILL"—which, in the in light of what he has already clearly intimated. i.e., that "WILL" is the province of the legislature—can be understood to mean that the courts should not assume a legislative function. That this is his meaning is even more evident from what he writes immediately following this assertion, namely, that should the courts "be disposed to exercise WILL instead of Judgment, the consequence would be the substitution of their pleasure to that of the legislative body."[25]

Constitutional morality and enforcement

By modern standards the role marked out for the courts by Hamilton and the early advocates of judicial review who preceded him is extremely narrow: that is, the fundamental law line of reasoning that justifies judicial review also sets limits on the nature and scope of judicial power. When we add to this consideration the subsequent "morality" set forth in Federalist essay no. 78 regarding its proper use—a morality whose purpose, it would appear, is to keep the courts from acting in a manner contrary to the fundamental law—it seems unlikely that the Framers expected the courts to nullify legislation with any frequency. In fact, this morality can be viewed as leading directly to what James B. Thayer in his classic article on the origins and scope of judicial review termed a judicial "rule of administration." This rule, which Thayer notes was more or less followed from the time of founding to the late 19th century, hold that the courts "can only disregard" an act of the legislature "when those who have the right to make laws have not merely made a mistake, but have made a very clear one,—*so clear that it is not open to rational question*." "That is the standard of duty," he continues, "to which the courts bring legislative Acts; that is the test which they apply—not merely their own judgment as to constitutionality, but their conclusion as to what judgment is permissible to another department which the constitution has charged with the duty of making it." In this process, the "rule" obliges the judges to recognize that what "will seem constitutional to one man, or body of men, may reasonably not seem so to another; that there is often a range of choice and judgment; that in such cases the constitution does not impose upon the legislature any one specific opinion, but leave open this range of choice."[26]

As Thayer's remarks indicate, his rule or principle takes the form of a "constitutional morality" that the judges ought to follow in keeping with the character of the fundamental law which entrusts the law making function to the legislature. The same is true with the injunctions set forth by Hamilton regarding the role and functions of the courts; namely, they also comprise a constitutional morality, unwritten rules designed to insure the operation of the constitutional order in keeping with its basic or underlying principles. But we find nothing in the Constitution that would compel the judges to observe them or, what might be more feasible, a means to discipline judges who ignore them. On the contrary, their observance turns almost entirely on the knowing and willing compliance of the judges.

Now the fact is that almost from the outset of the Republic, there has been no effective means by which these principles could be enforced even in the most extreme circumstances. To see why this is so, we need only to return to Hamilton and *The Federalist*. To set about enforcing Hamilton's constitutional morality, we would first have to distinguish between "WILL" and "JUDGMENT" and then convince others of the soundness or cogency of our distinction. We might be able to do this in the abstract, that is, as a purely intellectual enterprise, but honoring it in actual court decisions, particularly in those cases in which passions have been aroused and where its strict observance is perhaps most needed, would probably not be possible. Indeed, the partisanship surrounding the judiciary, the involvement of vested interests and ideologues of various persuasions, and the fact that any distinction would have some "wiggle room," all operate to allow interests and passions to dominate to the detriment of the WILL/JUDGMENT principle as either a measure of proper judicial decision making or an ethic that judges are able to follow. Presume, nevertheless, that these difficulties can be overcome and we find judges consistently exercising WILL. What remedy does Hamilton provide? In essay no.78, after acknowledging that judges exercising "WILL" are usurping the function of the legislative body, he answers—as we have noted—that this state of affairs, "if it proved anything, would prove that there ought to be no judges distinct from that body."[27] A sound observation, to be sure, but no real remedy for transgressions of this nature in an ongoing system. In Federalist essay no. 81, he takes up the closely related contention, initially set forth by Brutus, that the Supreme Court will interpret "the laws according to the *spirit* of the constitution" and "mould them into whatever shape it may think proper." To this he responds, "there is not a syllable in the plan" which "directly empowers" the courts to interpret the law in this fashion and, moreover, this difficulty confronts "every constitution that attempts to set bounds to legislative discretion."[28] After arguing the merits of judicial as opposed to legislative determinations of the constitutionality of legislative acts, he returns to problem of judicial encroachment on legislative authority only to downplay the possibilities of such encroachments given the comparative weakness of the judiciary and "its total incapacity to support its usurpations by force." In the last analysis "complete security," he contends, is provided by Congress's power to impeach and remove judges who abuse their authority in this fashion because, he reasons, they would not undertake "deliberate usurpation on the authority of the legislature," knowing that "this body was possessed of the means of punishing their presumption, by degrading them from their stations."[29] While there is some evidence to believe that at the time of founding the possibility of impeachment and removal might have served to restrain judges in the manner Hamilton suggests, we know that the acquittal of Supreme Court Justice Samuel Chase in 1805 set a precedent that has subsequently become a fundamental part our constitutional morality, namely, judges should not be impeached for the decisions they render from the bench.[30] In sum, given the difficulty of differentiating between will and judgment coupled with the Chase "rule," there are no institutional and procedural means to impose even those limitations on the judiciary that are called for by the reasoning that justifies judicial review. The result is that while the courts may operate to confine the legislature to the terms of the fundamental law, there is no recognized or accepted procedure to so confine the judiciary.

In suggesting the possibilities of impeachment as a salutary restraint on judges, we have some reason to believe that Hamilton was simply working his way out of a tight spot since by all evidences, as a staunch advocate of a truly independent judiciary, he would have supported the Chase "rule." Moreover, the Constitution itself stipulates removal only for "treason, bribery, or other high crimes and misdemeanors," a stipulation that leaves some latitude for interpretation but, nevertheless, would seem to rule out removal for reasons related to constitutional interpretation. Thus, the question arises: Why did the Framers, most of whom shared the views of Madison and Hamilton on the need to keep each of the branches within their proper sphere lest the system degenerate into tyranny, fail to provide any effective check against judicial usurpation? To be sure, the comparative weakness of the judiciary, stressed by Hamilton, may be one reason; that is, checks simply weren't necessary because the judiciary was too feeble to pose any danger. Moreover, the Framers were preoccupied in keeping the Congress within its bounds for reasons that Madison's commentary in essay no. 48 makes abundantly clear. Consequently, and understandably, they were almost exclusively concerned with fortifying the coordinate branches against congressional assaults rather than with any usurpation of congressional powers. Still another reason might well have been a prevailing and firm consensus within the society as a whole relative to the proper role and function of the judiciary; an understanding that precluded judges from even entertaining the idea of intruding on the prerogatives of the legislature. Thayer's discussion and analysis, alluded to above, would lend credence to this view.

The Ascension of the Modern Courts: Substantive Due Process

What we have said to this point provides only a point of departure for understanding how it has come to pass that the courts have reached a new pinnacle of power our system. To put this otherwise, the absence of effective external restraints along with the gradual decline of the internal restraints have simply opened up avenues for the expansion of judicial power not envisioned by the Founders—or, for that matter, even by Brutus. Whereas, for example, Hamilton could declare that the courts can take "no active resolution," this is far from the case today. Even supporters of judicial activism would find common ground with its staunchest critics who point out that "in terms of issues that determine the nature and quality of life in society, the Supreme Court has become our most important institution of government."[31] The Court's decisions on abortion, quotas, public morality, libel and slander, apportionment, capital punishment, prayer in schools, aid to religious schools, the takings clause, and, *inter alia,* busing are abundant evidence to this effect.

It is beyond my purpose here to explore these and other areas where the courts have intervened. Rather, I want to highlight the development in judicial thinking over time that account for the Supreme Court's ascension to its present position or, to put this somewhat differently, to exam the ways in which the

Court has proceeded to use its freedom from both internal and external restraints to claim and justify its current powers.

In this endeavor the first thing we must note is that the judges have always operated within the confines of the theoretical framework that justifies judicial review. This is to say, they regard the Constitution as fundamental law in the same sense as Varnum or Iredale, i.e., as representing the constitutive will of the people that limits the powers of both the state and national governments. And the major controversies surrounding the growth of judicial power that have taken place since the time of founding are best understood in this context. This can be seen with the introduction of the concept of "substantive due process" that occurs at the national level on the second occasion when the Court exercised judicial review, *Dred Scott v. Sanford* (1857); a case in which Chief Justice Taney, writing for the majority, maintained that the terms of the Missouri Compromise enacted by Congress deprived an individual of his property (in this case a slave)[32] in violation of the due process clause of the Fifth Amendment. In no sense was "due process," strictly speaking, the issue; the propriety of the process by which the Missouri Compromise had become law was not in question. Nevertheless, the statute was held to be a deprivation of property in violation of the due process clause of the Fifth Amendment, "nor [shall any person] be deprived of life, liberty, or property without due process of law," and thus contrary to the fundamental law. Taney's understanding of the due process clause that allowed such a conclusion is and was, to say the least, highly controversial since "due process" had traditionally been understood to provide procedural guarantees in a narrower and different context, mainly for those accused of a crime.[33] In any event, it was also well established in the American tradition that "life, liberty, and property" could be restricted and regulated by legislatures in light of the common good. What is important to note, however, is the manner in which Taney circumvents Hamilton's "manifest tenor" admonition by reading into the fundamental law an understanding concerning the limits of legislative power that has its foundations or justifications, not in the language of the Constitution, but instead, it would seem, in its "spirit." Likewise, given the traditional understanding of the due process clause, Taney's decision could not possibly pass muster on Hamilton's "irreconcilable variance" test or Thayer's "rule"; that is, there were clearly ample and legitimate grounds to uphold the law.

Substantive due process is similarly employed in *Lochner v. New York* (1905), a case which has served over the decades as the Progressive's prime example of judicial overreach. In this case, Justice Peckham holds that the "liberty" of the due process clause of the 14th amendment includes "liberty of contract," a position essential to his justification for overturning a New York statute regulating the working conditions of bakers. Simply put, on his showing, the statute arbitrarily, without rational foundations, encroached upon the bakers' liberty of contract. Here, just as Taney had done in the Dred Scott decision by including slaves within the definition of property, Peckham places "liberty of contract" within the confines of "liberty," and then, again like Taney, reasons that the due process clause places limits on legislative authority. What we see in this process is that substantive due process is predicated on the fundamental law, albeit with very questionable additions to its substance. Beyond this, the reasoning underling the fundamental law theory that renders it such an effective justification for judicial review hardly lends support to the Court's use of substantive due process since, as remarked above, critical questions unavoidably arise over whether the Court itself has not violated the fundamental law by straying outside the domain intended for it by the constitutive will of the people.

Despite the harsh criticisms of the uses to which substantive due process has been put, particularly in Dred Scott and Lochner, it is now part of the judicial arsenal and, barring a highly unlikely and basic change among the legal elite concerning the proper role of the judiciary, will remain so. What is more, there seem to be no rules or guidelines that serve to dictate when it will be invoked. In recent decades, for instance, a majority of the Court has looked with favor on the position that the liberty guaranteed by due process cannot be confined to any code or specific provisions of the Bill of Rights; that "the best that can be said is that, through the course of the Court's decisions, it has represented the balance which our Nation, built upon postulate of respect for the liberty of the individual, has struck between that liberty and the demands of organized society."[34] This description of judicial balancing, it should be remarked, seems indistinguishable from what would ordinarily be considered the proper function of a legislative body. Consequently, it should come as no surprise that bitter controversy often ensues when the Court overturns the legislature's balancing for its own. More importantly, since substantive due process is now a given, the growth of judicial power necessarily depends on the content the Court gives to "life, liberty, and property," particularly "liberty" since it is most frequently at the center of litigation. As the Court finds or recognizes more "rights," this is to say, judicial authority is bound to expand, largely at the expense of the legislatures both state and national.[35] Indeed, this judicial expansion might even proceed without any acknowledged limits if the Court were to interpret constitutional provisions in light of a "higher law" to which the founding generation presumably subscribed.[36]

The Commands of Fundamental Law

Not unrelated to substantive due process is a further development that has elevated the Court to a new plateau of power.[37] This development involves the Court identifying a right or condition whose realization the fundamental law "commands" or enjoins and then mandating what is required to realize it. This process is what characterizes modern judicial activism: It goes beyond substantive due process to new level of judicial power wherein the Court sets forth what the other branches are obliged to do in order to achieve the state of affairs presumably required by the fundamental law. Put otherwise, the Supreme Court in relatively recent decades has undertaken "active resolution" by way of specifying the conditions necessary for compliance with what it perceives as "demands" arising from of the Constitution or fundamental law. And since our modern constitutional morality holds that the Court is the final arbiter concerning the meaning of the fundamental law and that the other branches, as well as the states, are obliged to honor its decisions, our present system, many contend, is one of judicial supremacy.[38]

The Court's decision in *Roe v. Wade* (1973)[39], which legalized abortion, perhaps best illustrates this development. In this case we encounter the use of substantive due process in the form of a "right to privacy," a right which is not expressly set forth in the Constitution. Justice Blackmun, however, writing for the majority, finds three sound constitutional bases for this right: "in the penumbras of the Bill of Rights"; "in the Ninth Amendment's reservation of rights to the people"; "the concept of liberty" in the Fourteenth Amendment.[40] These foundations clearly do not rest upon "manifest tenor," but ultimately rest upon what Blackmun perceives to be the "spirit" of the Constitution; that is, the thoughts, ideals, and ends which it implicitly embodies and which are supportive of and conducive to a right of privacy that, in turn, "encompass a woman's decision whether or not to terminate her pregnancy."[41]

To this point, this decision follows the path of *Lochner*. Where the two cases differ is that in Lochner the Court simply nullified the legislation in question, whereas in Roe the Court, having determined that the right of a woman to terminate a pregnancy was not absolute, assumes an essentially legislative function by undertaking the task of setting down guidelines dictating what the state legislatures can and cannot do in regulating this right: In the first trimester of pregnancy, the decision to terminate "must be left to the medical judgment of the pregnant woman's attending physician"; in the second trimester, the state "may, if it chooses, regulate the abortion procedure in ways that are reasonably related to maternal health"; and in the third, it "may . . . regulate, and even proscribe . . . abortion except where it is necessary . . . for the preservation of the life or health of the mother."[42] As might be expected, what has followed over the decades since this decision is a flood of litigation in which the Court has had to refine its guidelines in light of state efforts to regulate, e.g., What is the scope of "maternal health"? What constitutes regulation "reasonably related to maternal health"? The result is that these decisions, taken as a whole, represent a body of rules and regulations that resembles a legislative code, dictating in great detail what state legislatures (and the Congress, for that matter) may or may not do in regulating a woman's right to choose. For this reason, and given the intense controversies that have arisen over this issue, individuals of widely different political persuasions have contended that the Court should not have taken the issue of abortion out of the legislative arena in the manner it did.[43] But, whatever the merits of this position, what is clear is that the modern court, contrary to what Hamilton maintained relative to the judiciary of his day, can now undertake an "active resolution": the Court sets forth a right that it derives from the "spirit" of the Constitution and then it dictates to the legislature what this right requires by way of implementation or realization.

The Court's move from simple nullification into this active resolution mode can be viewed as the natural outgrowth of radical transformations in thinking about its role and function in our constitutional system. Whereas Hamilton and the early proponents of judicial review clearly emphasized its primary function as insuring that the laws comply with the Constitution, today the prevailing view, at least in academic legal circles, is far more expansive. One of the main pillars and inspirations for this expanded conception is the famous footnote in the Carolene Products case which, in effect, opened up new horizons for the Court in the exercise of judicial review by observing that "prejudice against discrete and insular minorities may be a special condition" that casts doubt on the legitimacy of decisions arrived at through "those political processes ordinarily to be relied upon to protect minorities."[44] Thus, increasingly over the decades, largely through the "equal protection" clause of the Fourteenth Amendment, the Court has set forth standards, quite apart from the traditional constitutional guarantees, that must be met for legislation dealing with such minorities (and women) to pass constitutional muster. Through this process the Court has had an enormous impact on practices and policies in both the public and private sectors—e.g., hiring and firing policies, university admission policies, legislative apportionment.

Added to this is the receptiveness in legal circles of an even more expansive vision of the judicial function that derives from viewing the Constitution as a "living document," whose meaning and "spirit" must be determined in light of contemporary circumstances and thought. As Justice Brennan put it in his famous Georgetown lecture, "the Constitution rests not in any static meaning it might have had in a world that is dead and gone, but in the adaptability of its great principles to cope with current problems and current needs."[45] Integral to this understanding is also the proposition that the intention of those who drafted the Constitution was not "to preserve a preexisting society," but rather "to make a new one, to put in place new principles that the prior political community had not sufficiently recognized."[46] While this formulation clearly stresses the impermanence of meaning that attaches to the Constitution over time, it simultaneously holds that underlying its provisions are permanent values and goals which, to Brennan's way of thinking, come down to security "the freedom, the dignity, and the rights of all person within our borders."[47] He stresses, in particular, "human dignity," a goal that, as he explores its meaning, embraces freedom and rights; a goal that, moreover, "will be an eternal quest" and whose "demands . . . will never cease to evolve."[48] We need not dwell on the particulars of this understanding, which in most respects closely resembles others that envision an expansive judicial function, to appreciate the latitude it provides for the Court in preserving or advancing human dignity. The Massachusetts Supreme Court, for instance, effectively mandated same sex marriages in 2003 on grounds that the Massachusetts Constitution of 1780 "affirms the dignity and equality of all individuals."[49] At the very least, an expansive conception of human dignity can easily serve to channel legislation along judicially determined lines,

Finally, by way of gauging the extent to which the power of the Court has grown in recent decades, we can recur to that original fundamental law theory elaborated by Iredale, Varnum, Hamilton and others. For openers, it is apparent that the more expansive role of the Court is fueled by interpreting the constitutional language in the context of a wider and more embracing philosophical construct. This mode of interpretation bears more than a cousinly resemblance to Brutus's concern that the Court would interpret the Constitution in keeping with its "spirit." At the same time, in interpreting the Constitution from a broader philosophical perspective, the Court has seen fit to reject the legislative understanding of the fundamental law, even when reconciliation between the two was possible. Even the more advanced theories of judicial interpretation also fashion the fundamental law in light of its "spirit," though these theories provide far more expansive grounds—e.g., human dignity, toleration, equality—for judicial intrusion into the legislative domain. If anything, as evidence by Brennan's views, these modern, more activist theories invoke the "higher spirits" of the Constitution;[50] that is, overarching values, goals, principles that can be applied to a wide and indeterminate range of social concerns.

The Demise of the Philadelphia Constitution: Concerns and Solutions

As the foregoing clearly shows, the constitutional morality that originally served to circumscribe judicial power is no longer operative. The effects of this are sufficient to alter fundamentally the character of that Constitution which emerged from the Philadelphia Convention. Today, for example, it is not uncommon to hear even members of Congress publicly assert that the Constitution established "three equal and coordinate branches of government."[51] This understanding of our system carries with it a picture of three branches; each equally entitled to employ the resources and authority of the government to make decisions binding on the people. For this reason, perhaps, it is not uncommon to hear, particularly from judicial activists, that the Court has an obligation to correct the "political failures" of Congress when it fails to advance values allegedly embedded in the fundamental law. Yet reading the Constitution with an innocent eye does not support this understanding. Nor does a reading of *The Federalist* in which the theoretical foundations for the separation of powers and the threats thereto are dealt with at length. As we have seen, it is precisely because the branches are not equal that life tenure for judges is provided for. Life tenure, it is crucial to note, was not intended to "equalize" the branches, but to provide protection for the judiciary from encroachments on its legitimate domain by the other branches, principally the legislative.

Legitimate concerns arise over the power of the modern Court, concerns that are not entirely unlike those raised by Brutus with which Hamilton felt obliged to deal. Hamilton could perceive that allowing for judicial legislation or even an unwarranted judicial intrusion into the legislative sphere would undermine the system in two critical ways. The republican character of the Constitution, he perceived, is violated by judicial nullification of perfectly legitimate legislative action. Beyond any doubt, he would see an even greater danger in the judicial legislation that has characterized decisions of the modern Court. He was also keenly aware that far more than republicanism was at stake: any merger of judicial and legislative powers constituted tyranny by opening up the avenues for an arbitrary and capricious government inimical to liberty. The potential for this state of affairs, it should be emphasized, increases almost exponentially as the Court assumes legislative powers based upon values and principles, not at all evident from or closely related to the text of the Constitution, but upon those theoretically abstracted from a broader conceptual "understanding" compatible with continually changing social circumstances and thought.

The charges against the Court's judicial activism are, indeed, weighty and they prompt the question of what can be done to curb its powers. Any number of proposals have been set forth by the Court's critics, ranging from limiting its jurisdiction to fixed terms for the justices. In recent decades both supporters and critics of the Court seemed to have settled on a "political" solution; that is, concentrating their efforts on securing the appointment of judges whose philosophy is most compatible with their views. Hence the intense and often bitter politics surrounding the confirmation process and the increasing importance attached what kind of nominees the candidates for president would nominate for the Court.

It is far beyond our purpose here to canvass the means that have been set forth to check judicial power. From our vantage point the political support necessary for any substantial alteration of the Court's power is lacking, mainly because the Court, as an institution, is largely venerated by the American people.[52] Nor, we must note, does the tactic of appointing judges who favor judicial restraint seem to hold out much prospect for a permanent solution to judicial overreach. Why so? Simply because the very issue of the Court's proper role and functions has now been thrust into the political arena where it has become in a relatively short period of time a partisan political issue of the first order. Consequently, at best we should expect that the Court's activism will wax and wane, depending solely upon the fortunes of the political parties.

Any permanent solution to judicial aggrandizement would seem to require recourse to Hamilton's understanding of the place of the judiciary within the constitutional order and its role within that order. We have previously termed this understanding a "constitutional morality"–a morality that sets forth the unwritten rules that are necessary for the constitutional system to operate in a coherent manner faithful to intentions of its drafters. This morality rests upon an understanding and appreciation of the respective roles of the three branches and of the underlying fundamental law theory which gives rise to judicial review as a means of preserving its integrity. It rests as well upon a conception of republicanism that allows wide latitude for the people to make critical decisions for the society, which, in turn, means that the judiciary should make every effort to confine itself to the exercise of JUDGMENT associated with precedent, impartiality, application of acknowledged rules of interpretation, fidelity to the text, and the like. Or, to put this in other terms, the morality rests upon judges avoiding the exercise of WILL, that entails, to return to Judge Thayer's formulation, a principled deference to the legislature. In sum, if followed, the injunction against the exercise of WILL—an injunction intimately connected to other elements of the morality—would itself put an end to the most disturbing aspects of judicial activism.

We may speculate that at the time Hamilton was writing Federalist no.78 he believed, along with others of the founding generation, that a clear and firm understanding concerning the proper role of judges prevailed within the legal community; a role that embraced the main elements of this constitutional morality. Thus, as we have intimated above, they may have tacitly relied on judicial self-restraint, the natural outgrowth of this understanding, as a barrier to judicial aggrandizement. This might, as we have suggested, account for the absence of effective constitutional checks on the judiciary that might curb the judicial activism that has come to pass. Whatever the case may have been, however, we know that today this understanding no longer prevails; that, to the contrary, our leading law schools are havens for the most radical proponents of judicial activism. Is there, then, any hope that the earlier morality can be resurrected as an effective barrier to judicial excesses? Probably not. The controversies surrounding the Court and its place within our constitutional system have taken on partisan overtones which serve to preclude an acceptance of this morality to the extent and at the level necessary for it to operate as an effective check. While it will never entirely disappear as an alternative to judicial activism, the chances of its establishing deep roots and prevailing within the profession or among the judges seem remote.

If my analysis is essentially sound, then what is the future of the Court? While all such projections are obviously fraught with perils, there is every reason to believe that the Court, to the extent it continues to practice judicial activism, will continue to be drawn by degrees into the purely political vortex. At some point it is conceivable that, by way of reaction to one or more of its excesses, it might become a third elected branch along the lines of a super-Senate with the justices elected for terms of fifteen or twenty years. But this or like prospects are not relished by even the severest critics of the modern Court for then we must say "farewell" to any hopes for a enduring *constitutional* republic.

ENDNOTES

1. I acknowledge at once that some would deny this conclusion. Such denials are usually based on the premise that the powers of the modern Court are not inherently any greater than they were when John Marshall assumed the power of judicial review or that, in any event, if there has been any augmentation of judicial power it is evolutionary, the natural outgrowth of the give and take characteristic of American politics. In what follows, I will endeavor to show in some detail how, over the course of the Twentieth Century, the Court has moved well beyond its intended role. Among the extended analyses that in my mind convincingly bear out this contention see: Christopher Wolfe, *The Rise of Modern Judicial Review: From Constitutional Interpretation to Judge-Made Law* (New York: Basic Books, 1986); Robert H. Bork, *The Tempting of America: The Political Seduction of the Law* (New York: The Free Press, 1990); Raoul Berger, *Government by Judiciary: The Transformation of the Fourteenth Amendment* (Cambridge, Massachusetts: Harvard University Press, 1977).

2. This is not to say that the debate over the Framers' intention regarding judicial review has been resolved. While this matter is beyond the scope of my concerns, there are, indeed, legitimate reasons for denying that judicial review was intended by the founding generation. The question that is relevant to my inquiry is what kind of reasoning what used to justify judicial review at the time of founding and how this reasoning bears upon what powers the courts can legitimately exercise.

3. Over the years one of the first questions asked of nominees to the Supreme Court is

whether they accept the reasoning of *Marbury v. Madison* concerning the role of the Court. The presumption in asking the question seems to be that this decision is the foundation of the Court's authority to exercise judicial review. But see note 1, *supra*.

4. Here Marshall notes that among those reasons why the Bill of Rights does not apply to the states is that they were adopted "In compliance with a sentiment" of the founding era that the powers of the national government "might be exercised in a manner dangerous to liberty." *Barron v. Baltimore*, 7 Peters 243.

5. Charles G. Haines's classic, *The American Doctrine of Judicial Supremacy* (New York: Russell and Russell, 1939) surveys the roots of judicial review and cites eight instances of its exercise prior to the adoption of the Constitution.

6. Not all scholars agree about the number of instances of judicial review prior to the Constitution, but even Brent Bozell, who was highly skeptical of all such precedents, concluded that these two cases have by far the strongest claims. See: *The Warren Revolution* (New Rochelle, New York: Arlington House, 1966). In any event, these two cases are most frequently cited as examples of early judicial review. While we have no records of the arguments presented in the courts in these cases, we do have a brief written later by James Varnum and the letters of James Iredale clearly providing their arguments and reasoning that apparently proved decisive in these cases.

7 Gerald Stourzh, "Fundamental Laws and Individual Rights in the 18th Century Constitution," in *The American Founding: Essays on the Formation of the Constitution*, ed. J. Jackson Barlow, *et al.* (New York: Greenwood Press, 1988), 177.

8. Quoted in Haines at 106 and 108.

9. Quoted in Haines at 115.

10. For an overview of this development see "Introduction" to *The Federalist: The Gideon Edition*, ed. George W. Carey and James McClellan (Indianapolis: Liberty Fund, 2000). All subsequent references to *The Federalist* are to this edition with essay number followed by page number.

11. *The Federalist*, 47:249.

12. He writes to this effect that "it is against the enterprising ambition of this department [the legislature], that the people out to indulge all their jealousy, and exhaust all their precautions." *The Federalist*, 48:257. Hamilton expresses similar warnings when he remarks on "The propensity of the legislative department to intrude upon and absorb the powers, of the other departments." *The Federalist*, 73:380.

13. *The Federalist*, 78:401. Emphasis in the original.

14. *The Federalist*, 78:402.

15. *The Federalist*, 78:403. It seems clear that in using the expression "manifest tenor," Hamilton is using the word "tenor" in the legal sense which, according to the Webster Encyclopedic Dictionary, refers to "a copy of the exact claims of a document, as a transcript" This understanding is supported by his other use of the word "tenor" in this essay: "There is no position which depends on clearer principles, than that every act of a delegated authority, contrary to the tenor of the commission under which it is exercised, is void" (78:403).

16. *The Federalist*, 78:404.

17. *The Federalist*, 78:406.

18. *The Federalist*, 78:404.

19. Of course, by clear implication, all branches are obliged to obey the constituent will. The legislators and executive are obliged to consider the constitutionality of measures that come before them and to reject those that contravene the fundamental law.

20. When I ask my undergraduate students whether the Court can do anything unconstitutional, I usually get a look of bewilderment. This, I think, indicates the degree to which the Court has come to enjoy a special status, a more privileged status, so to speak, than either Congress or the executive. The current view of the Court seems to be that it can occasionally make mistakes – i.e., render decisions that are "wrong" for various reasons – but that it cannot act *ultra vires* because it, in effect, is the judge of the constitutional the limits of its operations.

21. *The Anti-Federalist: Writings by the Opponents of the Constitution*, ed. Herbert J. Storing (Chicago: University of Chicago Press, 1985), 165.

22. *The Anti-Federalist*, 169.

23. *The Anti-Federalist*, 168.

24. *The Anti-Federalist*, 169.

25. *The Federalist*, 78:405.

26. James B. Thayer, "The Origin and Scope of the American Doctrine of Constitution Law" in *Taking the Constitution Seriously*, ed. Gary L. McDowell (Dubuque, Iowa: Kendall/Hunt, 1981), 57 (emphasis added). In this connection Thayer believes that "one who is a member of a legislature may vote against a measure as being, in his judgment, unconstitutional; and, being subsequently placed on the bench, when this measure, having been passed by the legislature in spite of his opposition, comes before him judicially, may there find it his duty, although he has in no degree changed his opinion, to declare it constitutional." Ibid.

27. *The Federalist*, 78:405.

28. *The Federalist*, 81:418.

29. *The Federalist*, 81:420.

30. As Alfred H. Kelly and Winfred A. Harbison write, the failure to remove Chase constituted "the abandonment of impeachment as a political device" in bringing the judiciary to heel. The *American Constitution: Its Origins and Development* (3rd ed.; New York: W.W. Norton, 1963), 236.

31. Lino Graglia, "How the Constitution Disappeared," in *Interpreting the Constitution*, ed. Jack N. Rakove (Boston: Northeastern University Press, 1990), 36.

32. Holding slaves to be property is, of course, another controversial aspect of the decision. It is, however, analytically separable from the concept of substantive due process.

33. Due process and the due process clause have a long history dating back to the Magna Carta where it was understood to be "law of the land"; that is, no individual could be

deprived of life, liberty, or property "unless . . . by law of the land." Thus, throughout history, due process has been associated with procedure or process, not substance. For an exhaustive survey of the meaning attached to the due process clause to the end of the Nineteenth Century see: Charles A. Shattuck, "The True Meaning of the Term 'Liberty' in Those Clauses in the Federal and State Constitution Which Protect 'Life, Liberty, and Property,'" *Harvard Law Review* 4(1891). See also George W. Carey, "Due Process, Liberty, and the Fifth Amendment" in *In Defense of the Constitution* (Indianapolis: Liberty Fund, 1995).

34. Justice Harlan (dissenting from dismissal on jurisdictional grounds) in *Poe v. Ullman*, 367 U.S., at 542 quote approvingly in *Planned Parenthood of Southeastern PA v. Casey*, 505 U.S. 833 (1992).

35. Many shudder at the prospect of the Court "opening up" the Ninth Amendment. To view the Ninth Amendment as a fertile source of rights that the federal courts should enforce is predicated on a misunderstanding of the reasons why the amendment was added to the Constitution. The Bill of Rights was added at the insistence of the Anti-Federalists who wanted to limit the national government. The problem that arose with these limits was articulated by Hamilton in Federalist essay no. 84, namely, some of them sought to prevent the national government from doing that which the national government, being one of delegated powers, had no power to do in the first place. The addition of such amendments, therefore, carried with it the implication that rather than being a government of delegated and limited powers, the national government possessed plenary powers. Thus, to get around this understanding, the necessity of both the Ninth and Tenth Amendments. See Raoul Berger, "The Ninth Amendment," in *Selected Writings on the Constitution* (Cumberland, Virginia: James River Press, 1987).

36. Some contend, for instance, that ends and values embodied in the Declaration of Independence, mainly those found in its second paragraph, represent the American creed and the basic principles upon which the Constitution is grounded. For this reason, they would argue that, when appropriate, the Court can and should take cognizance of them in its decisions. See, for example, Harry Jaffa, Original Intent and the Framers of the Constitution: A Disputed Question (Chicago: Regnery, 1993). See, also, Robert Bork's review of this work in *National Review*, 7 February, 1994 and the subsequent exchange between him and Jaffa in *National Review*, 21 March 1994. In this connection, Joseph J. Ellis writes that the language of the Declaration and its "open ended" statement of individual rights signifies that "Jefferson" was, in effect, "urging each new generation to interpret his famous words anew." Thus "gay rights" and single sex marriage find sanction in the language and sentiment of the Declaration. "A New Topic for an Old Argument," *New York Times*, 29 February 2004, A24.

Still others contend that "For the generation that framed the Constitution, the concept of a 'higher law,' protecting 'natural rights,' and taking precedence over ordinary positive law as a matter of political obligation, was widely shared and deeply felt . . . at the same time, it was generally recognized that written constitutions could not completely codify the higher law. Thus in the framing of the original American constitutions it was widely accepted that there remained unwritten but still binding principles of higher law." Thomas C. Grey, "Do We Have an Unwritten Constitution?" 27 *Stanford Law Review*, 703. The Court, from this perspective, is entitled to employ the "unwritten . . . higher law" when it sees fit.

37. The term "new plateau" to indicate the qualitative expansion of judicial power was

first used by Charles S. Hyneman, *The Supreme Court on Trial* (New York: Atherton Press, 1963).

38. In *Cooper v. Aaron* (1958), 358 U.S. 1, as Charles Hyneman notes, the Court asserted that what the Court "says the Constitution means is exactly what the Constitution does mean, and all other public officials and branches of government, national and state, shall respect [the] Court's statements of what the Constitution means, no matter what other interpretations may seem to them to be clearly implied by the words of that document." Hyneman, 78. Hyneman goes on to remark that neither he nor Edward S. Corwin, the distinguished constitutional scholar, could find any previous pronouncements by the Court that its constitutional interpretation is binding on the other branches. The net effect of Cooper v. Aaron is that the Constitution is now what the Court says it is and the other branches are constitutional obliged to accepts its interpretations as binding.

39. 410 U.S. 113 (1973).

40. Id. at 152.

41. Id. at 153.

42. Id. at 164–65..

43. Cass Sunstein, for instance, hardly the harshest critic of the modern Court, maintains that "In the Court's first confrontation with the abortion issue [i.e., Roe v. Wade], it laid down a set of rules for legislatures to follow whenever that issue arose. The Court decided far too many issues too quickly. The Court should have allowed the democratic processes of the states more time to adapt and to deliberate, and to generate solutions that might be sensible but that might not occur to a set of judges." *One Case at a Time: Judicial Minimalism on the Supreme Court* (Cambridge: Harvard University Press, 1999), 57.

44. *United States v. Carolene Product Company*, 304 U.S. 144, 152 n. 4 (1938).

45. "The Constitution of the United States: Contemporary Ratification," speech delivered by William J. Brennan at Georgetown University, 12 October 1985 in *Interpreting the Constitution*, ed. Jack N. Rakove (Boston: Northeastern University Press, 1990), 27.

46. Brennan, 28.

47. Brennan, 30.

48. Brennan, 32.

49. *Goodrich v. Massachusetts Department of Public Health* (2003). The Massachusetts Supreme Court did allow the Massachusetts legislature 180 days "to take such action as it may deem appropriate in light of this opinion." The Court subsequently held that legislation authorizing "civil unions" would not satisfy the constitutional requirement, thereby leaving constitutional amendment as the only means of reversing its decision. The Canadian Supreme Court in December of 2004 rendered an advisory opinion at the request of the Canadian parliament on the constitutionality of same sex marriages. Its reasoning paralleled that of the Massachusetts Court citing the values of "tolerance, respect, and equality" emanating from the fundamental law. However, the advisory opinion, unlike the Massachusetts decision, only cleared the way for a legislative determination of the issue. See: Joanna Grossman, "The Canadian Supreme Court's Same-Sex Marriage Decision," <http:writ.news.findlaw.com/grossman/20041214.html>

50. In this vein, the Court could declare "at the heart of liberty is the right to define one's

own concept of existence, of meaning, of the universe, and of the mystery of human life." *Planned Parenthood of Southeastern Pennsylvania v. Casey*, 505 U.S. 833 (1992). This is indicative of the relative abstract nature of "rights" now derived from the "spirit" of the Constitution or its presumed animating principles. By itself such a formulation is without effect or impact, but it does expand the reach of the judiciary does in setting down boundaries to the behavior that results from this liberty.

51. To paraphrase George Orwell, the situation at the present time might be put as follows: All the branches are equal, but the Supreme Court is more equal than the others.

52. I have treated at length of the obstacles to Congress exercising control over the Court, not the least of these being the abysmal ignorance of the American people about their Constitution and how it was designed to operate. See: George W. Carey, "The Philadelphia Constitution: Dead or Alive?" in *The End of Democracy II: A Crisis of Legitimacy*, ed. Mitchell S. Muncy (Dallas: Spence Publishing, 1999).

Two
The Judicial Assault on Human Dignity
by Jack Wade Nowlin

Our constitutional order is founded upon the principles articulated in the Declaration of Independence: That all men are created equal and endowed by their Creator with unalienable rights to life, liberty, and the pursuit of happiness. The very purpose of the U.S. Constitution in establishing a framework of government and placing it under constitutional limits is ultimately to secure these natural rights from both private violence and governmental tyranny. The right to life is the most basic of these fundamental rights and it extends to all men (i.e., human beings), including, of course, the unborn and the infirm. Abortion and physician-assisted suicide are inconsistent with a proper respect for human life and are grave acts of injustice striking at the moral foundations of the Constitution. Therefore, all the institutions of government—the federal courts as well as Congress and the fifty state legislatures—should act to secure the right to life for all human beings. The pursuit of this goal by the institutions of government is constrained only by the various limits on their constitutional powers—such as the structural principles of the separation of powers and federalism that demarcate each governmental institution's proper sphere of authority. Alas, the federal judiciary has respected neither the fundamental right to life nor the constitutional limits of the judicial power in the American constitutional design.

Precursors of the Judicial Assault on the Right to Life: *Dred Scott*, Slavery, and African-American Citizenship

The contemporary judiciary's assault upon human dignity in decisions such as *Roe v. Wade*,[1] which created a constitutional right to abort unborn children, was foreshadowed in important ways by *Dred Scott v. Sandford* (1857),[2] the first great judicial assault on human dignity. *Dred Scott* is widely regarded as one of the worst decisions in the history of the Supreme Court because of its extreme judicial activism and its hostility to the basic rights of African-Americans.[3] Thus *Dred Scott*—in both its activist violation of the constitutional limits of the judicial power and its substantive moral iniquity—is *Roe v. Wade*'s clearest precursor.

The operative facts of *Dred Scott* are relatively simple: Scott, held in bondage in Missouri, sued for his freedom, claiming that he was no longer legally a slave because his owner had voluntarily taken him into a free state (Illinois) and a free federal territory (the Wisconsin territory) to reside for a significant length of time.[4] Dred Scott initiated his claim in Missouri state court, and most state courts, including several in the South, would have ruled in Scott's favor under well-established principles of law.[5] In fact, the predominant view at this time was that slavery could exist only as creature of positive law and that a slave owner who took a slave into a free state or territory (where the positive law failed to recognize or affirmatively prohibited slavery) to reside for substantial time thereby emancipated the slave.[6] Indeed, the rejection of this position by courts would have allowed slave owners to import the institution of slavery into areas where it was legally unrecognized or even prohibited, an obviously untenable view. This well-established position was also that of the courts in Missouri, but the Missouri Supreme Court ruled against Scott, reversing over twenty years of Missouri precedent and justifying that reversal in part as an affirmative judicial measure against the growing "dangers" of abolitionism.[7]

Dred Scott then sued in federal court, asserting what is known as "diversity" jurisdiction, the constitutional and statutory power of a federal court to hear a dispute if the plaintiff and defendant are citizens of different (i.e., "diverse") states.[8] Scott could claim this jurisdictional ground because he, Scott, was a resident of Missouri and Sanford, the defendant named in the litigation, resided in New York.[9] Scott, however, ultimately lost in federal district court. The judge there ruled that Scott's status as a (non-)slave was to be determined by Missouri law and that the Missouri Supreme Court had conclusively settled that question in favor of Sanford, Scott's putative slave-master, ruling that Scott remained a slave. Scott then appealed directly to the Supreme Court.[10]

The Supreme Court eventually heard Scott's case in 1857, and its opinion in *Dred Scott v. Sandford* fills over 200 pages in the Supreme Court reports, making it one of the longest cases in the history of the Supreme Court. All nine Justices wrote individual opinions—including two dissents—and their public reading by the members of the Court took two full days.[11] The Supreme Court ultimately rejected two options consistent with traditional nineteenth century conceptions of judicial restraint and the properly limited role of the Court among the institutions of government in our constitutional system: The Court could have ruled in Scott's favor in light of the well-established principles of law discussed above,[12] or, following the federal district judge's decision, the Court could have simply deferred to Missouri's resolution of the case out of respect for the constitutional principle of federalism.[13] Instead, Chief Justice Taney in his opinion for the Court abandoned judicial restraint and attempted to use the decision as an activist vehicle for settling by judicial fiat the central political question of the day—slavery—in favor of slaveholding, while also racistly denying the citizenship of even free African-Americans.

Chief Justice Roger Taney's opinion, styled the opinion of the Court,[14] first stated that no African-American descended from slaves, whether slave *or free*, could ever be a U.S. citizen or a citizen of a state for federal purposes.[15] This was asserted as a matter of the "original intent" of the framers of the Constitution[16]—despite the fact that free African-Americans were recognized as citizens in many states at the American Founding and were qualified to vote in the Philadelphia Constitution's ratification conventions, as was vigorously pointed out in the Court's dissenting opinions.[17] Taney thus asserted—in the face of facts clearly to the contrary—that free African-Americans in the United States historically "had no rights which the white man was bound to respect."[18] Taney's politically-motivated misinterpretation of the word "citizen" in the Constitution meant that Scott, even if free, as an African-American descended from slaves, could not be a "citizen" as that word is used in Article III and therefore could not sue in federal court. This activist and racist attempt to exclude free African-Americans from the political community of Americans is a stark example of the judicial assault upon the dignity of man.

Chief Justice Taney's first ruling, on African-American citizenship, would appear to have deprived the federal courts—including the Supreme Court itself—of jurisdiction to hear Dred Scott's suit and therefore required dismissal of the case. Despite this, Taney went forward to address Dred Scott's claim to emancipation, a move viewed by many as an inappropriate discussion of the actual merits of the case which Taney had claimed the Court had no jurisdiction to hear.[19] On this question, Taney asserted that the Constitution forbade the federal government from prohibiting slavery in the federal territories.[20] This ruling meant that the famous Missouri Compromise of the 1820s, limiting the extension of slavery into new U.S. territories, was invalid under the Constitution. Taney justified this position in part by asserting that the Due Process Clause of the Fifth Amendment contained a substantive right to own property in slaves.[21] Taney's position is indefensible because the Fifth Amendment prohibits the denial of "life, liberty, or property," only if done *without* due process of law," plainly allowing for denials of life, liberty, and property (including "property" in slaves) *with* due process of law.[22] Taney thus asserted that a *procedural* clause, which allows for the denial of property with due process of law, operated as a *substantive, non-procedural* bar against federal legislation prohibiting ownership of property in slaves even if the proper procedures for such a denial of property were granted or complied with by the federal government.

This marks the first appearance in U.S. Supreme Court history of the notorious doctrine known as "substantive due process," which holds that a plainly procedural provision of the Constitution has a plainly non-procedural, substantive content despite its clear language to the contrary.[23] It is quite revealing that Taney made no attempt to defend this obvious and deliberate misreading of the text and history of the Fifth Amendment Due Process Clause but merely stated it in a baldly conclusory fashion.[24] Nor did Taney make any serious attempt to reconcile this ruling with the long tradition of federal prohibitions of slavery in the federal territories dating back to the Northwest Ordinance of 1787 and thus predating even the ratification of the Constitution and the Bill of Rights. This activist and racist declaration of a constitutional right of one individual to enslave another is also a stark example of the judicial assault upon the dignity of man.

Why did the Court do what it did in *Dred Scott*? As an intensely politicized and hyper-activist decision, *Dred Scott* may be partially explained in terms of both the politics of the justices and the political climate of the nation in the 1850s. Significantly, seven of the nine justices deciding Dred Scott had been appointed by slave-owning Southern presidents.[25] And five of the nine justices were Southerners, all from slave-owing families.[26] In fact, only one justice, Benjamin Curtis, was neither a Southerner nor an appointee of a Southern, slave-owning president.[27] Therefore the Court's prejudice in favor of slavery is not surprising, though the unprecedented willingness to translate that prejudice into judicial policy-making may be. As for the political climate of the nation in the 1850s, it is worth noting that slavery was tied to both Southern economic self-interest and to Southern "nationalism" or identity politics. A court dominated by Southerners and appointees of Southerners faced a very real temptation both to protect the Southern slave-economy and to establish itself as friend of the "authentic" (i.e., pro-slavery and racist) South. Finally, the Democratic Party of the 1850s feared that its internal disagreements over slavery would divide— perhaps even destroy—the Party, and thus had a intense interest in removing the issue from the ordinary political area, something which many Democrats hoped that a judicial decision such as *Dred Scott* could do.[28] Notably, eight of the nine justices had been appointed by Democratic presidents, and seven of the justices continued to identify with that party affiliation.[29]

Dred Scott, of course, contained the seeds of its own destruction. The decision moved the United States further down the path to the Civil War, a conflict which ultimately led to the Reconstruction Amendments both abolishing slavery and guaranteeing African-American citizenship. But the *Dred Scott* decision, as judicial hyper-activism in violation of the constitutional limits of the judicial power and an assertion of an iniquitous substantive moral position at odds with America's Founding principles, did not die as fully as it deserved. Instead, the "spirit" of *Dred Scott* has found contemporary expression in the Supreme Court's abortion jurisprudence.

The Judicial Assault on the Right to Life: *Roe* and Abortion

Echoes of *Dred Scott* abound in the contemporary judiciary's assault upon the right to life and the broader American constitutional order in the U.S Supreme Court's infamous decision in *Roe v. Wade* (1973),[30] which first declared a putative constitutional "right" to abort (i.e., kill) unborn children, and in *Roe*'s progeny cases, including *Planned Parenthood v. Casey* (1992),[31] which reaffirmed the "central holding" of *Roe*. In *Roe*, as in *Dred Scott*, the Court both asserted a substantive due process right to violate another person's moral rights (in *Roe*, the right to abort an unborn child rather than to own a person as a slave) and interpreted the Constitution to exclude some individuals from the community of those entitled to equal concern and respect in the United States (in *Roe*, unborn children rather than African-Americans).

The operative facts of *Roe v. Wade* are as follows: "Jane Roe" (whose actual name was Norma McCorvey) was a poorly-educated, impoverished, and unmarried young woman who wanted to abort her unborn child, an act which was prohibited by law in the State of Texas where she lived.[32] With the aid of her attorney Sarah Weddington, Roe/McCorvey sued Henry Wade, district attorney for Dallas County, seeking to overturn the more than one-hundred year old Texas law that prohibited abortion and protected the life of unborn children except when necessary to save the life of the mother.[33] Weddington hoped to use the case to establish a broad constitutional right of a mother to kill her unborn child.[34]

The creation of such a broad right, of course, would require the invalidation of laws protecting the unborn in almost all fifty states.[35] Many of these laws were a century old and more[36] and had modified even older legal doctrines reaching centuries back to the English common law which viewed the killing of an unborn child after "quickening" (the common law term for the stage of fetal development when the mother first begins to feel fetal movement, usually occurring at about 16 to 18 weeks after conception) as a serious crime.[37] The moral insight which formed the basis for these laws was a growing awareness that each individual member of the human species—at whatever age or stage of physical development—is entitled to basic human rights to life, liberty, and the pursuit of happiness.[38]

"Jane Roe's" case was heard initially in federal court by a three-judge panel, which issued a surprisingly hyper-activist and morally obtuse opinion declaring unconstitutional the venerable and common-place Texas pro-life statute under the Fourteenth Amendment.[39] Notably, the three-judge panel asserted that the Constitution contains a "fundamental right" to have an abortion,[40] though, of course, no such right appears in the text or history of the Constitution. In fact, the Texas law protecting the unborn predated the Fourteenth Amendment by several years and had coexisted with it essentially unchanged for over a hundred years.[41]

The three-judge panel's decision was appealed to the U.S. Supreme Court, and the Court voted 7-2 to overturn centuries of legal tradition protecting the unborn and fabricate a new and broad constitutional right to kill unborn children, Justice Blackmun writing the majority opinion.[42] The Supreme Court's callous violation of the right to life of the unborn in *Roe* rested on *Dred Scott*'s doctrine of substantive due process, now with the doctrine extended from the Fifth Amendment Due Process Clause (which limits the federal government) to the Fourteenth Amendment's Due Process Clause (which limits the fifty states).[43] The Court in *Roe* also combined the doctrine of substantive due process with another judicial fabrication, the "right to privacy" created in *Griswold v. Connecticut*.[44]

Eight years before *Roe*, the Court in *Griswold* had created a novel and ill-defined "right to privacy" without a specific or clear foundation in the text of the Constitution[45] and rejected the Constitution's limitation of the right to privacy to the traditional rights protected by specific provisions of the Constitution—such as the Fourth Amendment with its prohibition of unreasonable searches of persons, houses, papers, and effects.[46] The Court located the "right to privacy" cryptically in what it called a "penumbra[], formed by emanations" from the Bill of Rights,[47] an odd phraseology and even odder form of constitutional analysis. The *Griswold* Court then invoked this newly-minted and textually-ungrounded right to privacy to invalidate a Connecticut statute criminalizing the use of contraceptives by married couples.[48] Justice Black, in his celebrated *Griswold* dissent, suggested that the Court in *Griswold* was adopting a method of constitutional analysis exceeding the judicial authority in violation of the separation of powers and federalism.[49] As Justice Black observed:

> There is no provision of the Constitution which either expressly or impliedly vests power in this Court to sit as a supervisory agency over acts of duly constituted legislative bodies and set aside their laws because of the Court's belief that the legislative policies adopted are unreasonable, unwise, arbitrary, capricious or irrational. The adoption of such a loose, flexible, uncontrolled standard for holding laws unconstitutional, if ever it is finally achieved, will amount to a great *unconstitutional* shift of power to the courts which I believe and am constrained to say will be bad for the courts and worse for the country. Subjecting federal and state laws to such an unrestrained and unrestrainable judicial control as to the wisdom of legislative enactments would, I fear, jeopardize the separation of governmental powers that the Framers set up and at the same time threaten to take away much of the power of States to govern themselves which the Constitution plainly intended them to have.[50]

In *Roe*, the Court stated in a baldly conclusory fashion that *Griswold*'s activist "right of privacy," now understood as part of the putative substantive content of the due process clause under *Dred Scott*'s doctrine,[51] is "broad enough to encompass a woman's decision whether or not to terminate her pregnancy"[52] (i.e., a mother's decision whether or not to kill her unborn child) and invalidated the laws that had traditionally protected the life of unborn children in at least 46 states.[53] The Court here also rejected traditions of judicial restraint that had grown up around the doctrine of substantive due process since *Dred Scott* in an effort to cabin its activist nature and harmonize the doctrine with the constitutional limits of the judicial power and the popular sovereignty foundations of the Constitution. In particular, the Court rejected the well-established *Palko* test that requires a substantive due process right to be "so rooted in tradition and the conscience of our people as to be ranked as fundamental."[54] Obviously abortion, which had been predominantly *criminalized* by statute for much of the nineteenth and twentieth century, an extension of earlier common law prohibitions, was not a "right" deeply rooted in the nation's tradition and conscience.

The Court in *Roe* applied a constitutional test known as "strict scrutiny" requiring that any restriction on abortion to be "necessary" to serve a "compelling state interest."[55] The Court applied this test along a sliding scale of both fetal development and evolving state interests. Applying strict scrutiny in this manner, the Court, in an openly-legislative fashion, crafted a trimester framework for abortion regulations: in the first trimester of pregnancy, the Court allowed no restrictions on abortion; in the second trimester of pregnancy, the Court allowed only those restrictions designed to promote the health of the mother; and in the third trimester, the Court allowed restrictions designed to protect the life of the unborn child as long as such restrictions contained an exception for the preservation of the life and health of the mother.[56]

In a companion case decided the same day as *Roe*, *Doe v. Bolton*,[57] the Court observed that the "factors [that] may relate to health" and thus to the health exception to third-trimester abortion restrictions include "all factors—physical, emotional, psychological, familial, and the woman's age—relevant to the well-being of the patient."[58] The Court in *Doe* also invalidated review procedures which required that an abortion performed to protect the life or health of the mother be approved by a hospital staff abortion committee and that the performing physician's medical judgement be confirmed by the independent examination of two other physicians.[59] Thus the "health exception" mandated by the Supreme Court appears to extend to beyond physical health into the nebulous realm of "emotional health," and the performing physician's judgment as to whether the preservation of the mother's "health," physical or emotional, requires an abortion appears to be a largely unreviewable exercise of his or her medical discretion. In sum, then, the Court's "health exception" is sweeping in its scope and largely vitiates the *Roe* Court's apparent allowance of abortion restrictions to protect the life of the unborn in the third trimester. Echoing *Dred Scott*, the Court ruled that there is a substantive due process right of one person to abort (i.e. kill) another, very similar to *Dred Scott*'s ruling that there is a substantive due process right of one person to hold another in bondage.

But what of the rights of unborn children under the Constitution? In *Dred Scott*, the Court ruled that free African-Americans descended from slaves could not be citizens as that term is used in the U.S. Constitution even if they were recognized by their states as citizens, thus in effect expelling African-Americans from the American political community. In the context of abortion, the rights of unborn children and their membership in the moral community of persons in the United States are implicated in at least two distinct ways: First, there is the question of whether fetuses are persons within the meaning of the word "person" in the Fourteenth Amendment and, second, there is the question of whether the protection of fetal life is a sufficiently compelling state interest to justify a broad prohibition of abortion—if abortion is indeed the kind of "fundamental right" which requires such a state interest to justify any restriction, as the Court asserted wrongly in *Roe*.

On the first question, the Fourteenth Amendment guarantees to all "person[s]" the "equal protection of the laws"[60] including the equal protection of the homicide laws. Of course, unborn children might be viewed as "persons" within the meaning of the Fourteenth Amendment and thus entitled to the protection of the homicide law.[61] Additionally, on the second question, even if unborn children were not viewed as persons as that term is used in the Fourteenth Amendment, they might be considered persons for purposes of the state justification for restrictions on abortion.[62] As noted, the Court in *Roe* applied a form of the constitutional test known as "strict scrutiny" to abortion restrictions and under this test should have upheld any restriction on abortion "necessary" to achieve a "compelling state interest." Protecting the life of unborn persons, of course, could easily be viewed as a "compelling state interest" and abortion restrictions could easily be viewed as "necessary" to serve that state interest. Thus unborn children could be viewed as persons for purposes of constitutional "state interest" analysis in the application of strict scrutiny under the Fourteenth Amendment, a view which would result in the judiciary upholding even under strict scrutiny those restrictions on abortion which states choose to enact as regulations "necessary" to serve the "compelling state interest" of protecting the life of unborn persons.

In *Roe*, reflecting the "spirit" of *Dred Scott*, the Supreme Court excluded unborn children from the moral community of persons in the United States, at least in the context of abortion. First, the Court held that the word "person" in the Fourteenth Amendment does not include unborn persons and thus unborn children have no rights under the Fourteenth Amendment, such as the right to the equal protection of the laws that might have required states to extend the protection of their homicide laws "equally" to unborn child.[63] While this narrow view of the meaning of "person" in the Fourteenth Amendment can be plausibly defended as an exercise in judicial restraint, it is notable that the Court's reading of the due process clause in *Roe* was neither narrow nor restrained. Thus the Court was strategically restrained in reading the word "person" in the Fourteenth Amendment to deny the rights of the unborn and strategically active in reading the word "liberty" in the Fourteenth Amendment as a matter of substantive due process to create a legally-ungrounded right to abortion.[64]

Secondly, the Supreme Court held that the protection of unborn children is not a compelling state interest justifying restrictions on abortion prior to the third trimester[65] and even in the third trimester, as noted above, abortion restrictions must have an open-ended health exception likely rendering futile any state attempt to protect the life of the unborn.[66] Thus the Court concluded that states may not consider unborn children "persons" under state law if the legal effect of that consideration is to restrict abortion in ways prohibited by the Court in *Roe*.

An unborn child, then, clearly an actual person entitled to basic human rights, is not a "Fourteenth Amendment" constitutional person entitled to the equal protection of the laws and cannot be considered a "state interest" constitutional person presenting a sufficient state interest for purposes of justifying abortion restrictions under the holdings of *Roe*. In sum, paralleling *Dred Scott*, the U.S. Supreme Court ruled that unborn children are not persons for purposes of constitutional analysis in the context of abortion, an attempt to expel the unborn from the moral community of persons entitled to equal concern and respect very similar to *Dred Scott*'s ruling on the question of African-American citizenship.

In *Roe* and *Doe*, then, the Supreme Court, without legal foundation and by simple super-legislative majority vote of unelected justices, established what amounted to a regime of abortion on demand in the United States. As Justice White described the decision in dissent, it was an "exercise of raw judicial power" utterly unsupported by the "language or history of the Constitution" with "scarcely any reason or authority behind it."[67] Since the Court's decision in *Roe*, the United States has often averaged well over a million abortions a year. The loss of human life in the decades following *Roe* is simply staggering—and rivals the mass murders committed by totalitarian regimes such as the Soviet Union and Nazi Germany in the twentieth century. Not surprisingly, *Roe v. Wade* generated tremendous controversy just as *Dred Scott v. Sandford* did before it. *Roe*, as with *Dred Scott*, combines both judicial hyper-activism in violation of the Constitution's governmental design with a callous disregard for the basic rights of vulnerable members of the human family, a callousness at odds with the founding moral principles of American constitutional government: that all men are created equal and endowed by their creator with unalienable rights to life, liberty and the pursuit of happiness.

The Judicial Assault on the Right to Life: *Casey* and Abortion

In 1992, after nineteen years of intense post-*Roe* controversy, the Supreme Court narrowly voted to reaffirm the judicially-fabricated right to abortion in *Planned Parenthood v. Casey*.[68] Significantly a plurality of the Court made up of Justices O'Connor, Kennedy, and Souter—each of whom had been appointed by pro-life and anti-*Roe* presidents—wrote a joint opinion "reaffirming" *Roe*'s "central holding" while replacing *Roe*'s complex trimester framework with an new approach linking the scope of the abortion license to fetal viability, the stage of development at which a fetus is capable of survival outside the womb. The *Casey* joint plurality opinion provided the crucial "swing" votes between the two justices who advocated strict adherence to *Roe* and the four justices who advocated overruling *Roe*. The *Casey* plurality opinion therefore determined the actual legal conclusions in the case.

On the question of substantive abortion law, the *Casey* plurality asserted that any restriction placing an "undue burden" on the right to abortion prior to fetal viability is unconstitutional, and it defined an "undue burden" as any abortion regulation with the "purpose or effect" of "plac[ing] a substantial obstacle in the path of a woman seeking an abortion."[69] Under this test, the plurality voted to uphold a number of minor regulations on abortion—such as a 24-hour waiting period, a requirement of informed consent, and a parental consent requirement with a judicial bypass option—but made plain that more significant restrictions would be declared unconstitutional.[70] Notably, the plurality voted to strike down a spousal notification provision as an "undue burden" on the grounds that husbands in some cases might attempt to deter their wives from having abortion with threats of financial or physical retaliation.[71] The plurality also asserted that after the fetus achieves viability the state may prohibit abortion to protect the life of the unborn, but that such prohibitions must have an exception for the health and life of the mother.[72] Again, in light of *Doe v. Bolton*'s sweeping definition of the abortion "health" exception it is unlikely that any meaningful restrictions on abortion protecting the life of the unborn will be considered constitutional by the federal courts and thus unlikely that states may provide any real protections for the unborn from the mothers and doctors who may choose to kill them.

In reaching its legal conclusions, the *Casey* plurality strongly reaffirmed both *Dred Scott*'s doctrine of substantive due process and *Roe*'s repudiation of any restrained methodology which would link substantive due process rights to long-standing American legal traditions thereby moderating its activist effect. Instead, the *Casey* plurality, as with the *Roe* court, adopted an approach allowing for the creation of new rights the justices may happen to find politically attractive without any requirement of a legal foundation. Indeed, in defense of its reaffirmation of *Roe*'s anti-life and legally-ungrounded holding, the plurality articulated a sweeping new judicial invention, a "mega-right" to antinomian individual autonomy expressed in what critics have often called the "mystery passage": "At the heart of liberty is the right to define one's own concept of existence, of meaning, of the universe, and of the mystery of human life. Beliefs about these matters could not define the attributes of personhood were they formed under compulsion of the State."[73] As shall be discussed, this conclusory, sweeping, and philosophically illiterate statement of hyper-libertarian individual autonomy—one inconsistent with centuries of communitarian morals legislation in the Anglo-American world and unsupported by constitutional text, history, and tradition—has implications not only for abortion but also for other life issue such as that of physician-assisted suicide.

The Casey plurality also defended its reaffirmation of *Roe* with a novel form of *stare decisis* analysis. *Stare decisis* is the legal doctrine concerning adherence to precedents, and it is based on the simple view that it is sometimes more important that the law be settled than that it be right—for obvious reasons of legal stability, continuity, and predictability.[74] Thus *stare decisis* principally concerns the question of when a court should adhere to a judicial decision that is either mistaken or potentially mistaken in the interest of legal settlement rather than overrule and thus unsettle the decision in order to correct it. The Supreme Court has routinely said that *stare decisis* is at its weakest in cases interpreting the Constitution (as opposed to, say, cases interpreting statutes) because the only means of correcting judicial mistakes in constitutional cases is constitutional amendment or an overruling by the judiciary.[75] If the latter means of correction were usually foreclosed by a strong form of *stare decisis*, mistaken constitutional decisions could be overturned only by the unwieldy mechanism of constitutional amendment and thus (eventually) a great number of mistaken constitutional decisions would be permanently entrenched in American constitutional law.

Despite the traditional view of the weakness of constitutional *stare decisis*, the *Casey* plurality invoked the doctrine in a surprisingly strong form, citing multiple reasons for reaffirming *Roe* even if *Roe* was wrong as originally decided, as the plurality's very invocation of *stare decisis* suggests one or more of its members may have thought. The plurality's first reason for adhering to *Roe* was their view that *Roe*'s doctrine had not proved "unworkable" or difficult to apply.[76] The *Casey* plurality asserted this position despite the fact that the plurality was itself replacing *Roe*'s trimester framework with a new framework of analysis, both suggesting the earlier framework was problematic and undercutting the plurality's broader reliance on *stare decisis*.[77] The *Casey* plurality also asserted a second reason for reaffirming *Roe*: The importance of the reliance interests of individuals who had organized their sexual activities in light of *Roe*—and who were depending "on the availability of abortion in the event that contraception should fail."[78] This assertion is refuted by the simple fact that such reliance must be at least *reasonable* for purposes of *stare decisis*,[79] and no one could have relied reasonably on the continued availability of abortion under *Roe* in light of its controversality and the continuing litigation on the question, as the Court's own five-to-four vote narrowly retaining the right to abortion in *Casey* itself conclusively demonstrates.

A third reason in the plurality's view for adhering to *Roe* was the absence of any evolution in the law suggesting a doctrinal erosion of *Roe*.[80] This view is insupportable in light of the *Bowers* decision in 1986,[81] a case in which a majority of the Court endorsed a narrow tradition-based form of substantive due process analysis incompatible with *Roe*'s broad ahistorical approach,[82] a clear case of doctrinal erosion of the legal foundation of *Roe* and one that was inexplicably ignored by the plurality. A fourth reason for adherence to *Roe* asserted by the plurality was that *Roe* had been subject to intense criticism since 1973 and that "to overrule under fire in the absence of the most compelling reason to reexamine a watershed decision would subvert the Court's legitimacy beyond any serious question."[83] Note that this last point suggests—paradoxically—that the *more* criticism a mistaken judicial decision receives from the citizenry and their elected officials, the *less* likely the Court is to overrule it in the putative interest of preserving judicial "legitimacy." The reverse view—that courts which make mistakes and dig in their heels in the face of justified public criticism erode their legitimacy much more than courts which admit error and correct their mistakes—apparently did not strike the plurality as persuasive.[84] Nor did the plurality consider the Supreme Court's own earlier suggestion that judicial decisions that usurp legislative authority are entitled to limited precedential weight.[85]

The *Casey* plurality also described *Roe*'s legally-ungrounded fabrication of a constitutional right to abortion as "resolv[ing]" an "intensely divisive controversy,"[86] asserting that "the Court's interpretation of the Constitution [had] call[ed] the contending sides of a national controversy to end their national division by accepting a common mandate rooted in the Constitution."[87] This extraordinary mischaracterization of *Roe* prompted Justice Scalia to observe in his opinion that:

> [T]o portray *Roe* as the statesmanlike "settlement" of a divisive issue, a jurisprudential Peace of Westphalia that is worth preserving, is nothing less than Orwellian. *Roe* fanned into life an issue that has inflamed our national politics in general, and has obscured with its smoke the selection of Justices to this Court, in particular, ever since. And by keeping us in the abortion-umpiring business, it is the perpetuation of that disruption, rather than of any *Pax Roeana* that the Court's new majority decrees.[88]

As Justice Scalia also rightly observed, abortion has no serious claim to constitutionally protected status because "(1) the Constitution says absolutely nothing about it, and (2) the longstanding traditions of American society have permitted it to be legally proscribed."[89] In fact, *Roe*, far from enforcing a "mandate rooted in the Constitution," can itself be thought to have violated the constitutional structure by judicially "amending" the Constitution to create a right to abortion and usurping the legislative authority of Congress and the fifty states.[90] Finally, Justice Scalia acknowledged the obvious parallels between the Court's decision in *Roe* and its decision in *Dred Scott*, stating that *Dred Scott*, "covered [the Court] with dishonor and deprived [it] of legitimacy."[91] The same thing, Justice Scalia intimated, can be said for *Roe*—and for *Casey*.

In sum, after nineteen years of controversy and after seven post-*Roe* judicial appointments by Republican presidents,[92] the concerted reform efforts to restore the Constitution's true meaning and reestablish the authority of the Congress and state legislatures to protect the life of the unborn children failed—and *Roe*'s central holding was "reaffirmed" by a narrow five-to-four vote. Hundreds of thousands of abortions continued to be performed each year in the U.S., and

America's promise in the Declaration of Independence to protect the natural rights of all the members of the human family remains unfulfilled.

The Judicial Assault of the Right to Life: Partial-Birth Abortion

Partial-birth abortion is an especially gruesome abortion procedure in which a unborn child is partially-delivered feet-first and then brutally killed while his or her head remains within the mother's body—a procedure bordering on infanticide. This abortion procedure is also known as "dilation and extraction" abortion or "D&X" abortion. As Justice Kennedy describes it:

> [Partial-birth abortion] can be used, as a general matter, after 19 weeks gestation because the fetus has become so developed that it may survive intact partial delivery from the uterus into the vagina. In the D&X, the abortionist initiates the woman's natural delivery process by causing the cervix of the woman to be dilated, sometimes over a sequence of days. The fetus' arms and legs are delivered outside the uterus while the fetus is alive; witnesses to the procedure report seeing the body of the fetus moving outside the woman's body. At this point, the abortion procedure has the appearance of a live birth. As stated by one group of physicians, "[a]s the physician manually performs breech extraction of the body of a live fetus, excepting the head, she continues in the apparent role of an obstetrician delivering a child." With only the head of the fetus remaining in utero, the abortionist tears open the skull. According to Dr. Martin Haskell, a leading proponent of the procedure, the appropriate instrument to be used at this stage of the abortion is a pair of scissors. Witnesses report observing the portion of the fetus outside the woman react to the skull penetration. The abortionist then inserts a suction tube and vacuums out the developing brain and other matter found within the skull. The process of making the size of the fetus' head smaller is given the clinically neutral term "reduction procedure." Brain death does not occur until after the skull invasion, and, according to Dr. Carhart, the heart of the fetus may continue to beat for minutes after the contents of the skull are vacuumed out. The abortionist next completes the delivery of a dead fetus, intact except for the damage to the head and the missing contents of the skull.[93]

Growing awareness the barbaric practice of partial-birth abortion in the 1990s led over 30 states to pass laws prohibiting it.[94] The lower federal courts, following the activist lead of the U.S. Supreme Court in the area of abortion, typically struck down these popular legislative prohibitions of quasi-infanticide.[95]

In 2000, a majority of the Court in *Stenberg v. Carhart* adopted the *Casey* plurality's viability framework and invoked it to invalidate Nebraska's ban partial-birth abortion.[96] Justice Breyer, writing for the Court—in a startling display of inhumanity—affirmed that there is a constitutional right to "abort" or kill even partially-born children and speciously asserted that Nebraska's statute was unconstitutional.

The Court's analysis in *Stenberg* asserted two independent grounds for invalidating the Nebraska statute under the Court's *Casey* analysis. First, the Court held that the statute violated the abortion license because it lacked a "health" exception.[97] This view is untenable in light of the substantial evidence showing that partial-birth abortion is never a safer option than other abortion procedures and that, even if it were a safer option, alternative abortion procedures always provide for a "safe" abortion, thus making a health exception unnecessary.[98] Even so, the Court in the face of these persuasive arguments disingenuously demanded a "health" exception to any partial-birth abortion ban. It is, of course, unclear whether any meaningful restriction on partial-birth abortion could survive the creation of health exception if the Court invokes *Doe v. Bolton* as the standard, given that decision's extremely broad view of the health exception and the deference it accords to abortionists.

Second, the Court held that the Nebraska statute violated the judicially-mandated abortion license because its prohibition of abortion, as the Court (mis)read the statute, extended beyond the narrow class of partial-birth abortions to other very common forms of abortion—such as "dilation and evacuation" or "D&E" abortion—performed while the unborn child remains wholly in utero and involving the dismemberment of the fetus within the mother's body and removal of the fetus's body parts piece by piece.[99] Significantly, the Nebraska statute defined the "partial-birth" aspect of its prohibition of partial-birth abortion as "partially deliver[ing] a living unborn child" and also defined that latter term as "deliberately and intentionally delivering into the vagina a living unborn child, or a substantial portion thereof."[100] Justice Breyer for the majority wrote that: "We do not understand how one could distinguish, using this language, between D&E (where a [severed] foot or arm id drawn through the cervix) and D&X (where the body up to the head is drawn through the cervix)."[101] The Court thus held that such a broad restriction on abortion was an "undue burden" and thus violated the Constitution.[102]

Justice Kennedy and Thomas in dissent recognized that this reading of the Nebraska statute is implausible in the extreme given the statute's repeated use of the phrases "partial-birth abortion" and "partial delivery" of an "living born human child" in defining the form of abortion which it sought to prohibit, language clearly aimed at the D&X abortion procedure replicating the birth process until the final moment when the fetus is killed just short of actual birth.[103] This language seems clearly intended to exclude from the statute's prohibition abortions involving the wholly internal dismemberment of the unborn child and the removal of its severed body parts one at a time—a form of procedure which involves no "partial-birth" or "partial-delivery" of a living unborn child mimicking the birth process. The majority of the Supreme Court, however, preferred an implausible reading of the statute and the second ground for invalidation that that reading provided.

In dissent, Justice Scalia observed:

> I am optimistic enough to believe that, one day, *Stenberg* v. *Carhart* will be assigned its rightful place in the history of this Court's jurisprudence beside . . . *Dred Scott*. The method of killing a human child—one cannot even accurately

say an entirely unborn human child—proscribed by this statute is so horrible that the most clinical description of it evokes a shudder of revulsion. And the Court must know (as most state legislatures banning this procedure have concluded) that demanding a "health exception"—which requires the abortionist to assure himself that, in his expert medical judgment, this method is, in the case at hand, marginally safer than others (how can one prove the contrary beyond a reasonable doubt?)—is to give live-birth abortion free rein. The notion that the Constitution of the United States, designed, among other things, "to establish Justice, insure domestic Tranquility, . . . and secure the Blessings of Liberty to ourselves and our Posterity," prohibits the States from simply banning this visibly brutal means of eliminating our half-born posterity is quite simply absurd.[104]

In 2003, Congress—responding to the Court's decision in *Stenberg*—passed a federal ban on partial-birth abortion. This federal statute addressed the Court's stated concerns (i) by including a congressional finding of fact, based upon extensive congressional hearings, that a partial-birth abortion is never necessary to preserve a mother's health and (ii) by attempting to define "partial-birth" abortion with greater precision to minimize the danger of any potential misreading of the statute. In 2007, the Supreme Court upheld this federal ban by a narrow five-to-four margin in the case of *Gonzales v. Carhart*, Justice Kennedy delivering the Court's opinion.[105] It is notable that of the five justices who voted to invalidate the Nebraska law in *Stenberg*, four remained on the Court during the 2006–2007 term and all four voted to invalidate the federal statute as well. Of the four justices who voted to uphold the Nebraska law in *Stenberg*, three remained on the Court to consider the constitutionality of the federal ban and all three also voted to uphold it—joined by the Court's two newest justices, appointed by President George W. Bush, to make a five-justice majority.

In *Gonzales v. Carhart*, the Court held that the federal statute's lack of a health exception did not render the statute unconstitutional "on its face" (i.e., in its entirety). The Court reasoned that any medical uncertainty surrounding the issue of whether partial-birth abortion is medically necessary in some small number of cases to preserve a mother's health should not preclude a legislature from passing a general ban on the practice—especially in light of the availability of safe alternative forms of abortion.[106] The Court thus ruled that the federal ban should be upheld as a general matter, given its indisputably wide range of constitutionally-sound applications. The Court further ruled that some of the federal statute's more specific applications could be invalidated but only upon a demonstration that clearly-defined medical conditions exist which require the performance of a partial-birth abortion to preserve the mother's health.[107] If such medical conditions do exist and can be demonstrated, the federal ban would be held unconstitutional "as applied" to those conditions. The Court, in short, reasoned that the federal statute should not be invalidated as generally applied and that health-exception challenges should be limited to specific applications of the statute that might prove problematic as a matter of medical necessity upon closer examination. Future litigation, then, will determine whether and to what extent the federal ban is unconstitutional on medical necessity grounds in some of its specific applications to particular medical circumstances. It is, of course, unclear whether any such "as-applied" challenges will be successful or whether any "health exception" to the statute they may create will ultimately be narrow or broad in scope.

The Court further reasoned that the federal statute had avoided any potential imprecision in describing partial-birth abortion that may have been present in the Nebraska statute. This was so in part because the federal ban used the narrower phrase "deliver[y] [of] a living fetus," instead of the broader phrase "deliver[y] [of] a living unborn child, or a substantial portion thereof" and thus made even clearer than did the Nebraska statute that it was the partial extraction of an intact living fetus rather than removal of individual fetal body parts that the statute sought to prohibit.[108] The federal statute, unlike the Nebraska statute, also identified partial-birth by reference to "specific anatomical landmarks" to which the living fetus must be delivered—such as the fetal "trunk past the navel" in a breach (or feet-first) presentation—rendering even more implausible any (mis)reading of the ban as extending beyond the narrow category of partial-birth abortions to other forms of abortion that involve dismemberment of the fetus in utero and the removal of fetal body parts in pieces.[109] Moreover, the Court recognized that the federal ban requires that the partial-birth of the intact living fetus be intentional (not inadvertent) and be done for the purpose of performing an ultimate "overt act" designed to kill the fetus—such as piercing or crushing the fetal cranium.[110] The Court concluded that such an indisputably precise ban on partial-birth abortion could not be read to restrict in any way the most common forms of abortion—where nothing occurs which resembles an intentional partial birth past the navel of an intact living fetus for the purpose of performing an overt act in order to kill the fetus. Therefore the federal ban, restricted narrowly to partial-birth abortion, does not impose any "undue burden" on the abortion license in violation of the Court's abortion holdings.

In sum, the Supreme Court held that a very narrowly-crafted ban on the inhumane practice on partial-birth abortion is facially constitutional, though still subject to potential "as applied" challenges on health exception grounds. *Gonzales v. Carhart*, then, represents a small, but important, victory in defense of the sanctity of human life and provides an opportunity for state legislatures to adopt state bans on partial-birth abortion modeled on the federal ban approved by the Supreme Court. It is also notable that the Court's newest justices, Chief Justice Roberts and Justice Alito joined Justice Kennedy's opinion both upholding the federal ban on partial-birth abortion and applying the *Casey* decision's analysis, though without expressing any opinion as to whether *Casey* was rightly decided in 1992 or whether it should be adhered to as a precedent in future cases.[111]

The Judicial Assault on the Right to Life: Explaining the Abortion Decisions

Why has the Court created a broad and legally-ungrounded right to abortion in decisions such as *Roe* and *Casey*? These politicized, activist, and gravely unjust decisions may be explained, at least partially, in terms of judicial politics and the political dynamics at work between courts and elite opinion in the United States. The contemporary judiciary is especially sensitive to and reflective of elite opinion in the United States, and elite opinion both supports a broad substantive right to abortion and an activist judiciary which will impose elite values on the American people, two positions which converge in decisions such as *Roe* and *Casey*.

First, as Lawrence M. Friedman observes, the unelected and electorally-unaccountable Supreme Court " remain[s] a strongly independent body" from popular opinion and "its sensitivity to enlightened [i.e, elite] opinion" should not be underestimated.[112] John Hart Ely explains, this "sensitivity" to elite opinion is tied in part to the class-based policy preferences of judges, who naturally chose substantive values in constitutional interpretation that reflect their own preferences. As Ely writes:

> [T]here [is] systematic *bias* in judicial choice of fundamental values, unsurprisingly in favor of the values of upper-middle, professional class from which most lawyers and judges, and for that matter most moral philosophers, are drawn. People understandably think that what is most important to them is what is most important, and people like us [judges and lawyers and legal academics] are no exception. Thus the list of values the Court and commentators have tended to enshrine as fundamental is the a list with which readers of this book will have little trouble identifying: expression, association, education, academic freedom, the privacy of the home, personal autonomy, even the right not to be locked in a stereotypically female sex role and supported by one's husband.[113]

Or, as Justice Scalia, colorfully puts it: "When the Court takes sides in the culture wars, it tends to be with the knights rather than the villeins [i.e. "peasants"] —and more specifically with the Templars, reflecting the views and values of the lawyer class from which the Court's Members are drawn."[114] Thus built-in to the justice selection process—which favors the well-educated graduates of elite law schools—is a class bias towards the values favored by upper-middle professional and law-trained elites.

Second, upper-middle class professional elites in the United States, including lawyers and judges, are often strongly supportive of "progressive," antinomian values such as abortion rights, as Ely's statement above also suggests. In fact, as sociologist James Davison Hunter's study of the "culture wars" recognizes, "the progressive [political] alliances [in favor of abortion among other things] tend to draw popular support among the highly educated professionally committed upper middle classes, while the orthodox [i.e., socially conservative and pro-life] alliances tend to draw from the lower middle and working classes."[115] Indeed, as John C. Jeffries, Jr., biographer of Justice Lewis Powell, one of the justices joining Justice Blackmun's original *Roe* opinion, writes: The fact "[t]hat Lewis Powell personally opposed restrictions on abortion was almost predictable" because "he was a well-educated, non-Catholic, upper-class male—a group then, as now, overwhelmingly supportive of" abortion.[116] Moreover, progressive" attitudes toward sexual conduct and the role of women common—attitudes common among professional elites—are viewed by many, including Justices of the Supreme Court, as providing putative justifications for abortion.[117]

Indeed, the primary sources of the moral blind spot that afflicts so many contemporary progressives on the issue of the rights of unborn children may be found in two areas. The first of these is the obvious self-interest in engaging in sexual activity without incurring the risk unplanned childbearing, which tends to corrupt the moral sense on the question of fetal rights. This dynamic clearly parallels that of the Southern economic self-interest in the maintenance of slavery so corrupting to the Southern moral sense in the 1840s and 50s. The second of these is the misguided view that support of feminism (and solidarity with women) requires support for abortion, a view which also distorts progressive moral reasoning on the issue of fetal rights. There is also a clear parallel here to the link between the nascent Southern "nationalism" of the mid-nineteenth century and support for slavery.

Third, upper-middle class professional elites in the United States, especially lawyers and judges, are often strongly supportive of judicial activism. As Richard Parker notes, "in the minds and hearts of most American constitutional lawyers, an [a]nti-[p]opulist sensibility appears to predominate," a sensibility which views ordinary Americans and the legislatures they elect with deep distrust while viewing unelected federal judges much more favorably.[118] Or, as Mary Ann Glendon observes, the "[c]ommon [elite] attitude that the educated are better equipped to govern than the masses finds its institutional expression in a disdain for ordinary politics and the legislative process, and a preference for extending the authority of courts, the branch of government to which [elites] have easiest access."[119] This "progressive" tendency towards elitist, anti-populism—combined with the natural institutional self-interest of the judiciary in expanding its own political power—predisposes the federal judiciary in the direction of judicial activism.

In sum, it is not especially surprising that an unelected institution staffed with highly-educated upper-middle class professionals trained by elite law schools, who are predisposed to hold progressive values, would reflect progressive support for both the abortion license and judicial activism, combining those views in *Roe*, *Casey*, and *Stenberg*.

The Judicial Assault on the Right to Life: Physician-Assisted Suicide

The right to life, of course, concerns more than the value of the nascent human life of the unborn. The right to life also extends to those on the other end of life's natural spectrum—the aged, the infirm, and the dying. The Court's abortion jurisprudence has obvious implications for human life issues such as these, surrounding the so-called "right to die," involving issues of physician-assisted suicide and voluntary and involuntary euthanasia. Since *Roe*, the Supreme Court has located the "right to privacy" in the Due Process Clauses of the Fifth and Fourteenth Amendments, a version of *Dred Scott*'s original doctrine used to create a right to own slaves. As noted, this a form of the doctrine of "substantive due process," a view which asserts that the *procedural* clauses of the Fifth and Fourteenth Amendments somehow have a substantive content despite their clear language to the contrary (i.e, due *process*) which limit the provisions to procedural rights.

Importantly, the Court has not settled on a single methodology for determining the content of the substantive rights which it asserts are protected by the Due Process Clauses. In many cases, the Court has invoked a traditional and restrictive test intended to limit judicial discretion, requiring, for instance, that any substantive due process right be "deeply rooted in the nation's history and tradition" as specifically described.[120] In other cases, the Court has employed a more fluid methodology, one that maximizes the discretion of the Court to fabricate new rights a majority of the justices happen to find politically attractive.[121] *Roe* itself is an example of such a case, one in which the Court refused to allow legal tradition to determine the scope of abortions rights and instead simply asserted a series of political arguments in favor of abortion as the basis for its decision. Moreover, the "mega-right" articulated in *Casey*'s "mystery passage" provides precedential support (however itself legally-ungrounded) for the latter view, stating that the substantive content of the Due Process Clauses contains the "right to define one's own concept of existence, of meaning, of the universe, and of the mystery of human life."[122]

The Court's sweeping formulation of individual autonomy in the "mystery passage" in *Casey* provoked the Ninth Circuit in 1996 to invalidate the State of Washington's prohibition of physician-assisted suicide, holding that the decision of a terminally ill patient to commit suicide with a physician's aid was encompassed within the "right to define one's own concept of existence, of meaning, of the universe, and of the mystery of human life."[123] The Ninth Circuit relied on *Casey* and also on a earlier Supreme Court decision, *Cruzan*, which had assumed the existence of a substantive due process right—grounded in legal tradition—of a competent person to refuse unwanted medical treatment even if such refusal might cause that person's death.[124] Notably, the Ninth Circuit's ultimate decision was made by an eleven-judge *en banc* panel, which voted 8-3 to invalidate the Washington law.[125] It is remarkable that a decision so very activist in nature and so quick to reject the traditional moral condemnation of suicide achieved such a large majority of the *en banc* panel.

The Supreme Court in *Glucksberg* unanimously reversed the Ninth Circuit.[126] The majority employed the "deeply rooted in the nation's history and tradition" test to determine the constitutional status of physician-assisted suicide and concluded that the asserted right to physician-assisted suicide was not deeply rooted in America's history and tradition and therefore not a fundamental right entitled to heightened scrutiny.[127] As the majority rightly noted, physician-assisted suicide was not only *not* recognized as a traditional right, instead it had been traditionally criminalized for centuries, a tradition of criminalization that continued in 49 states at the time *Glucksberg* was decided and so continues today.[128] The Court pointedly refused to apply *Casey*'s sweeping "mega-right" with its invitation simply to decide the question of physician-assisted suicide as a matter of judicial policy-making without legal foundation[129]—implicitly recognizing that the latter approach would constitute an exercise of judicial discretion corrosive of the Constitution's separation of powers and federalism norms.[130] The Court also rightly questioned whether constitutionalizing a right to physician-assisted suicide might in fact create recurring situations where individuals felt pressured by doctors, family members, or others to commit suicide—and eventually in practice create a regime of involuntary euthanasia.[131]

The Supreme Court in *Glucksberg* also distinguished *Cruzan*, which concerned not a novel right to commit suicide, but rather the traditional right, "deeply rooted in the Nation's history," to refuse unwanted medical treatment, a right very different from a right to commit suicide.[132] In fact, the traditions of the English common law both criminalized suicide[133] and recognized a right to refuse unwanted medical treatment,[134] a position reflecting the traditional moral distinction between the immoral choice to end one's life (suicide) and the (potentially) moral choice to avoid burdensome life-sustaining medical treatments, a decision which might cause or hasten one's death as a collateral matter or side effect, but one which does not (necessarily) involve the kind of direct choice against life properly viewed as suicidal and immoral.[135] The Supreme Court in its *Cruzan* and *Glucksberg* decisions has followed this traditional moral and legal distinction, assuming that the traditional right to refuse medical treatment is a constitutional right while rightly refusing to constitutionalize any (non-traditional) right to commit suicide.

Glucksberg's holding, however, may be in some jeopardy. This is so for at least two reasons, one concerning doctrinal erosion and a second concerning the influence of elite opinion on the decisions of the Supreme Court. First, the Court's principal basis for rejecting a right to physician-assisted suicide was its use of the traditional and restrained "deeply rooted in the nation's history" substantive due process test.[136] The application of this test has been called into question by a recent decision, *Lawrence v. Texas* (2003), which invoked the *Casey* "mystery" passage approach to substantive due process and overruled *Bowers v. Hardwick* (1986), which had used the traditional "deeply rooted in nation's history" test.[137] In *Bowers*, the Court had rejected a claim that the due process clause contained a substantive right to sexual privacy including the right to engage in sodomitical sex acts, citing the predominant legal traditions criminalizing such behavior as evidence that the asserted interest was not a right "deeply rooted" in history.[138] The *Lawrence* Court, seventeen years later, was willing to create such a right and expressly overruled *Bowers,* rejecting its tradition-based and restrained substantive due process methodology.[139] Significantly, *Lawrence* failed even to mention *Glucksberg*, but the decision arguably erodes *Glucksberg's* principal rationale in a restrained and historically-oriented substantive due process methodology.

Second, there is substantial and likely growing support for physician-assisted suicide among progressive elites in the United States. For instance, an eminent and influential group of liberal legal and political philosophers—Ronald Dworkin, Thomas Nagel, Robert Nozick, John Rawls, Thomas Scanlon, and Judith Jarvis Thomson—wrote one of the amicus briefs in support of the right to physician-suicide filed in the *Glucksberg* litigation.[140] There is good reason to think that this prominent elite support for a "right to die" may be reflected ultimately in the decision-making of the courts. Again, it is notable here that the Ninth Circuit *en banc* panel voted 8-3 to declare a constitutional right to physician-assisted suicide in 1996. The recent case of Terry Schiavo should give us little enough confidence in the judgment of judges, either state or federal.

What is to be Done? Lincoln as a Guide

The U.S. Supreme Court's assaults on the right to life in decisions such as *Roe* and *Casey* undermine the American constitutional system in at least three conceptually distinct ways: First, these decisions simply misinterpret the Constitution—finding rights to abortion where none exist and entrenching constitutional mistakes in the case law of the Supreme Court. *Roe* and *Casey*, then, as mistakes about constitutional meaning—which have the force of law—do damage to the integrity of the Constitution rightly interpreted. Second, these decisions exceed the judicial authority granted to the Court by the Constitution and encroach on the spheres of legislative authority established for elected officials in Congress and the fifty states. Thus *Roe* and *Casey* violate fundamental constitutional structures—such as the separation of powers, federalism, and representative democracy—which limit the authority of the Supreme Court.[141] And, third, these decisions are acts of the gravest injustice directly conflicting with the moral foundations of the Constitution: the security of the equal rights of all human beings to life, liberty, and the pursuit of happiness. *Roe* and *Casey* therefore erode the moral legitimacy of the American constitutional order.

The doctrine of judicial supremacy holds that the Supreme Court is the ultimate institutional expositor of the meaning of the Constitution and its interpretations of the Constitution are to be followed by other governmental actors within the constitutional system—whether those interpretations are right or wrong.[142] Judicial supremacy is widely accepted today, though it was controversial at the Founding and throughout much of the nineteenth and even early twentieth century.[143] Still, even if one accepts judicial supremacy in some form, what are responsible citizens and their elected officials to do when decisions of the Supreme Court go beyond "mere" mistakes about constitutional meaning and involve judicial violations of constitutional norms that limit the judicial branch and/or conflict with the very natural rights the Constitution was created to protect? Should the doctrine of judicial supremacy be adhered to without qualification even in such extreme cases? Or may the president and

Congress, at least in some circumstances, act to protect the Constitution and its moral foundations from the un- or anti-constitutional decisions of the courts?[144]

Abraham Lincoln—a man who faced the first great judicial assault upon the dignity of man in *Dred Scott*—can provide valuable guidance on these questions. In the aftermath of *Dred Scott*, Lincoln often spoke on questions concerning the judicial power, the constitutional design, and the deference to which decisions such as *Dred Scott* are entitled. The following three passages from Lincon's speeches on the *Dred Scott* decision are representative of his views:

> If this important decision [*Dred Scott*] had been made by the unanimous concurrence of the judges, and without any apparent partisan bias and in accordance with legal public expectation, and with the steady practice of the departments throughout our history, and had been in no part, based on assumed historical facts, which are not really true or, if wanting in some of these, had been affirmed and reaffirmed, it might be factious, even revolutionary, to not acquiesce in it. But when we find it wanting in all these claims to public confidence, it is not resistance, it is not factious, it is not even disrespectful, to treat it as not having yet quite established a settled doctrine for the country.[145]

I do not forget the position assumed by some that constitutional questions are to be decided by the Supreme Court, nor do I deny that such decisions must be binding in any case upon the parties to a suit as to the object of that suit, while they are also entitled to very high respect and consideration in all parallel cases by all other departments of the Government. And while it is obviously possible that such decision may be erroneous in any given case, still the evil effect following it, being limited to that particular case, with the chance that it may be overruled and never become a precedent for other cases, can better be borne than could the evils of a different practice. At the same time, the candid citizen must confess that if the policy of the Government upon vital questions affecting the whole people is to be irrevocably fixed by decisions of the Supreme Court, the instant they are made in ordinary litigation between parties in personal actions the people will have ceased to be their own rulers, having to that extent practically resigned their Government into the hands of that eminent tribunal.[146]

If I were in Congress and a vote should come up on a question whether slavery should be prohibited in a new territory, in spite of that *Dred Scott* decision, I would vote that it should.[147]

Lincoln, in short, did not believe that a decision as gravely flawed as *Dred Scott* on issues as important as slavery and African-American citizenship should be accorded the deference that might be given to other decisions of the Supreme Court. Significantly, Lincoln, as President, signed into law in 1862 a bill banning slavery in the federal territories[148]—despite *Dred Scott*'s ruling forbidding federal prohibition of slavery in the territories; and the Lincoln administration issued patents and passports to free African-Americans as citizens of the United States[149]—despite *Dred Scott*'s ruling that African-Americans, slave or free, could not be U.S. citizens.

Lincoln—our greatest statesman and perhaps our greatest teacher on the moral foundations of the Constitution—believed that the political branches of the federal government have authority under the Constitution to check judicial decisions that undermine the Constitution and need not accord such decisions absolute deference or supremacy.[150] The Lincolnian response to *Dred Scott* should guide contemporary responses to *Roe* and *Casey*. While Lincoln obviously counsels caution in this endeavor, a counsel that should be followed, he is right that the political branches—in the interest of preserving the constitutional order—have the authority to oppose those decisions of the Supreme Court that subvert the Constitution. In sum, in response to decisions that are destructive of the foundations of the constitutional order and violative of the constitutional design, the president and Congress may follow their own oaths to uphold the Constitution and seek—with due caution—to limit and check the anti- and unconstitutional actions of the federal judiciary.

Conclusion

The Declaration of Independence, the document that first "constituted" the United States as a political community and stated the common-sense of the "American mind"[151] on foundational questions of political morality, teaches us that all men are created equal and endowed by their Creator with unalienable rights to life, liberty, and the pursuit of happiness. Our nation is dedicated to that proposition, and our constitutional system is designed to safeguard these natural rights from private violence and from governmental invasion. The right to life, of course, is the most basic of these natural rights, and it is the most basic purpose of government to protect it. Abortion and physician-assisted suicide are choices that directly conflict with the right to life. Each institution of government in the United States should act within its proper sphere of authority to protect the right to life and thus to prohibit anti-life actions such as abortion and physician-assisted suicide. As this chapter recounts, the U.S. Supreme Court has failed to respect the right to life in the context of abortion and has also failed to respect the constitutional limits on its own sphere of authority. As Virginia's revered Declaration of Rights tell us, "no free Government, or the blessing of liberty, can be preserved to any people but by a firm adherence to justice, moderation, temperance, frugality, and virtue, and by frequent recurrence to fundamental principles."[152] It is up to the American people and their elected representatives to restore the true meaning of the Constitution and to protect the life of America's unborn children. No one else can do it for us—or for them.

ENDNOTES

1. *Roe. v. Wade*, 410 U.S. 113 (1973).

2. *Dred Scott v. Sandford*, 60 U.S. (19 How.) 393 (1857).

3. See, e.g., Bernard Schwartz, *A History of the Supreme Court* (Oxford University Press, 1993), pp.105-106.

4. Ibid., p. 111.

5. See, e.g., Paul Finkelman, Dred Scott v. Sandford: *A Brief History with Documents* (Bedford/St. Martin's, 1997), pp. 20-22.

6. Ibid.

7. Ibid., p. 22; *Scott v. Emerson*, 15 Mo. 576 (1852), p. 586.

8. Article III, Section 2 of the Constitution states that "The judicial power shall extend to all cases . . . between citizens of different states."

9. See, e.g., Don E. Fehrenbacher, *The Dred Scott Case* (Oxford University Press, 1978), pp. 276-78. Notably, the defendant, John F.A. Sanford, spelled his name "Sanford," but because of an error by the court reporter the Supreme Court's decision is Dred Scott v. San*d*ford. See, e.g., Finkelman, supra, p. 22.

10. Finkelman, supra, pp. 25-26.

11. Schwartz, supra, pp 115.

12. See, e.g., *Dred Scott v. Sandford* 60 U.S. (19 How.) 393 (1857)(Curtis, J., dissenting)(McLean, J., dissenting). For an analysis of the *Dred Scott* dissents, see Fehrenbacher, supra, pp. 403-414.

13. See, e.g., *Dred Scott v. Sandford*, 60 U.S. (19 How.) 393 (1857)(Nelson, J., concurring). For an analysis of Justice Nelson's concurrence, see Fehrenbacher, supra, p. 390.

14. While Chief Justice Taney's opinion appears under the heading "the opinion of the Court," there is some dispute as to whether he actually spoke for a majority of the Justices on each major point of law. See, e.g., Fehrenbacher, supra, p. 322.

15. *Dred Scott v. Sandford*,60 U.S. (19 How.) 393 (1857), 403-431.

16. Ibid., pp. 405, 407-408.

17. See *Dred Scott v. Sandford*, 60 U.S. (19 How.) 393 (1857)(Curtis, J., dissenting), pp. 572-577.

18. *Dred Scott v. Sandford*, 60 U.S. (19 How.) 393 (1857), p. 407.

19. See, e.g., Finkelman, supra, p. 36.

20. *Dred Scott v. Sandford* 60 U.S. (19 How.) 393 (1857), 431-453. Chief Justice Taney also argued—absurdly—that the Territories Clause in Article IV ("Congress shall have Power to dispose of and make all needful Rules and Regulations respecting the Territory or other Property belonging to the United States") did not in fact confer power on Congress to make "rules and regulations" concerning the federal territories in general, but rather was confined to territories owned in 1787. Ibid., pp. 432-446.

21. Ibid., pp. 450.

22. The Fifth Amendment reads "No person shall be . . . deprived of life, liberty, or property, without due process of law."

23. See, e.g., Schwartz, supra, p. 117; Finkelman, supra, pp. 40-41.

24. *Dred Scott v. Sandford*, 60 U.S. (19 How.) 393 (1857), 450 (observing that "an Act of Congress which deprives a citizen of the United States of his liberty or property, merely because he came himself or brought his property into a particular Territory of the United States, and who had committed no offense against the laws, could hardly be dignified with the name of due process of law.").

25. Finkelman, supra, p. 29.

26. Ibid.

27. Ibid.

28. On the political context of the *Dred Scott* decision, including the improper contacts between Democratic president-elect James Buchanan and Democratic members of the Court while *Dred Scott* was pending, see Schwartz, supra, pp. 112-115.

29. Finkelman, supra, p. 29.

30. *Roe. v. Wade*, 410 U.S. 113 (1973).

31. *Planned Parenthood of Southeastern Pennsylvania v. Casey*, 505 U.S. 833 (1992).

32. Lucinda M. Finley, *The Story of Roe v. Wade: From a Garage Sale for Woman's Lib, to the Supreme Court, to Political Turmoil*, in *Constitutional Law Stories* (Foundation Press, 2004)(Michael C. Dorf, ed.) pp. 381-382

33. Ibid., p. 384.

34. Ibid.

35. See Gerald N. Rosenberg, *The Hollow Hope: Can Courts Bring About Social Change?* (University of Chicago Press, 1991), p. 175.

36. *Roe. v. Wade*, 410 U.S. 113 (1973)(Rehnquist, J., dissenting)(observing that "[a]s early as 1821, the first state [statute] dealing directly with abortion was enacted by the Connecticut Legislature" and that "[b]y the time of the adoption of the Fourteenth Amendment in 1868, there were at least 36 laws enacted by state or territorial legislatures limiting abortion."), pp. 175-176.

37. For instance, common law treatise writers were in general agreement that the killing of a quickened unborn child was a serious criminal offense. 2 Henry Bracton, *De Legibus et Consuetudiinbus Angliae* 279 (T. Twiss ed. 1879); Edward Coke, *Institutes* III *50; 1 William Blackstone, *Commentaries* *129-130. See also *Keeler v. Superior Court of Amador County*, 2 Cal. 3d 619 (1970)(Burke, J., dissenting)(observing that "although the common law did not apply the labels of "murder" or "manslaughter" to the killing of a quickened fetus, it appears that at common law this [offense] was severely punished.").

38. For a defense of the moral personhood of the unborn grounded in their existence as individual members of the human species, see Robert P. George, *The Clash of Orthodoxies: Law, Religion, and Morality in Crisis* (ISI Books, 2001) pp. 8-11.

39. *Roe v. Wade*, 314 F. Supp. 1217 (N.D. Tex. 1970).

40. Ibid., p. 1222.

41. See *Roe. v. Wade*, 410 U.S. 113 (1973)(Rehnquist, J., dissenting), 176-177.

42. *Roe. v. Wade*, 410 U.S. 113 (1973).

43. Ibid., p. 153.

44. *Griswold v. Connecticut*, 381 U.S. 479 (1965).

45. Ibid., p. 482-486.

46. The Fourth Amendment reads: "The right of the people to be secure in their persons, houses, papers, and effects, against unreasonable searches and seizures, shall not be violated, and no Warrants shall issue, but upon probable cause, supported by Oath or affirmation, and particularly describing the place to be searched, and the persons or things to be seized."

47. *Griswold v. Connecticut*, 381 U.S. 479 (1965), p. 484.

48. Ibid., pp. 485-486.

49. *Griswold v. Connecticut*, 381 U.S. 479 (1965)(Black, J., dissenting)(emphasis added) pp. 520-521.

50. Ibid.

51. *Roe. v. Wade*, 410 U.S. 113 (1973), p. 153.

52. Ibid.

53. See Rosenberg, supra, p.175.

54. *Palko v. Connecticutt*, 302 U.S. 319 (1937).

55. *Roe. v. Wade*, 410 U.S. 113 (1973), pp. 155-156.

56. Ibid., p. 164-165.

57. *Doe v. Bolton*, 410 U.S. 179 (1973).

58. Ibid., p. 192.

59. Ibid., pp.195-200.

60. The Fourteenth Amendment Equal Protection Clause reads "No state shall . . . deny to any person within its jurisdiction the equal protection of the laws."

61. In defense of this view, see Gerard V. Bradley, *Life's Dominion: A Review Essay*, 69 *The Notre Dame Law Review* 329 (1993), pp. 341-351.

62. Notably, the State of Texas argued that the protection of the unborn was a compelling state interest justifying abortion restrictions even under strict scrutiny. See *Roe v. Wade*, 410 U.S. 113 (1973), p. 159.

63. Ibid., pp. 156-169.

64. Gerard Bradley observes that "[a] deep prejudice against the unborn, obscured but still visible behind a methodological double standard, underwrites *Roe*." Bradley, supra, p. 341.

65. *Roe v. Wade*, 410 U.S. 113 (1973), pp. 159-165.

66. See *Roe v. Wade*, 410 U.S. 113 (1973), pp. 163-64; *Doe v. Bolton*, 410 U.S. 179 (1973), pp. 192-200.

67. *Roe. v. Wade*, 410 U.S. 113 (1973)(White, J., dissenting)

68. *Planned Parenthood of Southeastern Pennsylvania v. Casey*, 505 U.S. 833 (1992).

69. Ibid., p. 878.

70. Ibid., pp. 881-887, 899-900.

71. Ibid., pp. 887- 898.

72. Ibid., pp. 879.

73. Ibid., p. 851.

74. On the policy basis of *stare decisis*, see *Walton v. Arizona*, 497 U.S. 639 (1990) (Scalia, J., concurring in part and concurring in the judgment)(observing that "[t]he doctrine [of *stare decisis*] exists for the purpose of introducing certainty and stability into the law and protecting the expectations of individuals and institutions that have acted in reliance on existing rules.").

75. On constitutional *stare decisis* as weak *stare decisis*, see, e.g., *Agostini v. Felton*, 521 U.S. 203 (1997)(stating the *stare decisis* "reflects a policy judgment that 'in most matters it is more important that the applicable rule of law be settled than that it be settled right' and that "[t]hat policy is at its weakest when we interpret the Constitution because our interpretation can be altered only by constitutional amendment or by overruling our prior decisions.")(internal citations omitted).

76. *Planned Parenthood of Southeastern Pennsylvania v. Casey*, 505 U.S. 833 (1992), p. 855.

77. See *Planned Parenthood of Southeastern Pennsylvania v. Casey*, 505 U.S. 833 (1992)(Scalia, J., dissenting)(observing that "I confess never to have heard of this new, keep-what-you-want-and-throw-away-the-rest version" of *stare decisis*), p. 993.

78. *Planned Parenthood of Southeastern Pennsylvania v. Casey*, 505 U.S. 833 (1992), p. 856.

79. As the Casey plurality itself notes, "[t]he inquiry into reliance counts the cost of a rule's repudiation as it would fall on those who have relied *reasonably* on the rule's continued application." (Emphasis added) Ibid., p. 855.

80. Ibid., pp. 857-860.

81. *Bowers v. Hardwick*, 478 U.S. 186 (1986).

82. Ibid., pp.191-194.

83. *Planned Parenthood of Southeastern Pennsylvania v. Casey*, 505 U.S. 833 (1992), p. 867.

84. See *Planned Parenthood of Southeastern Pennsylvania v. Casey*, 505 U.S. 833 (1992)(Rehnquist, C.J., dissenting), pp. 957-964.

85. As the Court observed in *Erie,* the doctrine of *Swift v. Tyson*, concerning the creation of federal common law in violation of the federal structure of the Constitution, was "an unconstitutional assumption of powers by the Courts of the United States which no lapse of time or respectable array of opinion should make us hesitate to correct." *Erie R. Co. v. Tompkins*, 304 U.S. 64 (1938)(quoting *Black & White Taxicab & Transfer Co. v. Brown & Yellow Taxicab Transfer Co.*, 276 U.S. 518 (1928)(Holmes, J., dissenting).

86. *Planned Parenthood of Southeastern Pennsylvania v. Casey*, 505 U.S. 833 (1992), pp. 866-867.

87. Ibid., p. 867.

88. *Planned Parenthood of Southeastern Pennsylvania v. Casey*, 505 U.S. 833 (1992)(Scalia, J., dissenting), p. 980.

89. Ibid., pp. 995-996.

90. Cf. *Oregon v. Mitchell*, 400 U.S. 112 (1970)(Harlan, J., concurring in part and dissenting in part)("When the Court disregards the express intent and understanding of the Framers, it has invaded the realm of the political process to which the amending power was committed, and it has violated the constitutional structure which it is its highest duty to protect."), p. 203.

91. *Planned Parenthood of Southeastern Pennsylvania v. Casey*, 505 U.S. 833 (1992)(Scalia, J., dissenting), p. 998.

92. These appointments are: Justice John Paul Stevens by President Ford, Justice Sandra Day O'Connor by President Reagan, Chief Justice William Rehnquist by President Reagan (elevated from Associate Justice to Chief Justice), Justice Antonin Scalia by President Reagan, Justice Anthony Kennedy by President Regan, Justice David Souter by President George H.W. Bush, and Justice Clarence Thomas by President George H.W. Bush.

93. See *Stenberg v. Carhart*, 530 U.S. 914 (2000)(Kennedy, J., dissenting), p. 959-960.

94. Ibid., p. 979.

95. See *Richmond Med. Ctr. for Women v. Gilmore*, 224 F.3d 337 (4th Cir. 2000); *Planned Parenthood of Cent. N.J. v. Farmer*, 220 F.3d 127 (3d Cir. 2000); *Planned Parenthood of Greater Iowa, Inc. v. Miller*, 195 F.3d 386 (8th Cir. 1999); *Carhart v. Stenberg*, 192 F.3d 1142 (8th Cir. 1999); *Little Rock Family Planning Servs. v. Jegley*, 192 F.3d 794 (8th Cir. 1999); *Summitt Med. Assocs. v. Pryor*, 180 F.3d 1326 (11th Cir. 1999); *Women's Med. Prof'l Corp. v. Voinovich*, 130 F.3d 187 (6th Cir. 1997). But see *Hope Clinic v. Ryan*, 195 F.3d 857 (7th Cir. 1999) (en banc)(upholding a ban on partial-birth abortion).

96. *Stenberg v. Carhart*, 530 U.S. 914 (2000).

97. Ibid., pp. 930-938.

98. See *Stenberg v. Carhart*, 530 U.S. 914 (2000)(Kennedy, J., dissenting), pp. 964-972.

99. *Stenberg v. Carhart*, 530 U.S. 914 (2000), pp. 938-946.

100. Ibid., pp. 921-922.

101. Ibid., pp. 938-939.

102. Ibid., pp. 945-456.

103. See *Stenberg v. Carhart*, 530 U.S. 914 (2000)(Kennedy, J., dissenting), pp.972-979; *Stenberg v. Carhart*, 530 U.S. 914 (2000)(Thomas, J., dissenting), pp. 989-1005.

104. *Stenberg v. Carhart*, 530 U.S. 914 (2000)(Scalia, J., dissenting), p. 953.

105. Gonzales v. Carhart, 127 S. Ct. 1610 (2007).

106. Ibid., at 1636-1637.

107. Ibid., at 1638-1639.

108. Ibid., at 1630.

109. Ibid., at 1630.

110. Ibid., at 16329-1631.

111. Ibid., at 1626 (stating that the Court "assume[s]" the applicability of *Casey*'s principles "for the purposes of this opinion").

112. Lawrence Friedman, *American Law: An Introduction* (W.W. Nortion & Company, 1998), p. 211.

113. John Hart Ely, *Democracy and Distrust: A Theory of Judicial Reivew* (Harvard University Press, 1980), p. 59.

114. Romer v. Evans, 517 U.S. 620 (1996)(Scalia, J., dissenting).

115. James Davison Hunter, *Culture Wars: The Struggle to Define America* (BasicBooks, 1991), p. 63.

116. John C. Jeffries, Jr., *Justice Lewis F. Powell, Jr: Biography* (Charles Scribner's Sons, 1994), pp. 346-347

117. For instance, the *Casey* plurality endorsed this view, asserting that "for two decades of economic and social developments, people have organized intimate relationships and made choices that define their views of themselves and their places in society, in reliance on the availability of abortion in the event that contraception should fail. The ability of women to participate equally in the economic and social life of the Nation has been facilitated by their ability to control their reproductive lives." *Planned Parenthood of Southeastern Pennsylvania v. Casey*, 505 U.S. 833 (1992), p. 856.

118. Richard D. Parker, *"Here, the People Rule": A Constitutional Populist Manifesto* (Harvard University Press, 1994), p.65.

119. Mary Ann Glendon, *Rights Talk: The Impoverishment of Political Discourse* (The Free Press, 1991), p. 178.

120. See, e.g., *Palko v. Connecticutt*, 302 U.S. 319 (1937); *Bowers v. Hardwick*, 478 U.S. 186 (1986); *Washington v. Glucksberg*, 521 U.S. 707 (1997).

121. *Roe. v. Wade*, 410 U.S. 113 (1973); *Planned Parenthood of Southeastern Pennsylvania v. Casey*, 505 U.S. 833 (1992); *Lawrence v. Texas*, 539 U.S. 558 (2003).

122. *Planned Parenthood of Southeastern Pennsylvania v. Casey*, 505 U.S. 833 (1992), p. 851.

123. *Compassion in Dying v. Washington*, 79 F.3d 790, 798 (1996).

124. *Cruzan v. Direction, Missouri Department of Health*, 497 U.S. 261 (1990).

125. *Compassion in Dying v. Washington*, 79 F.3d 790, 798 (1996).

126. *Washington v. Glucksberg*, 521 U.S. 707 (1997).

127. Ibid., pp. 720-728.

128. Ibid., pp. 710-719.

129. Ibid., pp. 726-728.

130. Cf. *Griswold v. Connecticut*, 381 U.S. 479 (1965) (Black, J., dissenting), pp. 520-521.

131. *Washington v. Glucksberg*, 521 U.S. 707 (1997), pp. 729-736.

132. Ibid., pp. 724-726.

133. Ibid., pp. 711-713.

134. Ibid., pp. 724-726.

135. On the moral distinction between committing suicide and refusing unwanted medical treatment, see John Finnis, *Euthanasia, Morality, and Law*, 31 *Loyola of Los Angeles Law Review* 1123 (1998).

136. *Washington v. Glucksberg*, 521 U.S. 707 (1997), pp. 720-728.

137. *Lawrence v. Texas*, 539 U.S. 558 (2003), p. 574.

138. See *Bowers v. Hardwick*, 478 U.S. 186 (1986), pp 191-194. In addition to endorsing the legal tradition approach to substantive due process, the Court also observed in *Bowers* that "we [are not] inclined to take a more expansive view of our authority to discover new fundamental rights imbedded in the Due Process Clause. The Court is most vulnerable and comes nearest to illegitimacy when it deals with judge-made constitutional law having little or no cognizable roots in the language or design of the Constitution." Ibid., at 194.

139. *Lawrence v. Texas*, 539 U.S. 558 (2003), pp. 577-578.

140. This brief was published in the *New York Review of Books* under the title "Assisted Suicide: The Philosophers' Brief." See John Rawls, et al, *Assisted Suicide: The Philosophers' Brief*, Volume 44, No. 5, *New York Review of Books* (March 27, 1997). It can be found on line at http://www.nybooks.com/articles/1237.

141. A number of scholars have recognized that judicial decisions such as *Roe* actually violate the structure of the Constitution. See, e.g., George W. Carey, *In Defense of the Constitution*, 132-138 (Liberty Fund, revised and expanded ed., 1995)(drawing on *Federalist No. 78* to argue that the judicial exercise of an activist legislative "will" rather than restrained judicial "judgment" is violative of the republican structures of the Constitution and is therefore an unconstitutional judicial action); Raoul Berger, *Government by Judiciary: The Transformation of the Fourteenth Amendment* 273-274 (Liberty Fund, 2nd ed., 1997)(asserting that the judicial creation of substantive unenumerated rights "violate[s] the injunction of the separation of powers" and "encroache[s] on the sovereignty reserved to the States by the Tenth Amendment"); *See* Robert P. George, *Natural Law and the Constitution Revisited*, 70 FORDHAM LAW REV 243, 274 (2001). (contending that the positive law of the U.S. Constitution establishing the powers of the institutions of government does not grant the U.S. Supreme Court the authority to invalidate legislation on political grounds and thus that decisions such as *Dred Scott*, *Lochner*, *Griswold*, and *Roe*—given their lack of support in traditional legal materials and their basis in the political morality of the justices—are violations of the positive law of the Constitution by the Court).

142. *United States v. Morrison*, 529 U.S. 598 (2000)(asserting that "[n]o doubt the political branches have a role in interpreting and applying the Constitution, but ever since *Marbury* this Court has remained the ultimate expositor of the constitutional text.").

143. On judicial supremacy, see Robert A. Burt, *The Constitution in Conflict* (Harvard University Press, 1992).

144. A number of scholars have questioned whether unconstitutional judicial decisions bind the political branches with the same force as merely mistaken decisions. See, e.g., Carey, supra, pp. 135 (asserting that when the U.S. Supreme Court engages in an improper exercise of the judicial power in violation of the Constitution, "our obligation to respect or obey its power of judicial review is severed, and the other branches of government, principally the Congress, are entitled, nay *obliged*, to use the constitutional means at their disposal to curb, regulate, and control the Court in such a manner as to compel" the Court's adherence to the constitutional limits on its power); Robert P. George, *The Supreme Court 2000, First Things*, Oct. 2000, at 34 (rejecting a conception of judicial supremacy that requires the President and Congress to submit to "unconstitutional exercises of judicial power" by the Supreme Court that are destructive of the "constitutional order").

145. Abraham Lincoln, *Response to Douglas in Representatives' Hall in the Illinois State House* (June 26, 1857), in *The Living Lincoln: The Man, His Mind, His Times, and the War He Fought, Reconstructed from His Own Writings* (Paul M. Angle & Earl Schenck Miers eds., 1955)., p. 201.

146. Abraham Lincoln, *First Inaugural Address*, March 4, 1861.

147. Abraham Lincoln, *Speech at Chicago* (July 10, 1858), in *The Complete Lincoln-Douglas Debates of 1858* (The University of Chicago Press, Paul Angle ed., 1958), p. 36.

148. See David Herbert Donald, *Lincoln* (Simon and Schuster, 1995), p. 342.

149. See Hadley Arkes, *First Things: An Inquiry into the First Principles of Morals and Justices* (Princeton University Press, 1986), p. 421.

150. For a detailed discussion of Lincoln's views on (non-)deference to the Supreme Court, see Robert P. George, *Lincoln on Judicial Despotism, First Things*, No. 130, February 2003, pp. 36-40.

151. As Thomas Jefferson observed, the Declaration of Independence was "[n]either aiming at originality of principle or sentiment, nor yet copied from any particular and previous writing, it was intended to be an expression of the American mind." See Thomas Jefferson, *Letter from Thomas Jefferson to Henry Lee* (May 8, 1825), in *Thomas Jefferson: Writings* 1500-01 (Merrill D. Peterson ed., 1984).

152. *Article 15, Virginia Declaration of Rights* (1776)

Three
The Judicial Assault on the Family
by Allan W. Carlson

Visiting America in the 1830's, the German traveler Francis J. Grund found a land characterized by "early marriage," "the sanctity of the marriage vow," "rapid increase of population," and "domestic happiness." Indeed, he saw "the domestic virtue of the Americans as the principle source of all their other qualities," including democratic governance. Grund continued:

> No government could be established on the same principle as that of the United States, with a different code of morals. The American Constitution is remarkable for its simplicity; but it can only suffice a people habitually correct in their actions, and would be utterly inadequate to the wants of a different nation. Change the domestic habits of the Americans, their religious devotion, and their high respect for morality, and it will not be necessary to change a single letter of the Constitution in order to vary the whole form of their government . . . . : [T]he disparity which would then exist between the laws and the habits of those whom they are destined to govern, would . . . make a different government . . . absolutely necessary, to preserve the nation from ruin.[1]

While clear to a 19th Century visitor from Europe, this grounding of the American constitutional order in home, marriage, and family has not been a common object of discussion among Americans themselves. As legal scholar Bruce Hafen once put it, "[t]he 'family tradition' . . . has been such an obvious presupposition of our culture that it has not been well articulated, let alone explained or justified."[2] All the same, it is clear that family law in America has not only reflected these common assumptions and behaviors, but has also shaped them. Family law has performed a "channeling function," in Carl E. Schneider's words, where it "builds . . . institutions with norms" and offers people "models for organizing their lives" which have been successfully developed over time.

For example, "[t]he institution of marriage which the law recruits and shapes attempts to induce in spouses a sense of an obligation to . . . love and honor each other."[3] Legal theorist Martha Fineman agrees that "[s]tate policies can profoundly affect the form and functioning of the family."[4]

In recent decades, however, these powers to "channel" human behaviors and "shape" the form and functions of the family have taken a remarkable new course. "[I]t would not be wrong to talk of a revolution in family law," writes Lee Teitelbaum in the *Journal of Legal Education*.[5] "In the last few decades, family law has been transformed," explains Carl Schneider.[6] Importantly, these radical changes have not been primarily the result of popular social pressures coming from below. Rather, the driving force has been adoption by the U.S. Supreme Court and certain inferior courts of a new philosophy of marriage, family, and sexuality. As legal analyst Peter J. Riga notes:

> These judicial influences on family law have directly contributed to the change in marriage and family behavior and in the way people think about marriage and family . . . The educative force of law in America is so strong that people tend to draw moral conclusions for practical living from it which in turn influence social life itself.[7]

As this paper will explain, the Supreme Court's new social philosophy has aimed at nothing less than an embrace of the sexual revolution, the extinguishing of traditional marital structures, the elimination of the autonomous home, and the elevation of the state into a substitute for the family.

The Original Constitutional Order

To grasp the scope of this revolution in marriage and family law, one must first understand the roots and nature of the original American constitutional order.

The foundations of American family law lay in the social teachings of the early Christian Fathers, who crafted the moral basis of Western Christian civilization. Legal historian Charles Reid makes a compelling case that the "mental universe" of St. Augustine actually shaped the original American jurisprudence of marriage. Writing at the end of the fourth century, A.D., Augustine faced two challenges. On the one side stood the Manicheans, a heretical sect which so focused on the spirit that they practiced total abstention from reproductive intercourse. On the other side were the pagan Romans, among whom concubinage, prostitution, and easy divorce were common. Referring to the innate "sociability" of humankind and "a natural companionship between the sexes," Augustine defined the true "goods of marriage" as threefold: procreation; fidelity; and sacramental permanence. Rejecting both extreme ascetisin and hedonism, Augustine affirmed that "the marriage of man and woman is something good."[8]

These principles flowed into the making of public law. The Code of Justinian and his Novella 117 appeared in 542 A.D. and together they inaugurated the formal influence of Christianity on family law in the West.[9] They portrayed the family as a voluntary covenant union of a man and a woman resting on mutual fidelity and indissolubility. In 1140 A.D., the canonist Gratian compiled a vast and systematic legal treatise, the *Decretum*. Concerning marriage, he focused on its procreative purpose, condemning those who used the "poisons of sterility" to prevent conception. At the same time, he argued that it was the free consent of man and woman, not sexual intercourse, that made the marriage. A century later, Thomas Aquinas stressed that marriage rested on the natural law and was designed for procreation and the education of children. Through their vows, man and woman placed themselves in the power of the other, making their fidelity a matter of justice. Reid shows that while the Protestant Reformation denied the sacramental nature of marriage and introduced certain limited grounds for divorce, the Anglican canon law held on to Augustine's three "goods" of marriage. Canonist John Ayliffe (1676–1732), for example, embraced the "three fold matrimonial Good" in his description of marriage, while Richard Grey, writing in 1732, continued to emphasize the indissolubility of the marital bond.[10]

This tradition forcefully entered American law through the person of Chancellor James Kent (1763–1847), an early leader on the New York bench who had a profound impact on legal thinking in America. In an 1811 case, *Wightman v. Wightman*, Kent affirmed that the natural law underlay family law. He wrote: "by the law of nature I understand those fit and just rules of conduct which the Creator has prescribed to man, as from the deductions of right reason, though they may be . . . more explicitly declared by divine revelation." Writing several decades later, he underscored the transcendent value of the marital relationship:

The primary and most important of the domestic relations, is that of husband and wife. It has its foundation in nature, and is the only relation by which Providence has permitted the continuance of the human race. . . . It is one of the chief foundations of social order.[11]

Another early architect of American family law, Joel Bishop, also drew on the Anglican canons:

'As the first cause and reason of matrimony,' says Ayliffe, 'ought to be the design of having an offspring so the second ought to be the avoiding of fornication.' These two, observes Dr. Lushington, the law recognizes as its 'principle ends'; namely, 'a lawful indulgence of the passions to prevent licentiousness and the procreation of children according to the evident design of Divine Providence.'[12]

The American founders gave special attention to the family institution. They showed, in historian Nancy Cott's words, a "Christian common sense" in taking for granted "the rightness of monogamous marriage." In contrast, the founders associated polygamy with Oriental absolutism and the harem with tyrannical rule. Drawing from the Baron de Montesquieu's *Spirit of the Law*, they viewed monogamous marriage and republican governance as mirror images of each other. They reasoned that Christian monogamy and a free republic were both voluntary unions, premised on consent.[13] In this spirit, John Witherspoon, President of Princeton University and signer of the Declaration of Independence, cited "the absolute necessity of marriage for the service of the state, and the solid advantages that arise from it."[14] John Adams was even more adamant about the importance of strong homes to the nation:

[T]he foundations of national Morality must be laid in private Families. In vain are schools, Accademies [sic] and universities instituted, if loose Principles and licentious habits are impressed upon Children in their earliest years. . . . How is it possible that Christians can have any just Sense of the sacred Obligations of Morality or Religion if, from their earliest Infancy, they learn that their Mothers live in habitual Infidelity to their fathers, and their fathers in as constant Infidelity to their Mothers.[15]

Visitors to the new republic commented frequently on the special American attachments to marriage and family. Francis Grund, cited at the outset, emphasized how the American practice of early marriage brought prosperity. The successful merchants and shipowners, the leading manufacturers, and the owners of the largest farms and estates "are married men; and what is still more remarkable, have acquired their property, not before, but after, their marriage."[16] Grund's better known contemporary, Alexis de Tocqueville, found Americans unusually committed to strong and faithful unions:

> They consider marriage as a covenant which is often onerous, but every condition of which the parties are strictly bound to fulfil [sic], because they knew all those conditions before hand, and were perfectly free not to have contracted them. The very circumstances which render matrimonial fidelity more obligatory also render it more easy.

This observation led Tocqueville to a more sweeping conclusion:

> There is certainly no country in the world where the tie of marriage is more respected than in America, or where conjugal happiness is more highly or worthily appreciated. . . . While the European endeavors to forget his domestic troubles by agitating society, the American derives from his own home that love of order which he afterwards carries with him into public affairs.[17]

As had Grund, Tocqueville saw America's unique balance between liberty and order resting on a strong family system.

In the spirit of St. Augustine, court decisions among the states during the 19th Century underscored the importance of procreation. In 1847, the Pennsylvania Supreme Court ruled that "the paramount purpose of marriage [is] the procreation and protection of legitimate children, the institution of families, and the creation of natural relations among mankind; from which proceed all the civilization, virtue, and happiness to be found in the world."[18] The Supreme Judicial Court of Massachusetts reached a similar conclusion in 1862: "[O]ne of the leading and most important objects of the institution of marriage under our laws is the procreation of children, who shall with certainty be known by their parents as the pure offspring of their union."[19]

Controversy over the Mormon practice of polygamy brought the U.S. Supreme Court deeply into family law for the first time, and produced remarkable statements on the importance of monogamous marriage to the commonweal. In *Reynolds* v. *The United States*, the court linked polygamy to the despotic societies of Asia and Africa. In contrast, democratic "society may be said to be built" on monogamous marriage.[20] In *Murphy* v. *Ramsey*, the Supreme Court raised the tone still higher, arguing that no legislation could be "more wholesome and necessary" in the founding of a "free, self-governing commonwealth" than one which sees the family "as consisting in and springing from the union for life of one man and one woman in the holy estate of matrimony." This family model would be "the best guaranty of that reverent morality which is the source of all beneficent progress in social and political improvement."[21]

While dealing with divorce rather than polygamy, the Supreme Court in *Maynard* v. *Hill* affirmed the great import of matrimony in a still more powerful manner. Marriage "is something more than a mere contract," the Court ruled. While the consent of man and woman was of course essential, the marriage contract created a relationship between the two "which they cannot change." While other contracts could be "modified, restricted . . . enlarged," or even broken, "[n]ot so with marriage." Once formed, the law stepped in and enforced distinctive obligations and duties. This happened because marriage was "an institution, in the maintenance of which in its purity the public is deeply interested, for it is the foundation of the family and of society."[22]

The first seven decades of the 20th Century witnessed Supreme Court decisions that continued, in fine Augustinian fashion, to affirm the family as natural and autonomous. In 1923, the Court ruled in *Meyer* v. *Nebraska* that it was "the natural duty of the parent" to educate his child.[23] Two years later, the Supreme Court declared in *Pierce* v. *Society of Sisters* that the "child is not the mere creature of the State" and affirmed "the liberty of parents and guardians to direct the upbringing and education of children under their control."[24] In 1944, the Court recognized that "the custody, care and nurture of the child" resided first and foremost with parents whose primary functions and freedoms "the state can neither supply nor hinder." These formed "the private realm of family life which the state cannot enter."[25]

Other court decisions in the mid-20th Century remained faithful to the Augustinian "goods of marriage" embraced by the American founders. In *Skinner* v. *Oklahoma*, the Supreme Court struck down a mandatory sterilization act, declaring that "[m]arriage and procreation are fundamental to the very existence and survival of the race."[26] In 1957, California Justice Roger Traynor drew on the corpus of extant Supreme Court decisions and ably summarized the place of the family in American law:

> The family is the basic unit of our society, the center of the personal affections that ennoble and enrich human life. It channels biological drives that might otherwise become socially destructive; it ensures the care and education of children in a stable environment; it establishes continuity from one generation to another; it nurtures and develops the individual initiative that distinguishes a free people.[27]

Even after the revolution in family law had begun, some court rulings continued to reflect this prior line of thinking. In 1971, the Minnesota Supreme Court noted that "[t]he institution of marriage as a union of man and woman, uniquely involving the procreation and rearing of children within a family, is as old as the book of Genesis."[28] In *Wisconsin* v. *Yoder*, decided the same year, the U.S. Supreme Court elevated the "fundamental interest of parents" over that of the state relative to the education and rearing of children.[29] The Washington state Court of Appeals, in a 1974 case regarding claims to same-sex marriage, ruled that "the state views marriage as the appropriate and desirable forum for procreation and the rearing of children," adding "that marriage exists as a protected legal institution primarily because of societal values associated with the propagation of the human race."[30] As late as 1982, the Utah Supreme Court could argue that "[t]he rights inherent in family relationships—husband-wife, parent-child, and sibling—are the most obvious example of rights retained by the people." Indeed, such rights "are 'natural,' 'intrinsic,' or 'prior' in the sense that our Constitution presupposes them."[31]

"Privacy" and Legal Revolution

All the same, by the mid-1960s an alternate vision of family life and family law was taking form within the judiciary. It arose out of secular liberal thought as both a consequence and a reinforcement of the de-Christianization of American culture. This intellectual revolution proved to be particularly intense at American universities and law schools. In the name of equal protection and due process, this new vision would embrace the tenets of the sexual revolution, dismantle marriage, and subvert the autonomy of the home. The end result would be to magnify the power and sweep of the state.

Early straws in the wind came as dissents in *Poe* v. *Ullman*, a 1961 case involving a state of Connecticut ban on the use of contraceptives by married couples. For the first time, William O. Douglas claimed to see "the privacy that is implicit in a free society" residing within "the intimacies of the marriage relationship." In his dissent, John Harlan argued that the marital activity at issue involved not only procedural rights, but substantive rights as well. He believed that these rights should be applied in this case as the Court sought a balance between "respect for the liberty of the individual" and "the demands of organized society."[32]

In *Griswold* v. *Connecticut*, decided four years later, these appeals to "privacy" and substantive due process came together to begin the destruction of traditional American family law. In striking down the same measure it had ruled constitutional four years earlier, the Supreme Court cleverly appealed to the "sacred precincts of marital bedrooms." Writing for the majority now, Justice Douglas grounded the Court's decision in a constitutional "penumbra" of personal privacy that supposedly emanated from the Bill of Rights. He stated:

> We deal with a right of privacy older than the Bill of Rights. . . . Marriage is a coming together for better or worse, hopefully enduring, and intimate to the degree of being sacred. . . . It is an association for as noble a purpose as any involved in our prior decisions.[33]

According to legal scholar Peter Riga, this appeal to the sacred nature of marriage in *Griswold* "was at least logical and historical," even if the new right to privacy had no basis in the Constitution.³⁴ The moral and social revolution implicit in "privacy" only became apparent in the 1972 decision in *Eisenstadt* v. *Baird*, where the court struck down a ban on contraceptive use by the unmarried, as well. Rejecting its 1965 appeal to the "sacred precincts" of the marital bedroom, the court now ruled that "whatever the rights of the individual to access to contraceptives might be, the rights must be the same for the married and unmarried alike." The Court went on to weaken drastically the ability of a state or community to distinguish a married-couple family from other living situations. Upending over 1500 years of jurisprudence, the Court argued:

> It is true that in *Griswold* the right of privacy inhered in the marital relationship. Yet the marital couple is not an independent entity with a mind and heart of its own, but an association of two individuals each with a separate intellectual and emotional make up. If the right of privacy means anything, it is the right of the individual, married or single, to be free from unwarranted governmental intrusion into matters so fundamentally affecting a person as the decision to bear or beget a child.³⁵

Through these words, the U.S. Supreme Court essentially enlisted in the Sexual Revolution.

According to Riga, the *Eisenstadt* decision was "radical," "confusing," alien to the "rooted traditions" of the American people, and without any foundation in constitutional law.³⁶ All the same, its logic flowed into a series of decisions that dismantled key functions and most legal protections of the family. In the 1973 abortion cases, for example, the new right of a woman to abort a child during the first trimester of pregnancy was rooted in the same appeal to privacy. Significantly, relative to family relations, the Court's ruling made no distinction between Jane Roe, the unmarried plaintiff, and Mary Doe, who was married.³⁷ The Supreme Court's 1976 decision in *Planned Parenthood of Missouri* v. *Danforth* stripped the father of an unborn child—whether married to the mother or not—of any right to affect the mother's abortion decision.³⁸ A year later, the Court also stripped parents and state governments of any controls over the sale or gift of contraceptives to minor children. Here again, "privacy" trumped family autonomy and parental rights, with the Court ruling that "it is clear that among the decisions that an individual may make without unjustified interference are personal decisions,"³⁹ including the use of birth control.

In a subsequent case denying a parental veto over an abortion by a minor, the radical antinomianism flowing out of *Eisenstadt* became starkly clear. Denying any notion of natural law or moral order, and rejecting over a millennia of Christian influence on the law, the U.S. Supreme Court reasoned that "[a]t the heart of liberty is the right to define one's own concept of existence, of meaning, of the universe, and of the mystery of human life."⁴⁰ In 2003, the Court used the same gnostic thinking to strike down the Texas anti-sodomy law, ruling that the right-to-privacy also encompasses the behavior of homosexuals: "Their right to liberty under the Due Process Clause gives them the full right to engage in their conduct without intervention of the government."⁴¹

Deinstitutionalizing Marriage

While the right to privacy provided cover for the Court's embrace of the Sexual Revolution, another line of cases between 1967 and 2005 transformed the nature of marriage in another way. The broad trend has been from a view of marriage as a social institution with binding claims of its own and with prescribed roles for men and women into a free association, easily entered and easily broken, with a focus on the needs of individuals. However, the ironical result of so expanding "the freedom to marry" has been to enhance the authority and sway of government.

The new moral relativism toward marriage first surfaced in Associate Justice Frank Murphy's dissent in the 1946 case, *Cleveland* v. *U.S.* While the majority of the U.S. Supreme Court ruled here that polygamy remained a practice of debauchery, lewdness, and immorality, Murphy took a new approach. Rather than being "odious," he said that polygamy was "one of the basic forms of marriage," to be found around the globe. Even if distasteful to Americans, polygamy was "a form of marriage built upon a set of social and moral principles" that deserved legal recognition.[42]

The marital revolution commenced in 1967 with *Loving* v. *Virginia*. Here, the U.S. Supreme Court struck down a provision that denied marriage to persons of different races. On the one hand, this action was a logical and welcome component of the civil rights and desegregation campaigns of the 1960's. However, the Court went beyond the simple logic of requiring "equal protection" of the laws, which would have sufficed here. Instead, it chose to recognize in sweeping language "the right to marry" as one of the "basic civil rights of man," fundamental to "our very existence and survival." This freedom to marry, the justices continued, was "one of the vital personal rights essential to the orderly pursuit of happiness by free men."[43] While such language seemed on the surface to elevate marriage, in practice it diminished the institution. *Loving* took a social institution, with its own rights and claims, and redefined it as a personal choice, a matter governed by the rights of the individual. According to Dean Robert Drinan, SJ, this decision mandated "a complete rethinking" of American marriage law, for it implied "that the state and the law should say as little as possible about who should marry whom."[44]

Subsequent decisions revealed the full logic of *Loving*. In *Boddie* v. *Connecticut*, decided in 1971, the Supreme Court struck down a provision placing certain financial requirements on indigent persons seeking divorce. Such measures, the Court reasoned, were impermissible burdens on the newly recognized freedom to end a marriage.[45] As legal scholar Carl Anderson comments, "[t]he original freedom to marry had now become the freedom to divorce without cost."[46] The Court's decision in *Eisenstadt*, as noted earlier in another context, denied to the states the power to differentiate between citizens of varying marital status.[47] In the celebrated case of *Marvin* v. *Marvin*, the California Supreme Court ruled that cohabiting couples could claim some of the legal financial obligations formerly attached only to marriage.[48] In effect, the distinction between marriage and non-marriage diminished again.

Other decisions followed. In 1979, the U.S. Supreme Court ruled in *Zablocki* v. *Redhail* that the state of Wisconsin could not place significant limitations on the acts of marriage, divorce, or remarriage. Justice Thurgood Marshall, writing for the Court, said that the "freedom to marry" allowed legislators to construct only "regulations that do not significantly interfere with" these decisions.[49] In *Turner* v. *Safley*, the Supreme Court defined the essence of marriage to be: "expressions of emotional support and public commitment"; an expectation of consummation; and "the receipt of government benefits." What began as an institution focused on procreation, fidelity, permanence, and social order had become instead a highly personalized extension of the welfare state.[50] As legal theorist Richard Posner has summarized, through this string of cases "the contemporary Court has simply 'deregulated' the family in much the same way that its discredited predecessors prevented states from regulating business."[51]

Recent "same-sex marriage" cases have further altered, and weakened the institution of the marriage-based family. In its 1993 decision in *Baehr* v. *Lewin*, the Hawaii Supreme Court took a minimalist view of marriage. Where the prior legal tradition understood marriage as pre-existing the state, this Court defined marriage as a "state conferred legal status." Where the prior tradition emphasized procreation, fidelity, and permanence, the new one saw marriage as simply "a partnership to which both parties bring their financial resources as well as their individual energies and efforts."[52] In a similar case, an Alaska judge relabeled the right to marry as "the right to choose one's life partner," completely abandoning the historic connections of marriage to children and civil society.[53] Turning to sentiment, the Supreme Court of Vermont ruled in *Baker* v. *State* that homosexuals asking for marriage were mere "Vermonters who seek nothing more, nor less, than legal protection and security for their avowed commitment to an intimate and lasting human relationship . . . a recognition of our common humanity." In an age of reproductive technology, and given the Vermont legislature's willingness to allow same-sex couples to adopt children, the Court could find no legally meaningful differences between same-sex and opposite-sex couples.[54] Rewriting history, the Massachusetts Supreme Judicial Court declared in *Goodridge* v. *Department of Public Health*:

> Simply put, the government creates civil marriage. In Massachusetts, civil marriage is, and since pre-Colonial days has been, precisely what its name implies: a wholly secular institution.[55]

Implying that marriage is good for the individual's self-esteem, the Court concluded that "[c]ivil marriage is at once a deeply personal commitment to another human being and a highly public celebration of the ideals of mutuality, companionship, intimacy, fidelity, and family."[56] Meanwhile, the Washington state Superior Court in *Anderson* v. *King County* further minimalized marriage, ruling in 2004 that "[t]o 'marry' means to join together in a close and personal way."[57] This was a far cry from Augustine's goods of marriage.

As early as 1979, Peter Riga could conclude that this de-institutionalizing process meant that marriage was no longer a legal category on which the state could predicate exclusive sexual relations, govern parent-child relations, regulate state financial assistance, or control the sexual conduct of minors. And there were consequences. Carl Anderson has traced how the Supreme Court's *Griswold* and *Loving* decisions gave direct impetus to the "no fault" divorce revolution, launched in California in 1969, and also advanced the radical Uniform Marriage and Divorce Act of 1970, drafted by the National Conference of Commissioners on Uniform State Laws.[58] In addition, it seems to be no coincidence that the *revolution* in marriage law, launched by *Griswold* (1965) and *Loving* (1967) and climaxing in *Eisenstadt* (1972), exactly coincides with the collapse of America's 20th Century culture of marriage. Consider the table below:

AMERICA'S MID-CENTURY "CULTURE OF MARRIAGE"

Year	Marriage Rate*	% Above Base Year (1932)
1932	56.0	0%
1936	74.0	+32%
1940	82.8	+48%
1944	76.5	+37%
1948	98.5	+76%
1952	83.2	+49%
1956	82.4	+47%
1960	73.5	+31%
1964	74.6	+33%
1968	79.1	+41%
1972 (*Eisenstadt* v. *Baird*)	76.5	+37%
1976	64.8	+16%
1980	61.4	+10%
1984	59.5	+6%
1988	54.6	-3%
1992	53.3	-5%
1996	49.7	-11%

*Marriages per 1000 Unmarried Women, 15 years & older

It shows the mid-century American "marriage boom," from a Depression-era low in 1932 (which is used as the base here) to a peak in the late 1940's, and revealing strength as late as 1972. The numbers fall sharply only after the *Eisenstadt* decision, and the boom finally disappears during the 1980's. While other forces and factors were surely involved, the American judiciary's philosophical choice of *Eisenstadt* over Augustine bore here very bitter fruit.

Deconstructing Parenthood

Over the same years, the federal courts also radically altered the meaning of parenthood. The primary targets here were the concepts of "legitimate" and "illegitimate" births. These distinctions were old. Indeed, they reached back into the early centuries of Western Civilization. The purposes behind them were simple and clear. First, a "legitimate" birth assured that the new child would have a permanent claim on a father's support because that father would be reasonably sure that the child was, in fact, his own. Second, laws built on these distinctions discouraged illegitimate births, encouraged marriage between a newly pregnant woman and her lover, and created incentives for parents to legitimize children already born. Third, these distinctions restrained the number of impoverished, mother-only households needing support from the community or state.

All the same, between 1968 and 1973, the U.S. Supreme Court essentially abolished "illegitimacy." In effect, the justices decided that the harm done to children labeled as "illegitimate" greatly outweighed such social purposes. Viewed from another angle, the public goals of family law were sacrificed once more to the pursuit of individual rights.

Both *Levy* v. *Louisiana* and *Glona* v. *American Guarantee and Liability Ins. Co.*, decided in 1968, involved a wrongful death statute in Louisiana. In *Levy*, the U.S. Supreme Court ruled that illegitimate children had the right to file a wrongful death suit over the demise of their mother. Writing for the majority, Justice Douglas underscored "that illegitimate children are not 'nonpersons.' They are humans, live, and have their being. They are clearly 'persons' within the meaning of the Equal Protection Clause of the 14th Amendment." He added that "it is invidious to discriminate against them when no action, conduct, or demeanor of theirs is possibly relevant to the harm that was done the mother."[59] For similar reasons, the Court ruled in *Glona* that the mother of an illegitimate child had the right to seek recompense for the wrongful death of her child.[60]

The Supreme Court returned to the issue in the early 1970's. At issue in *Weber* v. *Aetna Casualty Insurance Company* was a Louisiana statute that gave preference to legitimate children in the recovery of worker's compensation benefits. Again, the Court overturned the law. Writing for the majority, Louis Powell underscored the break being made with legal history:

> The status of illegitimacy has expressed through the ages society's condemnation of irresponsible liaisons beyond the bonds of marriage. But visiting this condemnation on the head of the infant is illogical and unjust. Moreover, imposing disability on the illegitimate child is contrary to the best interests of our system.[61]

The following year, in *New Jersey Welfare Rights Organization* v. *Cahill*, the Court reached a similar conclusion. At issue were welfare benefits paid only to married persons with children born in wedlock. A three-judge federal court had found the restriction to be rational, a way "to preserve and strengthen traditional family life." The Supreme Court reversed the decision, finding such a purpose irrelevant. Instead, the court insisted that children could not be penalized by unequal state treatment.[62]

Modern sensibilities, of course, focus sympathy on the child born out-of-wedlock. All the same, the consequences of eliminating "illegitimacy" are large. Through this act, marriage is both diminished and discouraged. The number of "out-of-wedlock" births predictably grows. As the table below indicates, the explosion in out-of-wedlock births among white women correlates precisely with the dismantling of "illegitimacy" as a legal concept through the 1968 *Loving* and *Glona* decisions (the rise in out-of-wedlock births among African Americans occurred earlier and was clearly driven by other causes, such as the legacy of slavery and the disorienting migration of rural Southern blacks to northern cities in the early 20th Century⁶³):

Births to Unmarried White Women
(as a percentage of all births)
1965:   4.0% [*Levy* v. *Louisiana* (1968)]
1970:   5.7%
1975:   7.3%
1980:   11.0%
1985:   15.0%
1990:   20.0%
1995:   25.3%
2000:   27.1%
Source: *Statistical Abstract of the United States*

Fatherhood, too, is diminished by the end to "illegitimacy" while the support willingly provided by fathers to children predictably falls. In consequence, welfare costs rise, as does the need for state apparati to track down absent fathers and collect child support. Children without fathers in their homes, particularly boys, also show much higher levels of school failure, criminality, illegal drug use, and incarceration. In the end, the only winner here is the welfare state.

Fate of the Republic

Married in 1972, just prior to the *Eisenstadt* decision, your author here stands as one of the last Americans to be bound in wedlock under the Augustinian dispensation. The revolution launched against it continues to our day. Some radical legal voices, who view the marital bond as slavery and happily married women as "the 'house niggers' of slave culture," urge the complete abolition of marriage.⁶⁴ More refined legal theorists, such as those at the American Law Institute (ALI), would achieve the same end through incremental steps. In 2000, for example, the ALI promulgated a new set of recommendations, *Principles of the Law of Family Dissolution: Analysis and Recommendations*. Key values driving the document include efforts to: "minimize reliance on stereotypes"; "preserve diversity in parenting arrangements"; eliminate "sexual orientation" and "sexual conduct" in determining child custody; recognize "de facto" parents as having claims on children equal to those of biological parents; and reduce marriage to a "legal formality" with no intrinsic claims.⁶⁵ As early as 1979, Peter Riga concluded that the "mental universe" behind *Eisenstadt* could find no state interest "forbidding simultaneous polygamy, or polyandry, since this has to do with the fundamental rights of privacy, marriage, and consenting adults."⁶⁶ And indeed, new polygamy cases are now moving their way through the federal court system: "the next frontier in the freedom to marry," advocates claim.

Freedom, though, will not be the result. As the American Founders understood, marriage and the autonomous family were the true bulwarks of liberty, for they were the principle rivals to the state. The English author G.K. Chesterton has made the same point. Writing nearly a century ago, he argued that "the institution of the home is the one anarchist institution.... It is the only check on the state that is bound to renew itself as eternally as the state, and more naturally than the state."[67] And surely, as the American judiciary has deconstructed marriage and the family over the last 40 years, the result has been the growth of government. Legal scholar Mary Ann Glendon describes "the modern attenuated nuclear family with loose blood and conjugal ties, where jobs and entitlements of various sorts are the most important forms of wealth, and a persons status in the 'feudalism of the new property' is derived from his occupation or his dependency relation with government."[68] Historian Nancy Cott concludes that marriage and family in America have already surrendered most authority to the state:

> . . . the interweaving or intrusion of government presence in the lives of individuals through their employment, schooling, immigration, taxation, social welfare, travel, and so on, has advanced so far that all are already in the state's grasp.[69]

In good Orwellian fashion, Americans have surrendered their liberty in the name of freedom.

Can these developments be reversed? Might a Supreme Court guided by Chief Justice John Roberts, with Samuel Alito, Antonin Scalia, and Clarence Thomas at his side, launch a counter-revolution in family law? Could they decouple the "right to privacy" from the sexual revolution? Might they overturn the "freedom to marry"? Could they restore "illegitimacy" as a concept of law? The odds are long. All the same, the future of what is left of the American Republic depends on the answers to these questions.

ENDNOTES

1. Francis J. Grund, *The Americans in their Moral, Social, and Political Relations* (New York and London: Johnson Reprint Co., 1968 [1837]): 170–72.

2. Bruce C. Hafen, "Puberty, Privacy and Protection: The Risks of Children's Rights,'" *American Bar Association Journal* 63 (Oct. 1977): 1383.

3. Carl E. Schneider, "The Channeling Function in Family Law," *Hofstra Law Review* 20 (Spring 1992): 506–07.

4. Martha Fineman, *The Autonomy Myth: A Theory of Dependency* (New York: The New Press, 2004): 63.

5. Lee E. Teitelbaum, "The Last Decade(s) of American Family Law," *Journal of Legal Education* 46 (Dec. 1996): 547.

6. Schneider, "The Channeling Function in Family Law," p. 513.

7. Peter J. Riga, "The Supreme Court's View of Marriage and the Family: Tradition or Transition?" *Journal of Family Law* 18 (#2, 1979–80): 306.

8. Charles J. Reid, Jr., "The Augustinian Goods of Marriage: The Disappearing Cornerstone of the American Law of Marriage," *The BYU Journal of Public Law* 18 (#2, 2004): 450–52.

9. Riga, "The Supreme Court's View of Marriage and the Family," p. 301; n.1.

10. Reid, "The Augustinian Goods of Marriage," pp. 454–58.

11. James Kent, *Commentaries on American Law, Vol. II*, (1838); in Reid, "The Augustinian Goods of Marriage," p. 460.

12. Joel Bishop, *New Commentaries on Marriage, Divorce, and Separation*; in Reid, "The Augustinian bonds of Marriage," p. 462.

13. Nancy Cott, *Public Vows: A History of Marriage and the Nation* (Cambridge, MA: Harvard University Press, 2000): 9–10.

14. "Letters on Marriage" (1775), reprinted in *The Works of the Rev. John Witherspoon* (Philadelphia: William W. Woodward, 1802): 166.

15. Entry for June 2, 1778; in Lyman H. Butterfield, ed., *Diary and Autobiography of John Adams, Volume 4* (Cambridge, MA: Belknap Press, 1962): 123.

16. Grund, *The Americans in their Moral, Social, and Political Relations*, p. 172.

17. Alexis de Tocqueville, *Democracy in America, Book Three,* Chapter XI.

18. *Matchin* v. *Matchin*, 6 Pa. 332, 337 (1847).

19. *Reynolds* v. *Reynolds*, 85 Mass. 605 (1862).

20. *Reynolds* v. *United States*, 98 U.S. 145, 165 (1878).

21. *Murphy* v. *Ramsey* 114 U.S. 45 (1885). See also *Davis* v. *Beason* 133 U.S. 333 (1890).

22. *Maynard* v. *Hill*, 125 U.S. 190, 210–11 (1888).

23. *Meyer* v. *Nebraska*, 262 U.S. 390 (1923).

24. *Pierce v. Society of Sisters*, 268 U.S. 510 (1925).

25. *Prince* v. *Massachusetts*, 321 U.S. 158, 166 (1944). On these cases, see also: William C. Duncan, "State, Society, and the Redefinition of Marriage," *The Family in America* 19 (September 2005): 3–4.

26. *Skinner* v. *Oklahoma*, 316 U.S. 1110, 1113 (1942).

27. *DeBurgh* v. *DeBurgh*, 39 Cal. 2nd 858, 250 P. 2nd 598 (1957).

28. *Baker* v. *Nelson*, 191 N.W. 2d 185 (Minn 1971).

29. *Wisconsin* v. *Yoder*, 406 U.S. 205, 232 (1972).

30. *Singer* v. *Hara*, 522 P. 2d 1187, 1195 (Wash. Ct. App. 1974).

31. *In re J.P.*, 648 P. 2d 1364, 1373 (Utah 1982).

32. *Poe* v. *Ullman*, 367 U.S. 497 (1960).

33. *Griswold* v. *Connecticut*, 381 U.S. 486 (1965).

34. Riga, "The Supreme Court's View of Marriage and the Family," p. 302.

35. *Eisenstadt* v. *Baird*, 495 U.S. 438, 453 (1972).

36. Riga, "The Supreme Court's View of Marriage and The Family," pp. 302–04.

37. *Roe* v. *Wade*, 410 U.S. 113 (1973); *Doe* v. *Bolton*, 410 U.S. 179 (1973).

38. *Planned Parenthood of Missouri* v. *Danforth*, 428 U.S. 52, 69 (1976).

39. *Carey* v. *Population Services International*, 431 U.S. 679 (1977).

40. *Planned Parenthood of Southeastern Pa.* v. *Casey*, 505 U.S. 833 (1992).

41. *Lawrence and Garner* v. *Texas*, 539 U.S. 558 (2003).

42. *Cleveland* v. *U.S.*, 329 U.S. 14 (1946).

43. *Loving* v. *Virginia* 388 U.S. 1 (1967).

44. Robert Drinan, "The *Loving* Decision and The Freedom to Marry," *Ohio State Law Journal* 29 (1968): 358, 367.

45. *Boddie* v. *Connecticut*, 401 U.S. 371 (1971).

46. Carl Anderson, "The Supreme Court and the Economics of the Family," *The Family in America* 1 (October 1987): 3.

47. *Eisenstadt* v. *Baird*, 405 U.S. 438, 453 (1972).

48. *Marvin* v. *Marvin*, 134 Cal. R. ptr. 815, 557. P. 2d 106 (Cal.1976).

49. *Zablocki* v. *Redhail*, 434 U.S. 374 (1978).

50. *Turner* v. *Safely*, 482 U.S. 78 (1987).

51. Richard Posner, *The Economics of Justice* (Cambridge, MA: Harvard University Press, 1981): 328.

52. *Baehr* v. *Lewin*, 852 P. 2d 44 (Haw.1993).

53. *Brause* v. *Bureau of Vital Statistics*, 1998 WL 88743 (Alaska Super. Ct. 1998).

54. *Baker* v. *State of Vermont*, 744 A.2d 864, 889 (Vt. 1999).

55. *Goodridge* v. *Department of Public Health*, 798 N. E.2d 954 (Mass. 2003).

56. *Id.*

57. *Anderson* v. *King County*, 2004 WL 1738447, #2 (Wash. Super. Ct. 2004).

58. Anderson, "The Supreme Court and the Economics of the Family," p. 3.

59. *Levy* v. *Louisiana*, 391 U.S. 68 (1938).

60. *Glona* v. *American Guarantee and Liability Ins. Co.*, 391 U.S. 73 (1968).

61. *Weber* v. *Aetna Casualty Insurance Company*, 406 U.S. 164, 175 (1972). See also: Lynn Wardle, "Fragile Families and Family Law," in Lori Kowaleski-Jones and Nicholas H. Wolfingers, eds., *Fragile Families and the Marriage Agenda* (Belin: Springer Verlag, Gmbh, 2005): 73–82.

62. *New Jersey Welfare Rights Organization* v. *Cahill*, 411 U.S. 619 (1973) (per curiam).

63. See: Daniel P. Moynihan, *The Negro American Family: The Case for National Action*, found in Lee Rainwater and William L. Yancy, eds., *The Moynihan Report and the Politics of Controversy* (Cambridge, MA: MIT Press, 1967); and Donna L. Franklin, *Ensuring Inequality: The Structural Transformation of the African American Family* (New York: Oxford University Press, 1997).

64. Dianne Post, "Why Marriage Should Be Abolished," *Women's Rights Law Reporter* 18 (Spring 1997): 312–13.

65. The American Law Institute, *Principles of the Law of Family Dissolution: Analysis and Recommendations* (Washington, DC: Matthew Bender and Co., 2002). For a thorough critique of the document, see: Dan Cere, *The Future of Family Law: Law and the Marriage Crisis in North America* (New York: Institute for American Values, 2005).

66. Riga, "The Supreme Court's View of Marriage and the Family," p. 326.

67. G.K. Chesterton, *What's Wrong with the World* [1910] and *The Superstition of Divorce* [1920]; in *Collected Works. Volume IV* (San Francisco: Ignatius Press, 1987): 67, 256.

68. Mary Ann Glendon, "The New Family and the New Property," *Tulane Law Review* 53 (1979): 709–10.

69. Cott, *Public Vows*, p. 213.

Four
The Judicial Assault on Religion
by Charles E. Rice

What we are observing here is not . . . a struggle of religion against no religion. It is instead a battle pitting one religion, broadly speaking, against another. On one side we have the biblical faith of Jews and Christians. On the other side, secularism. . . .

For each element of Judeo-Christian faith, secularism has its counterpart. . . . [S]ecularism promises eternal life—well, long life, which is the central point of the most common strain of secular faith and which explains the pop-cultural focus on moral commandments having to do with physical health: Thou shalt not smoke. Thou shalt not get fat. Thou shall fight global warming by taking the bus to work. Indeed, thou shalt vote for public subsidies for mass transit. In secularist doctrine, a fat person isn't merely unhealthy; he is a sinner in need of salvation. To address his situation, one secular gospel preaches the good news of the South Beach Diet, another that of the apostle Atkins. There is a secular creation account—evolution through random mutation and natural selection, a just-so story increasingly challenged by scientists. . . .

[I]n the controversies surrounding the Pledge of Allegiance and the LA. County seal, what we're seeing is an unacknowledged interreligious civil war. Centuries ago in Europe and the Middle East, intolerant faiths sought to suppress one another, erasing symbols of their rivals wherever possible. . . . Today the church of secularism agitates against its rival, the Judeo-Christian tradition. In the interest of honest debate . . . it would be of benefit to recognize secularism for what it is: an aggressive religion competing for converts, a faith lacking the candor to speak openly of its aims. [1]

David Klinghoffer, columnist for the *Jewish Forward*, wrote this comment in reaction to the campaign to erase "under God" from the Pledge of Allegiance and the decision in 2004 by Los Angeles County to remove a tiny cross from the

County seal. He describes a religious and cultural war in which the courts are engaged on the side of secularism.[2]

What are the origins of this conflict? "On the one hand," wrote Cardinal Joseph Ratzinger (now Pope Benedict XVI), "the modern age boasts of having discovered the idea of human rights . . . and of having proclaimed these rights in solemn declarations. On the other hand, these rights . . . have never been so profoundly and radically denied on the practical level. The roots of this contradiction are . . . in the Enlightenment theories of human knowledge and the vision of human freedom connected with them, and in the theories of the social contract and their idea of society. The fundamental dogma of the Enlightenment is that man must overcome the prejudices inherited from tradition; he must have the boldness to free himself from every authority in order to think on his own, using nothing but his own reason." [3]

Under that Enlightenment philosophy, "[r]eligion had to be purged from public life because, with the enshrinement of 'reason' as the guide of man, the experiences which inspired religious symbolisms were deemed unscientific [and] 'irrational' because they cannot be understood in scientific categories. Religion was valuable . . . only as a . . . device of social utility which compelled men to act in an orderly fashion. . . . [A]ny affirmations of the spirit such as prayer had to be eliminated as a precondition to progress in public life."[4]

The privatization of religion has been impressed on the law, not by elected representatives of the people, but by Supreme Court Justices, appointed for life. Those judicial edicts are enforced by state and lower federal courts and implemented in varying degrees by state and local officials. State courts, incidentally, have power to interpret state constitutions and laws so as to confer greater protection on individual rights than is afforded by the United States Constitution as interpreted by the Supreme Court of the United States. [5] State courts have employed this power to exceed Supreme Court mandates on issues of religion, marriage and other matters. [6]

The First Amendment's religion clauses provide: "Congress shall make no law respecting an establishment of religion, or prohibiting the free exercise thereof." Those provisions were designed to insulate the new, federal government from religious conflict by reserving the subject of religion to the states and by mandating neutrality among religious sects on the part of the federal government. The body of the Constitution reinforced that neutrality by providing that "no religious Test shall ever be required as a Qualification to Any Office or public Trust under the United States.[7]

The Free Exercise Clause forbids the federal government to interfere with the free religious exercise of all, whether believers in God or not.[8] The Establishment Clause had a limited purpose. "[T]he principal importance of the [First] Amendment," wrote Professor Edward S. Corwin, "lay in the separation which it effected between the . . . jurisdictions of state and nation regarding religion, rather than in its bearing on the . . . separation of church and state."[9]

Neither the Constitution nor the First Amendment precluded the new government from acknowledging the existence of God who had been explicitly recognized in the Declaration of Independence. The Establishment Clause required the government of the United States to maintain neutrality among religious sects, while permitting that government to encourage belief in God and in the general principles of Christianity:

> Probably at the time of the adoption of the constitution, and of the first amendment to it . . . the general, if not the universal sentiment in America was, that Christianity ought to receive encouragement from the state, so far as was not incompatible with the private rights of conscience, and the freedom of religious worship. An attempt to level all religions, and to make it a matter of state policy to hold all in utter indifference, would have created universal disapprobation if not universal indignation. . . .
>
> The real object of the amendment was not to countenance, much less to advance Mahometanism, or Judaism, or infidelity, by prostrating Christianity; but to exclude all rivalry among Christian sects, and to prevent any national ecclesiastical establishment which should give to a hierarchy the exclusive patronage of the national government.[10]

On September 22–24, 1789, both houses of the First Congress did two things. They approved the First Amendment; and they called on the President to proclaim a national day of "public thanksgiving and prayer, to be observed by acknowledging, with grateful hearts, the many signal favors of Almighty God, especially by affording them an opportunity peaceably to establish a Constitution of government for their safety and happiness."[11] The President did so, stating that "it is the duty of all Nations to acknowledge the providence of Almighty God, to obey His will, to be grateful for His benefits, and humbly to implore his protection and favor."[12] As discussed below, the Supreme Court now interprets the First Amendment to forbid all governments, state, federal and local, to affirm that, in fact, God even exists. The evident intent of the First Congress is to the contrary. Would Congress have approved an amendment to forbid governmental promotion of prayer and recognition of God on the same day it requested the President to proclaim a national day of prayer to that God? Not likely.

We have come a long way from the intent of that First Congress. Consider *ACLU v. Ashbrook*,[13] where a state court judge hung a framed poster of the Ten Commandments on his courtroom wall; on the opposite wall he hung a framed poster of the Bill of Rights. Also on display were posters and pictures featuring Jefferson, Madison, Hamilton and Lincoln. The District Court ordered the Commandments poster removed. When the Court of Appeals panel affirmed, Judge Alice M. Batchelder dissented and noted, approvingly, that the state court judge's brief had pointed out "the absurdity of this case, wherein a federal judge, sitting beneath 'a magnificent mural of the Ten Commandments flanked by two angels,' has ordered a state judge to remove from *his* courtroom a poster containing the plain text of the same Ten Commandments." Or imagine yourself as one of the students at Everett Middle School in Wheat Ridge, Colorado, when you hear the Pledge of Allegiance, as amended by the school guidance counselor, come over the intercom. "Instead of 'one nation, under God,' the voice said, 'one nation, under your belief system.' As one complaining mother said, the students never even got to 'indivisible.'"[14]

As discussed below, the Supreme Court interprets the Establishment Clause to require an official neutrality between theism and non-theism. That amounts in effect to an establishment of an agnostic secular religion which in, practice, is hostile to Christianity. In *Walz v. Egg Harbor Township Board of Education*,[15] the Court of Appeals upheld a public school district's order forbidding Daniel Walz, a pre-kindergarten student, to hand out, during a spring holiday gift exchange, "pencils to his classmates with the imprint, 'Jesus [Loves] The Little Children' (heart symbol). Mrs. Walz had purchased the pencils at a local store because she thought the pencils were 'pretty . . . and [Daniel] liked them. . . . We both thought that [the pencils] would be his little gift at Easter, at the Easter party or the spring party.'" What Mrs. Walz didn't count on, however, was the ability of liberal educators to regard the pencils as dangerous weapons and the readiness of courts to give the educators a blank check in that regard. In a revealing footnote the court said, "Elementary school marks a child's introduction to formal public education and requires parents to entrust their child's development to another adult mentor. . . . ('The public school is at once the symbol of our democracy and the most pervasive means for promoting our common destiny.'). During these formative years, elementary school educators must be able to structure an appropriate curriculum to achieve the desired pedagogical and behavioral goals."[16] Could that civic orthodoxy, excluding any mention of Christ, possibly evoke an image of the Hitler youth?

Perhaps the most visible manifestation of a governmental and cultural hostility to Christianity is the annual round of litigation and controversy over Christmas. As author John Gibson[17] describes it, the war on Christmas is really a war on Christians. "When I asked people," he said in an interview, "'Why did you ban this Christmas tree?' or, 'Why did you fire Santa?' . . . they would say, kind of just blandly, 'Because it's Christian.' They wouldn't say that about any other religion. There's this kind of accepted, casual bias against Christians, and I think it's mostly because of politics, because conservative Christians have gotten behind certain political questions, like abortion or gay marriage. People are opposed to them politically, and therefore they feel no compunction about transferring their hostility to the way they treat these holidays. You hear people say, 'Christians should take it indoors. We don't want you guys in our face'"[18]

A strong contender for the gold medal in the Christmas Obliteration Olympics has to be the incident described in a news story on the same page of the *Washington Times* as that interview of John Gibson quoted above. "Library officials in Memphis, Tenn., have banned Jesus, Joseph, Mary and the wise men from the Nativity display. . . . A member of the music ministry at Broadmoor [Baptist] Church wanted to include a small Nativity scene on the Memphis/Shelby County Public Library's community shelves, traditionally open to groups and individuals for announcements, as part of an announcement of the church's Christmas show. Library officials accepted [the] announcement but . . . told her she would have to remove the 'inappropriate' figures of Jesus, Joseph, Mary and the wise men from the Nativity scene and limit it to farm animals alone."[19] Perhaps only a politically correct bureaucrat—or academic—could envision a "Nativity scene" with nothing but a couple of donkeys staring at each other over an empty manger.

Judicial remedies for alleged infringements of the free exercise of religion can be difficult to obtain. In *Employment Division v. Smith*,[20] the Supreme Court held that a restriction on the free exercise of religion resulting from "generally applicable prohibitions of socially harmful conduct" will not be subjected to "strict scrutiny" requiring a "compelling government interest" but will be upheld if it satisfies the more lenient requirement that it have a rational basis. "The only decisions," said the Court, "in which we have held that the First Amendment bars application of a neutral, generally applicable law to religiously motivated action have involved not the Free Exercise Clause alone, but the Free Exercise Clause in conjunction with other constitutional protections, such as freedom of speech and of the press."[21] Unless a case involves "such a hybrid situation,"[22], a general law restricting an individual's free exercise of religion will be upheld on a showing merely of a rational basis.

Congress enacted the Religious Freedom Restoration Act (RFRA) to overturn the *Smith* decision. The Court held RFRA unconstitutional because it exceeded Congress' power to enforce the Fourteenth Amendment.[23] Congress responded by enacting, under the Spending and Commerce clauses of the Constitution,[24] the Religious Land Use and Institutionalized Persons Act (RLUIPA). RLUIPA required heightened scrutiny by the courts in religious exercise cases involving land use regulation and institutionalized persons. In *Cutter v. Wilkinson*, the Court held that the Establishment Clause was not violated by RLUIPA's provision that "No government shall impose a substantial burden on a person . . . in . . . an institution" unless the burden furthers "a compelling governmental interest" by "the least restrictive means."[25] The Court held merely that the provision was not void on its face under the Establishment Clause, leaving to further cases the constitutionality of that provision in specific situations. Nor did the Court decide whether the provision exceeds Congress' power under the Spending and Commerce clauses.

Federal courts have no monopoly on interpretations hostile to religious freedom, as seen in the ruling of the California Supreme Court in *Catholic Charities of Sacramento, Inc., v. Superior Court.*[26] The Women's Contraception Equity Act required that all health care plans providing prescription drug coverage must cover contraception as well. The law provided an exemption for "a religious employer." The WCEA defined "religious employer" "as "an entity for which each of the following is true: (A) The inculcation of religious values is the purpose of the entity. (B) The entity primarily employs persons who share the religious tenets of the entity. (C) The entity serves primarily persons who share the religious tenets of the entity. (D) The entity is a nonprofit organization as described in . . . the Internal Revenue Code. . . . "[27]

The court held that, despite the fact that the Catholic Church regarded Catholic Charities as part of its apostolate, Catholic Charities was not a "religious employer" because most of the people it serves are not Catholic. The only way Catholic Charities could get around the statute would be to cease offering prescription drug coverage to its employees. Justice Janice Rogers Brown, in dissent, raised the issue of whether the Free Exercise Clause should be interpreted to permit government to tell a religious organization that what that church defines as its religious activity is not religious. Justice Brown's analysis is worth an extended quote:

> After *Smith*, neutral, generally applicable laws do not have to survive compelling state interest review. Such laws require no justification no matter how severely they burden the individual religious claimant and no matter how inconsequential the government interest. . . . It is, however, far from self-evident, if or how, *Smith* applies to laws that . . . contravene the religious conduct of religious organizations. . . . [M]ay the government determine what parts of . . . religious organizations are religious and what parts are secular? And . . . may the government make such distinctions in order to infringe the religious freedom of that portion of the organization the government characterizes as secular? . . .
>
> To permit religious beliefs to excuse acts contrary to law, the *Smith* court reasoned, "'would be to make the professed doctrines of religious belief superior to the law of the land, and in effect to permit *every citizen* to become a law unto *himself.*" . . . Since *Smith* focused exclusively on the individual's free exercise of religion, some courts have reasoned that religious institutions are exempted entirely from the *Smith* analysis. . . .
>
> [T]he government may generally separate the religious from the secular to decide how it will dispense its benefits, but it cannot parse a bona fide religious organization into "secular" and "religious" components solely to impose burdens on the secular portion. . . .
>
> [G]overnment action may burden the free exercise of religion in two different ways: 'by interfering with a believer's ability to observe the commands or practices of the faith . . . and by encroaching on the ability of a church to manage its internal affairs.' . . . Catholic Charities would be a religious employer if the legislature had not designed the exemption narrowly enough to exclude it.[28]

To place these Free Exercise problems in context we have to examine the Court's interpretation of the Establishment Clause. The freedom of private persons and religious entities is the direct concern of the Free Exercise Clause. Governmental religious neutrality is the concern of the Establishment Clause. But individuals and religious entities can be involved in the public sector so as to be affected by Establishment Clause strictures as to what sort of speech or conduct government can allow in that public sector.

To put it simply, the Supreme Court has reinvented the Establishment Clause so as to restrict the free exercise of churches as well as individuals when their activities or speech intersect the public sector. The Court's reinvention of the Establishment Clause has had a decisive impact because of the Court's enlargement of its own role.

One reason for unpredictability in religion cases is the Court's treatment of its own constitutional interpretations as having the same authority as the words of the Constitution. Article VI provides that "this Constitution and the laws of the United States, which shall be made in Pursuance thereof . . . shall be the supreme Law of the Land, and the judges in every State shall be bound thereby." In 1816 the Supreme Court affirmed its rightful authority to review the judgments of state courts.[29] But not until 1958, in *Cooper v. Aaron*, a school desegregation case, did the Court claim that its decisions were on the same level of authority as the text of the Constitution itself. The Court in *Cooper* asserted "the basic principle that the federal judiciary is supreme in the exposition of the law of the Constitution. . . . It follows that the interpretation of the Fourteenth Amendment enunciated by this Court in [*Brown v. Bd. of Education*] is the supreme law of the land and Art. VI . . . makes it of binding effect on the States."[30] If it were literally true that each Supreme Court decision is "the supreme law of the land," the Court could never reverse its decisions; but it has done so numerous times. What *Cooper* signals instead is that the Court has appointed itself as a continuing constitutional convention. Judge Learned Hand's observation is pertinent, that "it would be most irksome to be ruled by a bevy of Platonic Guardians, even if I knew how to choose them, which I assuredly do not."[31] *Cooper v. Aaron* accounts in part for the general, but erroneous, assumption that the only corrective for a Supreme Court misinterpretation of the Constitution is a constitutional amendment.

In accord with the theory of *Cooper v. Aaron*, Supreme Court decisions on constitutional issues tend to focus on prior decisions of the Court rather than on the language and intent of the constitutional provisions themselves. The rule of *stare decisis* does require courts to follow the precedents of decided cases.[32] But that doctrine has less application to constitutional than to nonconstitutional cases.[33] "If the Court 'errs' on nonconstitutional matters, legislatures may respond by passing a new statute. Errors of constitutional dimension, however, need attention by the judiciary. . . . [E]rrors of constitutional doctrine require correction." [34] As Professor Gary Lawson has persuasively argued, the Supreme Court is bound to apply the Constitution rather than a conflicting prior judicial decision, just as it must choose the Constitution over conflicting legislation or executive action.[35]

A striking example of such "bootstrap jurisprudence," elevating the Court's own decisions over the intent of the Constitution, is the Court's misconstruction of the Fourteenth Amendment to incorporate and apply against the states virtually all of the first eight amendments of the Bill of Rights, including the Establishment Clause. The protections of the Bill of Rights, as the Supreme Court held in 1833, restricted the federal government and not the states.[36] For protection against state governments the people relied on state constitutions and state courts. The Supreme Court , however, began to rule in the 1920s that the Fourteenth Amendment guarantee of "liberty" makes the fundamental protections of the Bill of Rights, including the religion clauses of the First Amendment, binding on state and local governments.[37]

The Court uses this Incorporation Doctrine not only to enforce a broad range of rights the Court regards as fundamental, but also to invent new rights and enforce them against every state and local government, as with abortion, pornography, criminal procedure, etc. But even if the Incorporation Doctrine were legitimate, it should not include the Establishment Clause.[38] That clause was a demarcation of federal and state jurisdiction over religion rather than a protection of "liberty" such as freedom of speech. As Justice Clarence Thomas put it, "the Establishment Clause is a federalism provision which, for this reason, resists incorporation."[39] "If the Establishment Clause does not restrain the States," Thomas noted in restating the obvious, "then it has no application . . . where only state action is at issue."[40]

In *Elk Grove Unified School District v. Newdow*,[41] the Court held that the father of a public school child, who did not have custody of the child, lacked standing to challenge the inclusion of "under God" in the pledge of allegiance. In his concurring opinion, Justice Thomas explained his view that the Establishment Clause, unlike the Free Exercise Clause, does not protect any individual right and therefore, even if the Incorporation Doctrine were legitimate, the Establishment Clause should not be incorporated into the Fourteenth Amendment's protection of rights against state infringement:

> The Establishment Clause . . . probably prohibits Congress from establishing a national religion. . . . Perhaps more importantly, the Clause made clear that Congress could not interfere with state establishments. . . . Nothing in the text of the Clause suggests that it reaches any further. The Establishment Clause does not purport to protect individual rights. By contrast, the Free Exercise Clause plainly protects individuals against congressional interference with the right to exercise their religion. . . . The best argument in favor of incorporation would be that, by disabling Congress from establishing a national religion, the Clause protected an individual right, enforceable against the Federal Government, to be free from coercive federal establishments. Incorporation of this individual right, the argument goes, makes sense. . . . But even assuming that the Establishment Clause precludes the Federal Government from establishing a national religion, it does not follow that the Clause created or protects any individual right. [I]t is more likely that States and only States were the direct beneficiaries. . . . Moreover, incorporation of this putative individual right leads to a peculiar outcome: It would prohibit precisely what the Establishment Clause was intended to protect—*state* establishments of religion.[42]

Through the Incorporation Doctrine, the Court binds every unit of state and local government, and every public official, by the Court's own version of the Bill of Rights on virtually every imaginable issue capable of definition in terms of individual rights. In the process, the Court has given the Establishment Clause a new meaning that would have astonished the members of the First Congress. First, let us note Justice Thomas' appeal for a return to coercion as the touchstone of an Establishment Clause violation. In *Van Orden v. Perry*,[43] a Ten Commandments case, he said that, even if the Clause is incorporated into the Fourteenth Amendment, the Court should return "to the original meaning of the word 'establishment.' . . . The Framers understood an establishment 'necessarily [to] involve actual legal coercion.' . . . ('The coercion that was a hallmark of historical establishments of religion was coercion of religious orthodoxy and of financial support *by force of law and threat of penalty*.'] 'In other words, establishment at the founding involved, for example, mandatory observance or mandatory payment of taxes supporting ministers.' . . . *And 'government practices that have nothing to do with creating or maintaining . . . coercive state establishments* simply do not 'implicate the possible liberty interest of being free from coercive state establishments.'"[44]

Thomas went on to criticize the Court's decisions which "permit even the slightest public recognition of religion to constitute an establishment of religion. . . . [I]ndividuals frequenting a county courthouse have successfully challenged . . . a sign at the courthouse alerting the public that the building was closed for Good Friday and containing a 4-inch high crucifix." . . . [I]n a seeming attempt to balance out its willingness to consider almost any acknowledgment of religion an establishment, in other cases Members of this Court have concluded that the term or symbol at issue has no religious meaning by virtue of its ubiquity or rote ceremonial invocation. . . . But words such as 'God' have religious significance. . . . Much, if not all, of this would be avoided if the Court would return to the views of the Framers and adopt coercion as the touchstone for our Establishment Clause inquiry."[45] Interestingly, Justice Thomas, citing his *Newdow* opinion, said in *Van Orden* that "The declaration that our country is 'one Nation under God' necessarily 'entail[s] an affirmation that God exists."[46]

The Ten Commandments cases illustrate the Court's Establishment Clause theory. In 1980, the Court had ruled that a display of the Commandments in a public school classroom violates the Establishment Clause.[47] After 1980, and as of the time of the Chief Justice Moore controversy we will discuss below, lower courts had ruled both ways on the Commandments, with the result depending on the context. The general approach required that the display must have been placed for a secular purpose and its primary effect must not have been to advance religion. The display could recognize the Commandments as historical fact, but could not endorse religion or the Commandments.[48] In 2005 the Court confirmed this approach. *Van Orden v. Perry*[49] upheld the display of a monument inscribed with the Ten Commandments on the Texas State Capitol grounds. Chief Justice Rehnquist, in the plurality opinion, noted that there is "no evidence" of a "primarily religious purpose" in the placement of the monument. The monument was donated by the Eagles, a civic organization. The Court upheld the District Court's conclusions that the monument would not convey to a "reasonable observer . . . the message that the State was seeking to endorse religion" and that "the State had a valid secular purpose in . . . commending the Eagles for their efforts to reduce juvenile delinquency."[50] Rehnquist said:

> Our opinions, like our [Supreme Court] building, have recognized the role the Decalogue plays in America's heritage. . . . The Executive and Legislative Branches have also acknowledged the historical role of the Ten Commandments. . . . Of course, the Ten Commandments are religious. . . . But Moses was a lawgiver as well as a religious leader. And the Ten Commandments have an undeniable historical meaning. . . . Simply having religious content or promoting a message consistent with a religious doctrine does not run afoul of the Establishment Clause. . . . Texas has treated her Capitol grounds monuments as representing the several strands in the State's political and legal history. The inclusion of the Ten Commandments monument in this group has a dual significance, partaking of both religion and government."[51]

In the companion case of *McCreary County v. ACLU*,[52] the Court held unconstitutional the display on courthouse walls of the Ten Commandments surrounded by other documents because the purpose of the display was religious.

"[T]he First Amendment mandates governmental neutrality between religion and religion, and between religion and nonreligion. . . . When the government acts with the ostensible and predominant purpose of advancing religion, it violates that central Establishment Clause value of official religious neutrality."[53]

The Ten Commandments cases follow the path projected in the 1960s when the Court redefined the Establishment Clause's requirement of governmental neutrality among religious sects to mean that government must be neutral as between theism and non-theism. In *Torcaso v. Watkins*, the Court struck down Maryland's requirement that all public officials declare their belief in God because it invaded "freedom of belief and religion" and because the "power and authority of the State of Maryland thus is put on the side of one particular sort of believers—those who are willing to say they believe in the existence of God."[54] Nontheistic creeds were defined by the court to be religions. The court held that "neither a State nor the Federal Government can constitutionally aid all religions as against non-believers, and neither can aid those religions based on a belief in the existence of God as against those religions founded on different beliefs."[55] In a footnote to his opinion for the Court, , Mr. Justice Black said: "Among religions in this country which do not teach what would commonly be considered a belief in the existence of God are Buddhism, Taoism, Ethical Culture, Secular Humanism and others."[56]

In 1963, the Court adopted the Torraso neutrality principle as the rule for the Establishment Clause and ruled out the voluntary reading of the Bible and recitation of the Lord's Prayer in public school classrooms.[57] Justice William Brennan captured the essence of that ruling in his concurrence arguing that the words "under God could be kept in the" Pledge of Allegiance only because they "no longer have a religious purpose or meaning." Instead, according to Brennan, they "may merely recognize the historical fact that our Nation was believed to have been founded 'under God.'"[58] This supposed neutrality would logically prevent an assertion by any government official that the Declaration of Independence states the truth when it affirms the existence and providence of God. Suppose a pupil asks his public school teacher whether God exists, as the Declaration affirms. If the teacher says, "Yes," that is unconstitutional as a preference of theism; if the teacher says no, that is unconstitutional as a preference of atheism. The only answer the teacher can give, according to the theory of the Court, is to suspend judgment, to say, in effect, "I (the state) do not (or cannot) know." But this is an affirmation of a non-theistic religion—agnosticism. This suspension of judgment on the existence of God repudiates the American Founding, and specifically the First Congress, through the effective establishment of agnostic secularism as the national religion.

The law is an educator. The Court's expulsion of theistic affirmations, unless they are ceremonial and meaningless, from schools and other areas of the public square contributes to the secularization of the culture. It would be misleading, however, to pin the blame simply on the Supreme Court and other federal courts for the exclusion of religion from public life. The problem is primarily cultural and only secondarily constitutional. Local governments, public school, library and other officials have hastened not only to comply with court orders but to capitulate to demands of pressure groups that exceed any realistic bounds of such court orders. John Gibson, host of "The Big Story" on Fox News Channel, and author of *"The War on Christmas"* described the usual process:

> Q.: You write that ACLU has been providing the "legal muscle and pretzel logic" in the war. How are they doing that?
> A.: They threaten: "We're willing to litigate this. We realize the court has not said this is illegal, but we're willing to make a case for it nonetheless." And if you follow the trail of crumbs, you arrive at a conclusion that they say this and they get away with it because organizations like schools and libraries and so forth are just afraid of incurring litigation costs and, perhaps, losing and having to pay the ACLU's litigation costs.[59]

The judicial pressure on freedom of religion goes beyond the suppression of Christian expression in the public forum. As will be discussed in other chapters of this book, the displacement of Christian views can be seen in the treatment by state as well as federal courts of issues relating to marriage and the family which implicate religious principles. For example, on one day, August 22, 2005, the California Supreme Court casually redefined the state law on the family in three cases:[60] In *Elisa B.*, the court ruled that a woman who agreed to raise children with her lesbian partner, and held out as her own the twins resulting from her partner's artificial insemination by an anonymous donor, is the childrens' parent under the Uniform Parentage Act and has an obligation to support them. In *K.M. v. E.G.*, the plaintiff, who had donated her eggs so that her registered domestic partner could bear a child through *in vitro* fertilization, petitioned to establish her parental relationship with the partner's twin children after the relationship ended. The court held that: "both lesbian partners were parents of the children," and that "Family Code section 7613 . . . which provides that a man is not a father if he provides semen to a physician to inseminate a woman who is not his wife, does not apply when a woman provides her ova to impregnate her partner in a lesbian relationship in order to produce children who will be raised in their joint home."[61]

In *Kristine H.*, the court held that the biological mother of a child was estopped to challenge a judgment in which she had stipulated that both she and her lesbian partner, Lisa, were "the joint intended legal parents of the child, "and that Lisa "is the legal second mother/parent" of the child. [62] Interestingly, Kristine and Lisa stipulated in court their joint parenthood when Kristine was seven months' pregnant. Until delivery, would Kristine have had the right, under *Roe v. Wade*, to kill the child? Or would Lisa's consent, unlike that of a father, be necessary for the child to be killed by abortion?

A similar abrogation of legislature prerogative can be seen in *Goodridge v. Dept. of Public Health*,[63] where the Massachusetts Supreme Judicial Court construed "civil marriage to mean the voluntary union of two persons as spouses, to the exclusion of all others,"[64] and declared that "barring an individual from the protections, benefits, and obligations of civil marriage solely because that person would marry a person of the same sex violates the Massachusetts Constitution."[65]

Or consider the implications for the family of the Ninth Circuit decision in *Fields v. Palmdale School District*,[66] where children were questioned in their public elementary school, without parental knowledge, about topics such as the frequency of 'thinking about having sex' and 'thinking about touching other peoples' private parts.'"[] The questioning was part of a survey the school district was conducting regarding "psychological barriers to learning." The Court of Appeals held that parents have "no fundamental right . . . to be the *exclusive* provider of information regarding sexual matters to their children, either independent of their right to direct the upbringing and education of their children or encompassed by it. We also hold that parents have no . . . right to override the determinations of public schools as to the information to which their children will be exposed while enrolled as students."[67]

The Supreme Court's distortion of both religion clauses can create problems of conscience, especially for public officials. The case of Chief Justice Roy Moore illustrates that conscience problem and raises the issue of the legitimacy of Supreme Court doctrines that contradict the evident meaning of the Constitution. In 2001, Alabama Chief Justice Moore installed a 5,280 pound monument, featuring the Ten Commandments, in the rotunda of the Alabama State Judicial Building. The federal courts ordered it removed. When Moore refused, he was suspended and removed from office by the Alabama Court of the Judiciary. His removal was affirmed by the Alabama Supreme Court.[68]

In his trial testimony, Chief Justice Moore directly challenged the suspension of judgment on God required by the Supreme Court-mandated neutrality between theism and non-theism.[69] District Court Judge Myron H. Thompson rejected Moore's premise that the Constitution allows the state to recognize God: "Nowhere does the Constitution or the First Amendment recognize the sovereignty of any God, . . . or describe the relationship between God and the state. In fact, this country's founding documents support the idea that it is from the people, and not God, that the state draws its powers. . . . [T]he Declaration of Independence states that 'governments are instituted among Men, deriving their just powers from the consent of the governed,' and the Constitution begins with that immortal phrase, 'We the people of the United States . . . do . . . establish this Constitution'. . . . Even under the most narrow readings of the Establishment Clause, then, while the Chief Justice is free to keep whatever religious beliefs he chooses, *the state* may not acknowledge the sovereignty of the Judeo-Christian God and attribute to that God our religious freedom."[70]

Chief Justice Moore, incidentally, defined "religion" as "the duties we owe to our Creator and the manner of discharging those duties."[71] Judge Thompson declined Moore's invitation to provide the court's alternative to Moore's theistic definition and said "because the court cannot agree with the Chief Justice's definition of religion and cannot formulate its own, it must refuse the Chief Justice's invitation to define 'religion.'"[72]

Chief Justice Moore had a right to bring a test case to challenge the Supreme Court's Establishment Clause rulings. Having brought a test case, Moore implicitly committed himself to play by the rules and obey court orders. In any event, he lost any legal basis to keep the monument in the rotunda when, after the deadline set by the District Court's final removal order, the other justices on the Alabama Supreme Court withdrew his authority, under state law, over the monument and ordered the building manager to remove the monument from the rotunda..[73] The Court of the Judiciary played by the rules of the game in finding that Moore had violated the Canons of Judicial Ethics and in removing him from office.

Moore claimed that the order to remove the monument was unlawful and that he "was ethically bound by his solemn oath to comply with the Constitutions of the United States and of Alabama, and not [with] the unlawful court order."[74] The Alabama Supreme Court noted that "Moore states that the judgment of the Court of the Judiciary has in effect created an 'oath transfer rule'–that an oath taken by a public official is no longer to a constitution but to a court's opinion, even one contrary to the constitution."[75] Moore had a debatable point there, one that might have made sense to Thomas Jefferson and others of the founding generation who would not have been at home with the *Cooper v. Aaron* idea that Supreme Court decisions are the "law of the land." The Alabama Supreme Court, however, responded to Moore's contention according to the logic of the federal system as we know it today. That court stated that "the Court of the Judiciary correctly refused to . . . review . . . the merits of the federal court order, because . . . it . . . lacks the jurisdiction or authority to engage in such a review. . . . [T]he Court of the Judiciary did not hold . . . that the federal order was correctly decided. Rather . . . the correctness of a federal court's ruling is not reviewable by the Court of the Judiciary. . . . Only a superior federal court can review the merits of a ruling by a federal court. Chief Justice Moore exercised his right to obtain such a review in the federal system, and the federal appellate courts consistently upheld the order of the federal district court."[76]

The Alabama court gave the only possible answer under the Supremacy Clause of Article VI if federal court rulings are equated to "the law of the land."[77] There is logic in that equation. But Moore's position is not entirely illogical in the context of the federal system as it was designed by the framers of the Constitution.

Chief Justice Moore, as the Alabama Supreme Court noted, chose to play by the rules of the game, as it is played in the federal courts. Having chosen to play, he was morally as well as legally bound to play by those rules, including the penalty for unsportsmanlike conduct.

Moore's attempt to defy the federal courts on their own turf, playing by their rules, was a loser from the beginning. His stand on principle would have made more sense as an outright exercise of civil disobedience, as noted below. In any event, Moore rendered an important service by calling attention to two aspects of the constitutional revolution affected by the federal judiciary: the Incorporation Doctrine and the Court's claim that its own rulings are the "law of the land."

The Supreme Court's religion edicts are binding only on federal and state or local government officials or other state actors and not on private persons. The Court forbids state officials to affirm *as fact* that this nation is "under God." Instead, the Court requires them to avow implicitly a central tenet of the new

Court-decreed state religion—that law and government must be insulated from any factual, rather than merely symbolic, affirmation of the existence and sovereignty of God. Those officials are required to affirm implicitly that a profession by them of the truth of the Declaration of Independence, which identifies the "Creator" as the source of rights, would be not only irrelevant but also hostile to the governance of civil society. That secularist postulate which they are required to affirm is, of course, itself a religious position. Chief Justice Moore could fairly interpret the compulsion to make implicitly such a secularist but religious profession as a compulsion to violate the law of God. As St. Thomas Aquinas said, a law that compels one to do anything "contrary to the Divine law . . . must nowise be observed, because . . . 'we ought to obey God rather than men.'"[78]

Moore's position would have made more moral and practical sense if he had refused to remove the Ten Commandments monument simply as an act of civil disobedience of a government command that he assent to the false religious belief that the state may not affirm in fact the existence and sovereignty of God. He could have argued reasonably that he was acting in the tradition of the Christian martyrs, Gandhi, Martin Luther King, Jr., war protesters, et al. Instead, he lost the moral focus of his position by engaging as a supplicant in the judicial supremacy game ordained by the Supreme Court.

It is not an overstatement to conclude that the Supreme Court is ramming a religious dogma down the throats of the American people and their public officials. Is God, the "Creator," the source of rights? Is human law subject to "the Laws of Nature and of Nature's God"? These are more than quotations from the Declaration of Independence. They are intrinsically religious questions. The founders of this nation recognized God—the God of Abraham, Isaac and Jacob—as the essential source of morality, law and rights. The recognition of the sovereignty of God either is, or is not, indispensable to sound human governance. The Supreme Court not only forbids public officials to affirm as fact that this nation was founded "under God," but also the Court requires those officials to affirm by implication the secular religious dogma that official acknowledgment of the sovereignty of God is hostile to sound government.

We strive to live under the rule of law. No one can convincingly claim that the Supreme Court's Establishment Clause jurisprudence reflects a rule of law rather than the arbitrary rule of unelected oligarchs. What is a state official to do if he objects conscientiously to compliance with those court rulings? It would promote the rule of law for such state officials to suspend any voluntary deference to the Supreme Court's autocratic demand that those officials affirm a religious position contrary to the intent of the Constitution and contrary to their own conscience. And the people should regard those Court decrees as illegitimate and unworthy of their voluntary compliance. Those Supreme Court decisions have no moral authority. The officials should follow instead the plain historical meaning of the First Amendment. Neither James Madison nor the framers of the Fourteenth Amendment would have walked out of the stadium when the high school football teams gathered on the 50 yard-line for voluntary prayer. This is not to advocate anarchy. If federal judicial power is ultimately brought to bear to compel their compliance, the officials will have to decide whether to submit, resign or subject themselves to whatever penalties are imposed for noncompliance. But why should they volunteer to treat the Supreme Court rulings as anything other than the usurpations they are? Let the ACLU and the federal courts do their own dirty work.

ENDNOTES

1. David Klinghoffer, "Worshipers at the Secular Altar." *Los Angeles Times*, June 17, 2004, p. B15.

2. See, for example, *Buono v. Norton*, 371 F.3d 543 546 (9th Cir., 2004), requiring the removal of a cross, between five and eight feet tall and constructed of metal pipe painted white, from the federal Mojave Desert Preserve. The cross was originally placed on the site in 1934 by the Veterans of Foreign Wars in memory of military personnel who died in World War I. Plaintiff, a visitor to the Preserve, objected to the cross as "a religious symbol."

3. Cardinal Joseph Ratzinger, *Address* to Consistory of College of Cardinals, Apr. 4, 1991, "The Problem of Threats to Human Life", *L'Osservature Romano* (English ed.), Apr. 8, 1991, p. 2; 36 *The Pope Speaks* 332-43 (1991) [headings added].

4. William Smith, "The First Amendment and Progress," *Humanitas,* Summer 1987, 1, 5-6.

5. *Pruneyard and Shopping Center v. Robins*, 447 U.S. 74 (1980).

6. See discussion in Michael W. McConnell, John H. Garvey and Thomas C. Berg, *Religion and the Constitution* (2002), 196-200. See also, *Goodridge v. Dept. of Public Health*, 798 N.E.2d 941 (MA, 2003).

7. *U.S. Constitution, Art. VI, cl.3.*

8. See *Torcaso v. Watkins*, 367 U.S. 488 (1961).

9. Edward S. Corwin, "The Supreme Court as National School Board," 14 *Law and Contemp. Problems*, 3, 14 (1949).

10. Joseph Story, *Commentaries on the Constitution of the United States* (3rd ed., 1858), Secs. 1874, 1877.

11. Annals of Congress, I, 949-50.

12. James D. Richardson, *Messages and Papers of the Presidents,* 1789-1897 (1901), 64.

13. 375 F.3d 484, 507 (6th Cir., 2004) (Emphasis by Judge Batchelder).

14. *Wash. Times*, April 23, 2005, p. A2.

15. 342 F.3d 271 273 (3rd Cir., 2003).

16. 342 F.2d at 281, n. 7.

17. See John Gibson, *The War on Christmas: How the Liberal Plot to Ban the Sacred Christmas Holiday is Worse Than You Thought* (2005).

18. *Wash. Times*, Dec. 8, 2005, p.A2.

19. *Wash. Times*, Dec. 8, 2005, p.A2. See also, Joe Drape, "Increasingly, Football's Playbooks Call for Prayer," *N.Y. Times*, Oct. 30, 2005, Sec. 1, p. 1; Nancy Armour, "Teaming Up for Prayer," *Wash. Times*, Dec. 6, 2005, p. A1.

20. 494 U.S. 872 (1990).

21. 494 U.S. at 881. See *Church of Lukumi Babalu Aye, Inc., v. City of Hialeah*, 508 U.S. 520 (1993).

22. 494 U.S. at 882.

23. *City of Boerne v. Flores*, 521 U.S. 507 (1997).

24. Art. I, Sec. 8, cl.1 and cl.3.

25. 544 U.S. 709, 712, 125 S. Ct. 2113 (2005).

26. 85 P.3d 67. (Cal. 2004).

27. California Health and Safety Code, Sec. 1367, 25; 85 p.3d at 74, n.3.

28. 85 P.3d at 98-101.

29. *Martin v. Hunter's Lessee*, 14 U.S. (1 Wheat.) 304 (1816).

30. *Cooper v. Aaron*, 358 U.S. 1, 18(1958).

31. Learned Hand, *The Bill of Rights* (1958), 73.

32. See Samuel C. Damren, "*Stare Decisis: The Maker of Customs*," 35 N. Engl. L. Rev. 1 (2000); Henry P. Monaghan, "*Stare Decisis and Constitutional Adjudication*, 88 Colum. L. Rev. 723 (1988).

33. See *Glidden v. Zdanok*, 370 U.S. 530, 543 (1962).

34. Louis Fisher, *American Constitutional Law* (1995), 88.

35. Gary Lawson "*The Constitutional Case Against Precedent*," 17 Harv. J. of Law & Public policy 23 (1994). See also, Charles J. Cooper, "Stare Decisis: Precedent and Principle in Constitutional Adjudication," 73 *Cornell L. Rev.* 401, 410 ('1988), concluding that an erroneous constitutional decision should be followed only to avoid serious "harm to the body politic."

36. *Barron v. Baltimore*, 32 U.S. (7 Pet.) 243 (1833).

37. See *Gitlow v. New York*, 268 U.S. 652, 666 (1925); *Fiske v. Kansas, 274 U.S. 380 (1927);* Duncan v. *Louisiana,* 391 U.S. 145, 148-49 (1968); *Abington School District v. Schempp*, 374 U.S. 203 (1963).

38. See William K. Lietzau, "Rediscovering the Establishment Clause: Federalism and the Rollback of Incorporation," 39 *DePaul L. Rev.*., 1191 (1990); *Notes,* "Rethinking the Incorporation of the Establishment Clause: A Federalist View," 105 *HARV. l. Rev.* 1700 (1992); William P. Gray, Jr., "The Ten Commandments and the Ten Amendments: A Case Study in Religious Freedom in Alabama," 49 *Ala. L. Rev.*509 (1998); Robert R. Baugh, "Applying the Bill of Rights to the States: A Response to William P. Gray, Jr.," 49 *Ala. L. Rev.* 551 (1998); William P. Ray, Jr., "'We the People' or 'We the Judges': A Reply to Robert R. Baugh's Response,' 49 *Ala. L. Rev.* 607 (1998).

39. *Elk Grove Unified School Dist. V. Newdow*, 542 U.S. 1, 46 (2004).

40. *Van Orden v. Perry*, 125 S. Ct. 2854, 2865 (2005) (Thomas, J., concurring opinion).

41. 542 U.S. 1, 1245. Ct. 2301 (2004).

42. 542 U.S. at 50-51, 124 S. Ct. at 2331 (2004). (Emphasis by Justice Thomas).

43. 545 U.S., 125 S. Ct. 2854 (2005).

44. 125 S. Ct. at 2865 (Emphasis by Justice Thomas.)

45. 125 S. Ct. at 2866-67.

46. 125 S. Ct. at 2866.

47. *Stone v. Graham*, 449 U.S. 39 (1980).

48. See *Indiana Civil Liberties Union v. O'Bannon*, 259 F.3d 766 (7th Cir. 2001), cert. denied, 534 U.S. 1162 (2002); *Books v. City of Elkhart*, 235 F.3d 292 (7th Cir. 2000), cert. denied, 532 U.S. 1058.

49. 545 U.S., 125 S. Ct. 2854 (2005) .

50. 125 S. Ct. 2858-59.

51. 125 S. Ct. at 2863-64.

52. 125 S. Ct. 2722 (2005).

53. 125 S. Ct. at 2733.

54 *Torcaso v. Watkins*, 367 U.S. 488, 490 (1961).

55. 367 U.S. at 495.

56. *Ibid.*, n. 11.

57. *Abiangton School District v. Schempp*, 374 U.S. 203 (1963).

58. *Abington School District v. Schempp*, 374 U.S. at 304.

59. *Wash. Times*, Dec. 8, 2005, B.A2.

60. *Elisa B. v. Superior Court,* 117 P.3d 660 (2005); *K.M. v. E.G.*, 117 P.3d 673 (2005); *Kristine H. v. Lisa R.*, 117 P.3d 690 (2005).

61. 117 p.3d at 675.

62. 117 p.3d at 692.

63. 798 N.E.2d 941 (MA, 2003). *Lawrence v. Texas*, the Supreme Court held unconstitutional the Texas prohibition of consensual sodomy.

64. 798 N.E.2d at 969.

65. Ibid.

66. 427 F.3d 1197, 1200, 1201,M. 3, (9th Cir., 2005). (Emphasis in original).

67. See Comment, "'The Forgotten Child of Our Constitution': The Parental Free Exercise Right to Direct the Education and Religious Upbringing of Children." 54 *Emory L. J.* 641 (2005).

68. *Moore v. Judicial Inquiry Commission*, 891, So.2d 848 (2004); N.Y. *Times*, May 1, 2004, p. A10.

69.   Q.   [W]as your purpose in putting the Ten Commandments monument in the Supreme Court rotunda to acknowledge GOD's law and GOD 's sovereignty? . . .

     A.   Yes.

     Q.   . . . Do you agree that the monument, the Ten Commandments monument, reflects the sovereignty of God over the affairs of men?

     A.   Yes.

     Q.   And the monument is also intended to acknowledge GOD's overruling power over the affairs of men, would that be correct? . . . .

     A.   Yes.

     Q.   . . . [W]hen you say "GOD" you mean GOD of the Holy Scripture?

     A.   Yes. *Glassroth v. Moore*, 335 F.3d 1282, 1287 (11th Cir., 2003).

70. *Glassroth v. Moore*, 229 F. Supp. 2d 1290, 1310-12 (N.D. Ala., 2002) (Emphasis by Judge Thompson).

71. 229 F.Supp. 2d at 1312.

72. 229 F.Supp. 2d at 1314.

73. *Moore v. Judicial Inquiry Commission*, 853 So. 2d 848, 853 (Ala., 2004). Stan Bailey, "Monument Removed, but Protests Continue." Birmingham (Als) News, Jan. 14, 2004, p.A1.

74. 891 So.2d at 856.

75. 853 So. 2d at 857.

76. 891 So. 2d at 857.

77. See *Cooper v. Aaron*, 358 U.S.1 (1958).

78. S.T., I, II, Q. 96, art.4

Five
The Judicial Assault on Criminal Law
by Ronald J. Rychlak

I. Introduction

When a society criminalizes specific conduct, it is attempting to regulate its citizens by punishing or threatening to punish those who violate certain norms. Societies do not usually harm or threaten to harm their citizens, but if punishment lessens crime, then criminal laws and the associated punishment (harm) serve the common good. By requiring people to conform their actions to the demands of the law, society may protect itself from crime while at the same time helping individuals appreciate the advantages of approved behavior.

The legislature, as an elected, representative body, best reflects the society's judgment about improper conduct and appropriate punishment. For that reason, it typically falls to the legislature to define crimes and identify the range of potential sentences. Since different communities view criminal acts in different ways, American criminal laws have traditionally been drafted and implemented at the state or local level by the legislative bodies that are closest to the people in the relevant communities.

Beginning in the 1960s, the United States Supreme Court extended constitutional guarantees to state criminal defendants and suspects, removing much discretion from state lawmakers. Other state and federal courts extended these holdings in ways that permitted judges to impose their personal views on proper and improper conduct, appropriate punishments, standards of evidence, and conditions of imprisonment. Along the way, the courts have thwarted the will of the people closest to the criminal activity and made it harder to stop crime.

It is true, of course, that trial judges sometimes assist the prosecution in criminal cases.[1] State judges, who conduct most of the criminal trials in the United States, often have to stand for retention or reelection. They, therefore, may pay attention to what voters think about criminal cases, and that can lead to a pro-

prosecution bias at the trial level in some cases. At the appellate level, however, and especially in the federal courts, judicial actions related to virtually every criminal issue—from abortion to vagrancy—frequently invalidate policy choices that were approved by the people through the democratic process.

Even when the laws themselves have been upheld, many convictions have been overturned (or prosecutions thwarted) by judges who have held police and prosecutors to standards far above what most citizens would expect. Moreover, when the defendants are convicted, judges frequently impose sentences much lighter than the legislature has authorized. Ironically, the judges who make these rulings often appeal to an "emerging democratic consensus." By preempting the role of the legislature, however, they actually prevent the democratic consensus from being carried out.

Virtually all judges are moral people, and they often have insights to the criminal justice system that are not available to the general public. Many of the changes that they force upon the system might be for the good. It is not, however, their role to replace the democratic process with their personal judgment. If judges have insights and ideas, they should—like everyone else—test them through the political process. Unfortunately, judges have a tendency not to do that.

When judges exceed their role and bypass the democratic process—even in those cases when we might agree that they have a very good point—they go beyond the role given to them by the Constitution and enter the field of "judicial legislation." This can have very bad consequences for society and do much harm to the common good. Nevertheless, it happens all too frequently. To a large extent, it began in the 1960s and was led by the Supreme Court.

II. The Warren Court and the Federalization of Criminal Law

From the time that this nation was founded until today, the law of crime and punishment primarily has been a matter for the states. James Madison, in Federalist Paper 45, wrote that federal powers "will be exercised principally on external objects, as war, peace, negotiation, and foreign commerce.... The powers reserved to the several states will extend to all objects which, in the ordinary course of affairs, concern the lives, liberties, and property of the people, and the internal order, improvement, and prosperity of the state." Likewise Alexander Hamilton, in Federalist Paper 17, explained that state governments, not the federal government, would have the power of law enforcement: "There is one transcendent advantage belonging to the province of the State governments, which alone suffices to place the matter in a clear and satisfactory light—I mean the ordinary administration of criminal and civil justice." The Constitution specifically notes only a few categories of federal criminal laws, and for about 100 years after it was adopted the federal criminal code was limited to treason, bribery of federal officials, perjury in federal court, theft of government property, and revenue fraud.

There is a good deal of logic to leaving matters of criminal law to state and local authorities. It fits with the idea of subsidiarity—letting those closest to the problem handle it when possible.² If the public is not pleased with the way some law or procedure is working, it is much easier to influence local police and legislators than it is to influence decisions at the national level. As former Attorney General Edwin Meese observed: "Federal law-enforcement authorities are not as attuned to the priorities and customs of local communities as state and local law enforcement."³

The Bill of Rights, of course, set forth certain constitutional guarantees that were available to defendants in criminal cases. As originally understood, however, these guarantees were available only to defendants in federal prosecutions. Since the vast majority of criminal trials took place in state courts, the Bill of Rights originally did not have a significant impact on most criminal trials.

The end of the Civil War brought the 14th Amendment, which—unlike the Bill of Rights—imposed limitations on the authority of a state when it came to certain matters, including a criminal prosecution. Of most importance to state prosecutions, it provided:

> No state shall make or enforce any law which shall abridge the privileges or immunities of citizens of the United States; nor shall any state deprive any person of life, liberty, or property, without due process of law; nor deny to any person within its jurisdiction the equal protection of the laws.

As it was understood by those who drafted and ratified it, however, the 14th Amendment required only that states accord to defendants those fundamental rights that were deemed necessary to the very concept of ordered liberty.⁴ It did not mean that states had to abide by all of the limitations set forth in the Bill of Rights.

Under the 14th Amendment, as it was originally understood, states had to provide fair trials, but they did not have to provide jury trials or attorneys to the defendant in most criminal cases. States did not have to respect the defendant's right to remain silent,⁵ and evidence taken by state authorities pursuant to an unreasonable search or seizure was not necessarily excluded from evidence.⁶ Even the bar on double jeopardy did not apply against the states.⁷ States could offer such rights to defendants. If, however, a state wanted to protect its citizens in some other manner, the decision was left to the public and their elected representatives.⁸ This understanding of the 14th Amendment remained constant for almost 100 years after its ratification.

In the 1960s under Chief Justice Earl Warren, the Supreme Court developed a new way to read the 14th Amendment. Instead of asking whether a state law infringed on some right that was necessary to the very concept of ordered liberty, the new test asked whether the state law infringed on some right that was considered fundamental to the American scheme of justice. In other words, the test asked whether the infringed-upon right was considered fundamental by "Americans," and the politically-immunized judges were left to decide that issue, not democratically-elected representatives.

Using this new test, the Supreme Court reshaped state criminal legal systems. By the end of the 1960s, state criminal defendants received the benefit of the prohibition against cruel and unusual punishment;⁹ the right to assistance of counsel;¹⁰ the privilege against self incrimination;¹¹ the right to confront opposing witnesses;¹²

the right to remain silent or have an attorney present for questioning;[13] the right to a speedy trial;[14] the right to compel defense witnesses to appear at trial;[15] the right to a jury trial;[16] and protection against double jeopardy.[17] The *Miranda* warnings were a direct result of this new test,[18] the exclusionary rule was extended to cover prosecutions in state cases because of it,[19] and the Supreme Court developed a doctrine built upon an "expectation of privacy" that made it much harder for police to listen in on conversations involving suspects.[20] None of these constitutional rights applied to criminal defendants in state courts prior to 1961.

The dynamics of this dramatic period of activity for the Supreme Court have to be placed into context. State criminal laws had been established through the political process. In other words, the situation as it was before these Supreme Court cases reflected the will of the majority of persons living in that state or community. The reforms did not take place because most people wanted reform; it may be assumed that most people did not want these judicially-imposed reforms. This is evident when one examines the states' response to the Court's effort to outlaw the death penalty.

Since most of the issues decided by the Warren Court were held to be required by the Constitution, political action could not change the law absent a constitutional amendment. As to the death penalty, however, it was hard to deny that this punishment was authorized by the Constitution.[21] In 1972, the Court therefore ruled not that capital punishment was *per se* unconstitutional, but that it was being *applied* in an unconstitutional manner *in each and every state*.[22] This holding, of course, left open the possibility of a legislative effort to overturn it. By 1974, twenty nine states had done just that and acted to restore the death penalty.[23] Two years later, six more states (amounting to virtually every state that had the death penalty prior to the Court's action) had also restored it.

The death penalty had been suspended only because a majority of the nine justices wanted reforms, not because most people opposed it. The same was true with the other changes to the criminal law system. To most of the public, reforms meant that criminals were being set free by the courts, even when guilt was not in question. These reforms had very serious consequences: The average person's chances of becoming a victim of a violent crime increased dramatically during the 1960s.[24] Richard Nixon, in fact, focused much of his 1968 presidential campaign on the Supreme Court's lenient treatment of criminals.

The Warren Court's expansion of the Bill of Rights (via the 14th Amendment) to state crimes federalized significant aspects of criminal law, taking decision-making authority away from the people who were most directly affected by crime. Moreover, this expanded authority gave judges a great deal of discretion when it came to overturning democratically-enacted criminal laws. Perhaps the two most important and controversial rulings in this area relate to the extension of the exclusionary rule to the states and the *Miranda* warnings.

A. The Exclusionary Rule: Suppressing Evidence

One of the most important developments from the Supreme Court's Warren era came in the 1961 case of *Mapp v. Ohio*.[25] In this case, the Court interpreted the Fourth Amendment in a new way that changed the rules of evidence in state criminal cases. To most Americans, the new interpretation meant that courts often threw out clear evidence of guilt.

The Fourth Amendment to the U.S. Constitution prohibits the federal government from conducting or sponsoring "unreasonable searches and seizures" of the "persons, houses, papers, and effects" of citizens. Federal courts have long used the exclusionary rule to enforce the prohibition against unreasonable searches and seizures. This rule holds that evidence collected pursuant to an unreasonable search is inadmissible at trial. Since, however, there are relatively few federal crimes, and even fewer violent ones, the exclusionary rule had a relatively small impact on society when it was limited to federal courts.

State authorities were also prohibited from conducting unreasonable searches and seizures.[26] Before *Mapp v. Ohio*, however, states were free to develop their own ways to protect their citizens. A state might use internal police disciplinary proceedings, civil actions by those who were searched, or other ways to protect against unreasonable searches, but they did not have to use the exclusionary rule. The Supreme Court changed that in 1961.

In *Mapp v. Ohio*, the Supreme Court required states to adopt the same rule that federal courts followed in the case of a Fourth Amendment violation—the exclusionary rule. Henceforth, no state would be permitted to use evidence in court if that evidence had been obtained pursuant to a search subsequently deemed by a judge to have been unreasonable. That was true, regardless of how trustworthy the evidence might be or how crucial it might be to the prosecution's case.[27] Moreover, police officers were often left without guidance as to what would constitute a "reasonable" search. The exclusionary rule became the "bogey that haunts reasonable policing."[28]

To the average citizen, the exclusionary rule meant that criminals were being set free on a technicality. If a police officer entered a building, and it was later determined that he should have first obtained a warrant, the evidence that he found—whether it was a small amount of marijuana or a murder weapon—could not be used by the prosecution at trial. Rejecting such a rule in 1926, Judge Benjamin Cardozo famously asked: "Should the criminal go free because the constable has blundered?"[29] He explained:

> No doubt the protection of the statute [against unreasonable search and seizure] would be greater from the point of view of the individual whose privacy had been invaded if the government were required to ignore what it had learned through the invasion. The question is whether protection for the individual would not be gained at a disproportionate loss of protection for society.... [New York's existing rule] strikes a balance between opposing interests. We must hold it to be the law until those organs of government by which a change of public policy is normally effected shall give notice to the courts that the change has come to pass.[30]

In the 1960s, however, the Supreme Court decided that criminal should indeed go free because the constable had blundered.

Extending the exclusionary rule to the states made it harder for the police to capture criminals, and it made it harder to convict those who were caught. As one commentator explained:

> The exclusionary rule—which bars the use of evidence said to have been illegally obtained—was established in 1914 in *Weeks v. United States* but did little harm until it was applied to the states. So long as the *Weeks* rule was confined to federal cases, as Justice Rehnquist pointed out, its chief "beneficiaries . . . were smugglers, federal income tax evaders, counterfeiters, and the like." State crime is a profoundly different matter. Ninety-five per cent of hate crime committed in the United States, and virtually all violent crime, comes under the jurisdiction of the states. Once the *Weeks* rule was brought to bear against the states the result was uncounted thousands of robbers, rapists, and murderers set free.[31]

The law-abiding public also came to realize that the exclusionary rule did not provide much help to them. After all, when an innocent person was subjected to an unreasonable search, there would be no subsequent prosecution and to no evidence to suppress.

One of the most controversial suppression cases in recent memory was when U.S. District Court Judge Harold Baer suppressed a large quantity of narcotics recovered in the drug-infested Washington Heights section of New York City.[32] Police officers had seen several people, late at night, loading a duffle bag into the trunk of a car. When they approached the car, the people ran away. Judge Baer, however, concluded that running away from the police was a normal reaction in that community and it should not give rise to any suspicion. He threw out the evidence that the police had recovered as well as the subsequent tape-recorded confession given by the defendants.

Judge Baer was held up to much ridicule in the press and many politicians called for his removal from office.[33] Eventually, he granted a motion for reconsideration and subsequently reversed his decision.[34] For every case like that, however, there are hundreds if not thousands of other cases where judges reject and exclude evidence that is both relevant and trustworthy. They do this because they "continue to second-guess the most intense, spontaneous policing decisions at a time and place removed from the streets."[35]

The exclusionary rule was not (and still is not) popular with the public. It received a lot of blame for the dramatic increase in crime that took place in the 1960s and 1970s. There was, however, another innovation of the Warren Court that caused even more controversy and may have contributed more to the increased crime rates of that era: the *Miranda* rule.

B. Turning Police Officers into Defense Lawyers: *Miranda*

Five years after requiring states to exclude relevant, reliable evidence of guilt, the Supreme Court went further and required state courts to throw out confessions that were not obtained in an approved manner. The Court started by suggesting that suspects were entitled to counsel under the Sixth Amendment to the Constitution when they were at the police station or when they had become the focus of the investigation,[36] but ultimately, the Court switched direction and looked to the Fifth Amendment.

The Fifth Amendment to the Constitution provides that no person "shall be compelled in any criminal case to be a witness against himself." Prior to 1964, however, this provision did not apply in state proceedings.[37] Moreover, before *Miranda* (1966), "compulsion" to testify meant *legal* compulsion: refusal to do so would result in contempt, and a lie would result in perjury. It did not relate to the interrogation that a police officer might conduct with a recently-arrested suspect.

In *Miranda v. Arizona*,[38] the Supreme Court decided that the Fifth Amendment meant something that no one had realized in the first 180 years of the Constitution: it meant that state police officers had to take affirmative steps to protect criminals from the consequences of their own folly. In other words, the officers who were trying to make the arrests also had to give legal advice to the suspects to help them avoid incriminating themselves. As the author David Simon wrote in the book *Homicide*: "Get it straight: A police detective, a man who gets paid government money to put you in prison, is explaining your absolute right to shut up before you say something stupid."[39]

Under *Miranda*, a suspect is entitled to be informed of his or her rights before being subjected to custodial interrogation. Thus, if a police officer wants to ask questions of someone who is in custody (and this is defined by asking whether the suspect feels free to leave),[40] the officer must first inform the suspect of his or her right to remain silent and the right to have an attorney present for questioning. Failure to comply with this procedure results in the statements (and any evidence derived therefrom) being deemed inadmissible at trial.

The rational underlying *Miranda* "was to prohibit physical or serious mental coercion in the obtaining of a confession."[41] It has turned out to have a much bigger impact on the process of arresting criminals than that, however. "If the cops do anything halfway clever in eliciting a confession (like appealing to the defendant's conscience . . .) some court will rule this a violation of the defendant's rights."[42] Former law professor, now Judge Paul Cassell has estimated that *Miranda* warnings prevent police from solving up to 359,000 crimes each year.[43]

To the average Joe on the street, *Miranda* meant that fully-reliable confessions were being thrown out of court, along with other evidence of the suspect's guilt. Coming on the heels of the extension of the exclusionary rule, this was a double-whammy that deeply troubled many citizens. Every criminal who escaped punishment because of these rulings remained free to strike again, and it seems that many of them did.

In 1960 there were about 900,000 burglaries in the United States. The rate, however, started to increase dramatically, reaching about 1.3 million in 1965, 2.2 million in 1970, 3.3 million in 1975 and 3.8 million in 1980.[44] Violent crime also went up. Between 1960 and 1970, the murder rate almost doubled.[45] The number of rapes each year more than doubled. Thus, during the 20 year period between 1960 and 1980, the United States experienced tens of millions of extra crimes arguably due, at least in part, to the Supreme Court's handling of criminal matters.

Crime rates only went up a little bit more during the 1980s and early 1990s, peaking in the early-to mid-1990s. In 1994, about fourteen million serious crimes were reported to the police.[46] In a nation of 280 million people, that was about one crime for every twenty people. So, in 1994, an average citizen had about a one in twenty chance of being a victim of crime. That was about five times higher than the risk of being a victim was in 1960.[47] It is unlikely that Supreme Court holdings are responsible for this entire increase, but is it also unlikely that those holdings had no impact on the increase.[48] Moreover, the courts did not stop there.

III. The Judicial Assault on State Laws

Ever since the 1960s, when the Supreme Court first began re-writing the criminal codes of all 50 states, judges have used their expanded powers to overturn the laws that people put in place through their elected representatives. Usually the judges have a logical basis for resisting the democratically-enacted legislation, but they often lack a valid legal or constitutional basis for imposing their own will over that of the populace. Among the areas of law where judicial activism is most evident are felony murder, pornography, and sex-related crimes.

A. Felony murder

Evidence of judicial reluctance to enforce democratically-enacted criminal laws can be seen in the way courts have dealt with the felony murder rule. While state statutes vary slightly in language and scope, the essential elements of the felony murder rule are that: if a death occurs during the course of a felony, the felons can be convicted of murder.[49] Felony murder is typically the same grade of murder as premeditated murder. In many jurisdictions, it is a crime for which the death penalty can be imposed.[50]

The felony murder rule is found in most state criminal codes because it makes sense to most people that the felons be held responsible when someone dies during their crime. The victim would still be alive if the felony had not been committed. As such, most state legislatures have enacted laws providing that the felons are guilty of murder in that situation, even if they did not intend to kill.[51]

Of course, the felony murder rule can have very harsh consequences. Consider the case of *People v. Stamp*.[52] Two robbers, armed with a gun and a blackjack, entered the rear of the building housing the offices of General Amusement Company. They ordered everyone to lie on the floor while they collected the money. After 10 to 15 minutes, the robbers left, telling the employees to stay on the floor for five more minutes.

Carl Honeyman, the owner and manager of General Amusement Company, looked very frightened and pale during the robbery. He may have had a gun held to his back when the robbers entered his office. About 15 or 20 minutes after the robbery occurred, just as the police arrived to investigate, he collapsed on the floor. He was pronounced dead on arrival at the hospital. The coroner's report listed the immediate cause of death as heart attack.

Honeyman had suffered from advanced heart disease, but three doctors testified at trial that the heart attack was precipitated by the fear produced by the robbery. As such, the robbers, including a driver who never entered the building, were tried for and convicted of felony murder. The court set forth the traditional rule: "a killing committed in either the perpetration of or an attempt to perpetrate robbery is murder of the first degree."

The defendants' ignorance of Honeyman's heart problems and their failure to use actual force did not relieve them of responsibility for felony murder. There was evidence of causation and the court ruled that the felony murder rule is applicable "whether the killing is willful, deliberate, and premeditated, or merely accidental or unintentional, and whether or not the killing is planned as part of the commission of the robbery." In short, the court applied the felony murder doctrine in accordance with the will of the people—the way the legislature drafted the statute.

Of course, law professors and legal commentators can have a field day with a case like this. What if the defendants had not been armed? What about conspirators who never even went to the scene of the crime? What if the victim would have had a heart attack and died anyway? What if a police officer had mistakenly shot the victim? Suffice to say that there are enough questions and critical commentary to convince most first year law students that the felony murder rule is unjust. In a good year, a law professor can almost whip them into a frenzy.

I like to ask my classes why we don't we see more politicians running on this platform: "Vote for me and I'll be sure that felons are not automatically considered murderers just because someone died when they committed their felony." That usually brings a laugh, but then I ask the students to consider their parents. Would they consider the felony murder rule unjust? No, Mom and Dad would all pretty much consider the felony murder rule to be fair. The felony led to a death; the felons are responsible. This sense of common justice underlies the felony murder rule. Professors may pick it apart, but most people think it is just.

Citizens in almost every state have elected politicians who put felony murder laws on the books, but courts have found numerous ways to limit the application of these laws. One very logical limitation is the so-called merger rule. This rule holds that some felonies, because they involve a direct assault on the victim, cannot be used to support a felony murder conviction. To count any death that occurred during the course of an assault as felony murder would obliterate the distinction between murder and manslaughter. Every manslaughter (a felony) would automatically become a murder under the felony murder rule. Of course, this limitation is so fundamental that it is incorporated into many criminal codes. Legislators have recognized the problem and taken steps to correct it by specifically identifying those felonies that will support a felony murder charge.[53]

Other limitations on the felony murder rule have been developed by judges and are far more controversial. Consider, for instance, the "inherently dangerous felony" limitation. In *People v. Burroughs*,[54] a faith healer was convicted by a jury of second degree felony murder because he was practicing medicine without a license (a felony) and one of his patients died (perhaps due to the massages given by the defendant or more likely because he was dissuaded from seeking conventional treatment).

The California Supreme Court overturned the conviction, noting that the justices disfavored the felony murder rule and would strive to limit it as much as possible. The justices said that only an "inherently dangerous" felony could serve as the predicate for a felony murder conviction, and practicing medicine without a license was not inherently dangerous. The way that they evaluated the dangerousness of this felony left little doubt about the forgone nature of the conclusion.

The statute prohibiting practicing medicine without a license had two elements: 1) treating sick people; 2) under circumstances which create the risk of great bodily harm, serious illness, or death. In other words, it was not the kind of thing one would be convicted of for dispensing a couple of aspirins. It was a serious felony, and the jury convicted Burroughs of both the felony and felony murder.

The felony, as it was committed, was certainly dangerous. Someone died. The California Supreme Court, however, decided that a felony could not support a felony murder conviction unless it was inherently dangerous *in the abstract*. Moreover, this was a decision for the court itself to make, not the jury.

In order to make this decision, the court considered whether the offense could possibly be committed without a "high probability" of loss of life. As long as a judge could imagine a way that a crime could be committed without creating a substantial risk of death, the crime in question was not inherently dangerous and could not be used as the predicate offense for felony murder. Burroughs' felony murder conviction was overturned.[55] Since the statute made clear that it *could* be violated without a risk of death (so long as there were circumstances which created the risk of great bodily harm or serious illness), this felony could not be used to uphold a felony murder conviction.

Other cases further illustrate the way this "inherently dangerous" limitation can be used to undermine the felony murder rule.[56] *People v. Patterson* involved a death resulting from the sale and subsequent ingestion of a lethal amount of cocaine.[57] The California Supreme Court held that the sale of cocaine was not an inherently dangerous felony and could not support a felony murder conviction. The court explained that a "less stringent standard would inappropriately expand the scope of the felony murder rule reducing the seriousness of the act which a defendant must commit in order to be charged with murder." In perhaps an even more surprising result, a California appellate court, in *People v. Caffero*, held that felony child abuse was not an inherently dangerous felony to which the felony murder rule could be applied.[58] The victim in that case was a premature newborn who died as a result of severe neglect.

Other judges have used different doctrines to scale back the felony murder rule. In *People v. Washington*,[59] for instance, two men robbed a gas station. One of the robbers was shot and killed by the robbery victim. The surviving robber was convicted by a jury of robbery and felony murder. On appeal, the California Supreme Court reversed the conviction and invoked the "agency theory" of felony murder. This rule holds that a defendant can be held responsible for the actions of a co-felon, but not the actions of a victim or bystander.[60] Since the shooter was a victim of the felony, not a perpetrator, the felony murder rule could not be invoked.

Rather than focusing on who did the shooting to limit the felony murder rule, some judges look to who got shot. Under the "protected person" theory of the felony murder rule, felony murder does not apply unless the decedent was an innocent or "protected" person. It does not matter who does the killing, but if one of the felons is killed, there can be no felony murder conviction.[61] It is yet another judge-made way to limit the felony murder rule.

Even when the court does not adopt a rule that limits the effect of the felony murder rule across the board, judges often limit its application on a case-by-case basis. Thus, judges may consider the killing to be outside the scope or the time frame of the felony, so that the felony murder rule does not apply. Consider, for instance, *Franks v. State*,[62] in which the defendant killed a child in a car accident while fleeing from a supermarket robbery and an assault on a police officer. The court dismissed the felony murder charge because there was no causal nexus between the crimes and the death.

Of course, many courts combine numerous limitations on the felony murder rule. New Mexico, for instance, has five main limitations to its felony murder rule. First, the predicate felony must be the actual and proximate cause of the death.[63] Second, the predicate felony must be inherently dangerous.[64] Third, the felony murder rule does not extend to cases where the victim of the predicate felony kills the defendant's accomplice (a form of the "protected person" theory).[65] Fourth, there is a *mens rea* requirement that the defendant must possess at least the intent required for second degree murder.[66] Finally, the "collateral-felony" limitation (that state's version of the merger rule) dictates that the predicate felony may not be a lesser included offense of second degree murder.

The judges who have imposed these limitations on felony murder have their reasons. A good case can be made for many, if not all, of these limitations. The problem is that the case has not been made to the public though the democratic process. It may be, as some commentators have argued, that the felony murder is "unfair, unprincipled and inconsistent with other criminal and civil standards."[67] The problem is that if society agrees that the felony murder rule is bad, it should change it through the legislature, not by judges imposing their views outside of the democratic process.

As my students regularly assure me, Mom and Dad still think the felony murder is fair.[68] If Mom and Dad are wrong, they should lose through the democratic process, not because a court somewhere decides that it knows better and will decide the matter for the rest of the society.

B. Free Speech and Offensive Conduct

Parents in any community well understand the damage that is caused to their families when the community is bombarded with overt sexuality. Pornography and related sexualization can have a corrosive effect on the community and limit the ability of parents to influence the conditions of their children's development. It also dehumanizes women.[69] This can make it very difficult to bring about the type of society in which children learn to respect the dignity of others.[70]

Overt sexual activity can hurt family relationships, shatter marriages, and harm the social development of children.[71] Recent studies show that use of pornography is associated with several disturbing trends, including: infidelity, marital distress, separation, and divorce; decreased marital intimacy and sexual satisfaction; increased demand for more and more graphic forms of pornography; sexual activity associated with abusive, illegal, or unsafe practices; compulsive and addictive sexual behavior. The impact on youth is particularly troubling. There are an estimated 900,000 teen-age pregnancies in the United States each year, and the rate of sexually transmitted diseases is higher among teenagers than among adults. Sexually active adolescents are also at high risk for depression and suicide, and early sexual experience among adolescents has been associated with alcohol, marijuana, and other drug use.[72] Moreover, communities often find a close relationship between strip clubs and porn theaters on one hand and prostitution, drug use, and petty crime on the other.[73]

These negative effects are extremely difficult, if not impossible, for individuals or families to combat on their own. For this reason, communities often do things like prohibit live sex shows or closely regulate nude dancers. These regulations, however, often face tough challenges in court.

In a well-known case coming out of Indiana, *Barnes v. Glen Theatre, Inc.*, a public indecency statute was challenged on the basis that it violated erotic dancers' right of free expression under the First Amendment.[74] Dancers at the Kitty Kat Lounge in South Bend wanted to dance totally nude because they thought that they would make more money that way. A state statute, however, required them to wear pasties and a G-string. The dancers argued that the First Amendment's guarantee of freedom of expression prevented the State of Indiana from enforcing its public indecency law to prevent this form of dancing.

It is fair assume that most citizens of Indiana and elsewhere were quite surprised that the Supreme Court seriously considered the argument that this regulation was interfering with the strippers' free speech. The Court ruled against them—upholding the regulation—but it accepted the basic argument that this was an issue of free speech. Justice Scalia filed a separate opinion specifically rejecting the argument that the regulation interfered with free speech. He wrote: "In my view . . . the challenged regulation must be upheld, not because it survives some lower level of First-Amendment scrutiny, but because, as a general law regulating conduct and not specifically directed at expression, it is not subject to First-Amendment scrutiny at all."

The regulations were ultimately upheld, but the Court accepted the idea that our founding fathers wrote a Constitution that protects nude dancing as a form of free speech. That ended up being enough for other judges to find ways to use state constitutions to overturn city and state regulations designed to uphold morality and protect the community.

In September 2005, for instance, in a pair of rulings, the Oregon Supreme Court struck down a state law against conducting live sex shows and a local ordinance that required performers to stay at least four feet away from patrons at nude dancing clubs.[75] According to the court, both restrictions violated the Oregon Constitution's guarantees of free speech and free expression. Justice Michael Gillette, who wrote the majority opinions, said it "appears to us to be beyond reasonable dispute that the protection extends to the kinds of expression that a majority of citizens in many communities would dislike—and even to physical acts, such as nude dancing or other explicit sexual conduct that have an expressive component."

The Oregon state constitution, adopted in 1859, says: "No law shall be passed restraining the free expression of opinion, or restricting the right to speak, write or print freely on any subject whatever." A spokesman for the Oregon Attorney General said: "We don't believe framers of the constitution intended to limit the Legislature's authority to regulate sexual conduct in public." Dissenting Oregon Supreme Court Justice Paul De Muniz said that he does not believe that masturbation and sexual intercourse in a live public show "is a form of speech that the drafters of the Oregon Constitution sought to protect.... I cannot conclude that legislative regulation of public sex acts must stop at the theater door." Most Oregonians probably agree.

In what might be considered the flip-side of this issue, most Americans feel that the American flag is a precious symbol, worthy of protection. For more than 100 years, the federal government and as many as forty-nine states had laws to do just that. During the Civil War, public desecration of the American flag was punishable by death. It is difficult to believe that just a few years later, by passing the 14th Amendment, Congress intended to amend the Constitution so as to protect flag burning as "expressive conduct," yet that is what the Supreme Court said happened.

In 1989, the Supreme Court found that the Fourteenth Amendment gave protestors the right to burn the flag, and state criminal laws to the contrary were unconstitutional.[76] Polls at that time indicated that 80 percent of the American people wanted to retain these laws, and Congress responded by making the burning of an American flag a federal crime, but the federal law was also held unconstitutional.[77] A result like this never would have come through the democratic process. No politician would have been elected by proposing amending the Constitution to protect flag desecration, but the Court accomplished the same thing by amending its understanding of the Constitution without changing the text!

Perhaps of even greater concern to average Americans is the way judges have used the federal and state constitutions to overturn regulations prohibiting the most offensive forms of pornography. In particular is the case of *Ashcroft v. Free Speech Coalition*,[78] in which the U.S. Supreme Court struck down a law that was designed to prohibit "virtual" child pornography. This pornography looks like a photograph (or motion picture film), but it is manufactured on a computer. As one commentator explained:

> It is now possible to create sexually explicit images of "children" without actually photographing or filming a child. One could create the image from scratch, "morph" or combine an image of a child in a non-sexual situation with an adult in a sexual situation, or modify the picture of an adult so he or she looks like a child.

> The end result could be an image that looks exactly like the photograph of a child in a sexual situation.[79]

If the ultimate image were photographic in nature, its possession would constitute a felony. When, however, the image has been constructed on a computer, the Supreme Court decided that it would be protected under the First Amendment.

The Clinton and Bush administrations both defended the prohibition on virtual child pornography, explaining that it "helps to stamp out the market for child pornography involving real children." The Justice Department argued that virtual child pornography jeopardized real children by stimulating the market for illegal materials and by making it difficult for police to distinguish between what was legal and what was illegal. The Supreme Court however reasoned that "[t]hese images do not involve, let alone harm, any children in the production process."

In actuality, there is no telling how many children will be harmed by molesters who have their sexual appetite whetted by this pornography.[80] According to the National Center for Missing and Exploited Children, child pornography is very dangerous for several reasons:

> Pedophiles use child porn not only for sexual stimulation but also as a way to justify their sexual preference for children. If they expose themselves to pictures of children in sexual situations—especially if those images also involve adults—it tends to create the impression that such activity is somehow "normal" and maybe even acceptable. Child pornography can also be used to help lure a child into a sexual act. It is sometimes used by pedophiles to break down the resistance of children to sexual advances of an adult. Pedophiles have been known to send or show images of children and teens engaged in sex to potential victims as a means of convincing the young person that such activity is not all that out of the ordinary.[81]

Additionally, this decision makes it much harder to enforce laws against photographic child pornography, because it is hard for investigators, prosecutors, jurors, and judges to be certain which is photographic and which is not.[82]

Artists know that art can elevate and ennoble. Parents know that it can also degrade and corrupt. Yet, according to the Supreme Court, the free expression rights of the pornographers completely trump the risks to children associated with this kind of pornography. Once again, American parents can only shake their heads in disbelief. However society decides to deal with these issues, judges should not ignore the insight and the concerns of the mothers and fathers on this very important issue.

C. Sex Crimes

Worse even than justifying hard core child pornography as a matter of free speech is when judges trivialize sexual crimes. This issue may have had its genesis in legitimate concerns about the relative harshness in some cases of crimes like statutory rape. Laws prohibiting statutory rape are premised on the assumption that sexual intercourse without consent is rape and that people under a certain age (often 16) are incapable of giving legal consent. In its traditional form, a 17 year old boy who has sex with his 16 year old girlfriend is guilty of statutory rape. Since statutory rape is *rape*, it traditionally carries a very serious sentence.

As should be obvious, statutory rape could lead to very harsh results in some cases. For that reason, most states have taken steps through their democratic processes to amend the traditional form of statutory rape. One typical amendment is a "Romeo and Juliet" provision that mitigates or eliminates criminal liability when consensual sex takes place between young lovers who are close in age.

Unfortunately, some judges have taken it on themselves to modify other sexual laws that they deem to be unfair. There was, in fact, quite an uproar in early 2006 when Judge Edward Cashman, from Vermont, gave a 60-day sentence to a 34-year-old child rapist who admitted raping his close friend's daughter from the time she was six until she was ten.[83] The judge said he wanted to ensure that the defendant got treatment rather than punishment, and he did not think that treatment would be available unless the defendant was released from prison.

Defending his position, Judge Cashman said that when he first became a judge he handed down tough sentences, but he had come to believe that "it accomplishes nothing of value." He went on to explain: "It [punishment] doesn't make anything better; it costs us a lot of money; we create a lot of expectation, and we feed on anger." Talking to a courtroom packed with disappointed supporters of the victim, Cashman said: "The one message I want to get through is that anger doesn't solve anything. It just corrodes your soul."

Judge Cashman's actions, of course, attracted a great deal of attention. Within days, Vermont Governor James Douglas reported that more than 20,000 e-mails, phone calls and letters had poured into his office. The governor's spokesman said that "the outrage that the vast majority of Vermonters have here is shared by fellow countrymen." Governor Douglas called for Cashman to resign and several lawmakers suggested he be impeached. Television personality Bill O'Reilly told viewers as video of Cashman rolled: "You may be looking at the worst judge in the USA."[84]

Although he resisted for a while,[85] eventually Judge Cashman relented to the pressure and increased the sentence to from three to ten years. State legislators also proposed news laws that would require longer sentences for convicted sex offenders.[86] This in-state reaction, coupled with the national outrage that Judge Cashman's original sentence sparked might suggest that this case was unique. As several other cases from this same time period show, it wasn't.

In January 2006, a former high school teacher pleaded guilty to one count of rape of a child, one count of enticement of a child under 16, five counts of possession of child pornography, and one count of distribution of harmful material to a child. Prosecutors asked Suzanne V. Delvecchio, Chief Justice of the Massachusetts Superior Court, to give the defendant four to eight years in state prison, followed by five years probation. The judge, however, issued a suspended, 2 1/2-year jail term, followed by five years probation.[87]

Also in January 2006, the former choir instructor for the Parkview School District in Orfordville, Wisconsin pleaded no contest to one count each of disorderly conduct and misdemeanor fourth-degree sexual assault of a 16-year-old boy. Although the defendant had, three months before his arrest on the sexual assault charges, pleaded no contest to procuring alcohol for another minor, he received no jail time. He was sentenced to three years probation, required to pay a $1,000 fine, made to serve 30 hours of community service, and ordered have no contact with the victims.[88]

To be sure, most judges are strict when it comes to an adult sexual predator and a youthful victim, but these recent cases seem to be part of a larger trend. Many judges are very reluctant to punish those who are convicted of sexual crimes. Consider the following:

> those who speak loftily of "alternatives to incarceration" or who continue to rely on hopes of "rehabilitation" or "prevention" . . . engage in much hand-wringing about what to do with sexual predators. While many ordinary people would say that they should be locked up—and, if they are too dangerous to be at large, we should lock them up and throw away the key. But those whose whole sense of themselves is based on their presumed superiority to ordinary people can never go along with such ideas. They balk even at notifying the public when some convicted sexual predator is released into their neighborhood. Their thinking—if it can be called that—is that sexual predators who have been released from prison have "paid their debt to society" and so the slate should be wiped clean and these sadists allowed to hide their past. It is amazing how many innocent young lives have been sacrificed for a half-baked phrase.[89]

The basis for this kind of thinking was set forth by the U.S. Supreme Court in *Planned Parenthood v. Casey*,[90] in which the Court upheld the right to abortion.

In *Planned Parenthood v. Casey*, the Court set forth what has become known as the "sweet mystery of life" passage. The Court wrote that there is "a promise of the Constitution that there is a realm of personal liberty which the government may not enter." The Court continued to define this personal liberty: "At the heart of liberty is the right to define one's own concept of existence, of meaning of the universe, and the mystery of human life. Beliefs about these matters could not define the attributes of personhood were they formed under compulsion of the State."

The "sweet mystery of life" passage seems to suggest that the state's only interest in sexual matters (at least among consenting adults) is to protect the unfettered expression of personal autonomy. In other words, the most important thing for the Court when it comes to sexual matters is protecting the freedom of individuals to engage in it. That would seem to suggest that there could be no state law against prostitution, drug use, physician-assisted suicide, or same-sex marriage.

Consider how the Supreme Court reversed itself on the issued of sodomy. In the 1986 decision *Bowers v. Hardwick*,[91] the Court found that the practice of "homosexual sodomy" was not a "fundamental right." Therefore, Georgia's law making it illegal was constitutional. The Court pointed out that "sodomy was a criminal offense at common law and was forbidden by the laws of the original 13 States when they ratified the Bill of Rights."[92] It went on to observe that "in 1868, when the Fourteenth Amendment was ratified, all but 5 of the 37 States in the Union had criminal sodomy laws. In fact, until 1961, all 50 States outlawed sodomy."

Less than 20 years after upholding the Georgia law, the Supreme Court changed its mind and found Texas's anti-sodomy law unconstitutional in *Lawrence v. Texas*.[93] The Court held that the framers of the 14th Amendment's due process clause intended it to protect "liberty of the person both in its spatial and more transcendent dimensions." Justice Anthony Kennedy, writing the majority opinion, did not offer any proof to support his claim about the "more transcendent dimensions," but he did set forth the following facts:

> 1. In 1955, the American Law Institute promulgated the Model Penal Code, and it did not recommend or provide for "criminal penalties for consensual sexual relations conducted in private."
> 2. A committee advising the British Parliament in 1957 recommended repeal of laws punishing homosexual conduct. Parliament enacted the substance of those recommendations 10 years later.
> 3. In 1981, the European Court of Human Rights held that laws proscribing homosexual conduct were invalid under the European Convention on Human Rights.
> 4. In *Michigan Organization for Human Rights v. Kelley*, a trial court ruled Michigan's sodomy law unconstitutional under the state constitution.[94]

The Court essentially adopted the libertarian view that states do not have the authority to restrict conduct affecting only one's self and a consenting partner.

Until *Lawrence*, sex-related decisions usually noted the importance of marriage and recognized the legitimate purpose of laws designed to support it as an institution. On the other hand, courts usually treated extramarital sex as an evil. Since *Lawrence*, however, judges no longer have a reason to hold marriage out as having a special status.

Consider the ruling from U.S. District Court Judge Victor Marrero, who held that it was a violation of free speech rights for USAID to require organizations that try to eradicate AIDS to sign a pledge opposing prostitution in order to receive federal funds.[95] In May 2003, Congress passed the United States Leadership against HIV/AIDS, Tuberculosis, and Malaria Act (Global AIDS Act)[96] and in December 2003, it passed the Trafficking Victims Protection Reauthorization Act (TVPRA).[97] The Global AIDS Act bars the use of federal funds to "promote, support, or advocate the legalization or practice of prostitution or sex trafficking." TVPRA requires that recipient organizations of anti-trafficking funds pledge not to "promote, support, or advocate the legalization or practice of prostitution." In June 2005, USAID released a policy directive requiring all non-governmental organizations to have anti-prostitution and anti-sex trafficking policies before they were eligible to receive U.S. global AIDS funding.

The Alliance for Open Society International (OSI, funded by billionaire activist George Soros) and Pathfinder International brought suit against USAID, asserting that the policy was unconstitutional in that it required private organizations to adopt the government's position on prostitution. Judge Marrero agreed and issued a preliminary injunction preventing USAID from demanding such pledges, finding that the U.S. Supreme Court "has repeatedly found that speech, or an agreement not to speak, cannot be compelled or coerced as a condition of participation in a government program." He held that the pledge requirement "impermissibly discriminates based on viewpoint and compels speech . . . it also violates the First Amendment. . .

Given these circumstances, the court finds that plaintiffs have made the necessary showing of irreparable harm."

Another case reflecting this new post-*Lawrence* judicial philosophy can be found in a 2005 decision from the Kansas Supreme Court. Like many other states, Kansas criminalizes voluntary sex between adults and minors. In 1999 the state enacted a "Romeo and Juliet" law that set a lower penalty for a statutory rape involving an 18-year-old having sex with a 14- or 15-year-old.[98] The lighter punishment, however, applied only to "members of the opposite sex." The Kansas Supreme Court struck down the law, finding that it discriminated against homosexuals.[99] Under *Lawrence*, the court said, a state could not use its laws to express "moral disapproval" of homosexuality. The court concluded that there was no "rational basis" for drawing a distinction between homosexual and heterosexual acts.

The legislature probably should have extended the "Romeo and Juliet" exception to cover homosexual acts, but should a court really order a state not to express moral disapproval of particular types of sex? It there really "no rational basis" for distinguishing between homosexual acts and heterosexual acts? For thousands of years, societies have thought otherwise.

No one wants the government spying into the bedrooms of its citizens, and despite some of the laws that were on the books, this was not a problem before the *Lawrence* decision.[100] Similarly, violence against any group cannot be condoned. To the extent that homosexuals have been the victims of hate, *Lawrence* does not seem to have changed things much. People may, however, want the law to express their objections to certain kinds of lifestyles. They may want the laws to help provide moral guidance to their children. *Lawrence* seems to foreclose that possibility.

Judges are not better positioned to reflect the will of the populace or the emerging consensus of thought than is the legislature. Citizens should be free to structure their society through the democratic process in a way that will best serve their children and their families. Judicial attempts to mainstream alternative lifestyles can undercut that structure and do harm to the common good.

D. Victims' Rights

In a traditional criminal prosecution, the state and the defendant are both represented, but the victim is not. The theory is that the defendant has harmed society, not an individual victim. The victim's interests are reflected as a part of the larger society. That arrangement, of course, leaves much to be desired for the crime victim. As then-President Clinton said:

> When someone is a victim, he or she should be at the center of the criminal justice process, not on the outside looking in. Participation in all forms of government is the essence of democracy. Victims should be guaranteed the right to participate in proceedings related to crimes committed against them. People accused of crimes have explicit constitutional rights. Ordinary citizens have a constitutional right to participate in criminal trials by serving on a jury. The press has a constitutional right to attend trials. All of this is as it should be. It is only the victims of crime who have no constitutional right to participate, and that is not the way it should be.[101]

As this author knows from first-hand experience, a victim may plan to be at the trial, take the day off work, get downtown and find a parking place, only to find that the case has been postponed or—even worse—dismissed. The victim, in a traditional case, is not entitled to notice of calendar changes or the right to testify at trial or sentencing.[102]

Starting in the 1980s, state and federal legislatures tried to rectify this situation. In 1983, the U.S. Department of Justice created the Office for Victims of Crime, and the following year the Victims of Crime Act established the Crime Victims Fund to support state victim compensation and service programs. Later in the decade and into the 1990s, many states amended their constitutions and enacted legislation giving greater rights to victims of crime.[103] New statutes permitted crime victims to seek compensation, up to a limited amount, from state-funded accounts. Most states also gave victims the right to be notified about court proceedings and to be present, the right to communication with the prosecution, the right to be heard at sentencing in some cases, the right to restitution from the defendant, the right to read pre-sentence reports, and other rights.[104] By 2002, every state, Washington DC, Puerto Rico, and Guam had established some type of victim rights program.

Obviously, victim rights are important to average citizens. As one author put it, "a pragmatic politician would commit electoral suicide by opposing *any* 'Victims Rights' initiative."[105] Unfortunately, judges often overlook victims' rights. As U.S. Senator Dianne Feinstein (D-Calif.) reports on her web page: "The unjust treatment of crime victims has been widely recognized for more than 20 years, yet today's American criminal justice system continues to deny victims basic respect and fair treatment."[106] The senator goes on in her web page to discuss recent cases in which family members of murder victims were not permitted to be in the courtroom, victims were not permitted to make a victim impact statement ("VIS"),[107] victims were denied the right to be heard at trial, and victims were not informed about court dates.

There are probably different reasons for non-compliance with victim rights laws. In some states, the laws are on the books, but the programs are woefully under-funded. As the Congressional Victim's Caucus explains:

> there are still too many victims whose needs are not met. There aren't enough beds in domestic violence shelters to house women and children who are abused. There aren't enough counselors and support services for women, children and men who are raped. There are too many family survivors of homicide victims who can't afford to give their loved one a decent burial. And elderly crime victims—already worried about paying the rent and finding funds for prescriptions critical to their health—too often don't receive services to help them deal with the incredible trauma of crime and victimization.[108]

In other states, the problem seems to be simply a matter of inertia. Victims' rights are still new to most judges. Unfortunately, if the court fails to abide by the victim's rights law, there usually is no legal recourse.[109]

Judges would not stand for such callousness and disregard of the rights of defendants. Indeed, they have usually forced the issue and demanded that defendants' rights be respected when the legislature has failed to act or even when the legislature has resisted acting. It is too bad that they have not been equally vigilant when it comes to protecting the rights of victims.

IV. Sentencing

Some of the most controversial judicial holdings do not relate to the constitutionality of specific laws, but rather to the sentencing of convicted defendants. Too often, judges negate the seriousness with which society views criminal conduct by imposing minimal punishment. They are especially reluctant to impose the death penalty, even when it is clearly authorized by the statute in question. Due to the perceived reluctance of judges to impose strict sentences, many state legislatures as well as Congress have enacted mandatory sentencing laws.[110] These legislative correctives to perceived failings on the part of the courts are themselves, however, subject to judicial review. Courts have been very willing to overturn such laws, particularly when they are designed to remove discretion from a sentencing judge.

A. Three-Strikes and Mandatory Minimum Rules

In state after state, legislative initiatives have increased the penalties for criminal activity and at the same time they have tried to take discretion away from judges who are perceived to be soft on crime. The hope, of course, is that increased punishments will decrease crime by incarcerating recidivist criminals and by deterring others. Unfortunately, courts often thwart these efforts to create a safer society.

One of the more common legislative initiatives to limit judicial discretion is the so-call "three-strike" laws. As the name implies, this law created a system of escalating sentences based on each new felony. A second felony, or second "strike," leads to a stiffer sentence than would ordinarily be handed down for that felony. If a third felony is committed by the same individual, that constitutes the "third strike" and the offender is typically given a life prison term or something close to it.[111]

About half of the states now have "three strikes" legislation on the books. Almost all of the other states now have some type of "honesty in sentencing" law that is designed to decrease judicial discretion and increase the time that must actually be served by violent and serious felons. Even the federal government has taken several steps in this direction, beginning with the creation of the Federal Sentencing Commission in 1984. As political analyst Cokie Roberts explains:

> that body was charged with developing a uniform set of federal sentencing guidelines that would establish tough but fair sentences for every crime, including those involving drugs. The Sentencing Commission sought to eliminate unwarranted sentencing disparity by abolishing parole and establishing a range of sentences available for a particular offense based on the seriousness of the offense, the underlying criminal conduct, the offender's past, etc.[112]

Roberts also notes that despite criticism of mandatory minimum sentences from judges and commentators "the public, the voters who asked for these laws in the first place, overwhelmingly favor mandatory minimums. And the Congress, supported by each president since the laws started being passed, has increased the reach of the mandatory minimums."[113]

Sentencing is how society expresses its moral outrage at criminal conduct. When voters, through the democratic process, put these mandatory minimum sentences in place, they are expressing their outrage at crime (much of it drug-related) and their frustration with judges who seem unable or unwilling to express society's outrage by giving appropriately long sentences to convicted criminals.

Judges did not like to see their discretion limited. In an August 2003 speech at the American Bar Association's annual meeting, U.S. Supreme Court Justice Anthony M. Kennedy complained about the removal of discretion from judges and urged the ABA to speak out against mandatory minimum sentences, saying "our punishments are too severe and our sentences are too long. . . . I accept neither the wisdom, the justice nor the necessity of mandatory minimums. In all too many cases they are unjust."[114] Much to Justice Kennedy's credit, he noted the difference between what he thought was the better policy and a determination as to the constitutionality of the matter:

> The court on which I sit, on which I serve, and many other courts, have upheld very rigorous and severe sentencing schemes. But please remember that because a court has said something is permissible, it is not necessarily wise. And this is a mistake that we see all too often in our public and civic discourse. And in the accounts of what our court has done, in the press. It is simply not proper, as a matter of self governance, as a matter of exercising your political will, as a matter of discharging your political responsibility, to just pass off policy issues to the courts.[115]

Despite Justice Kennedy's observations, the general public overwhelmingly favors strict mandatory minimum sentencing.

The public likes strict punishment because they have seen the results; mandatory minimum sentences are designed to serve the common good by reducing crime, and they seem to work. As Congressman Asa Hutchinson (R-Ark) explained in 1999:

> the mandatory minimum penalties appear to be effective. Violent crime has declined seven years in a row. Murder is down thirty-one percent since 1991. Robbery is down thirty-two percent. And even [President Clinton] indicated that the continued downward trend over the past four years is further evidence that we are on the right track with increased community policing, tougher penalties, and greater juvenile crime prevention. Now, I'd underline that the tougher penalty has been a very important part of our effort to combat crime. There is widespread agreement that the stabilization of the crack epidemic, which has been a major focus of the mandatory minimums, and the Sentencing Guidelines, is a principal cause of the decline in violent crime rates. And so you have a cause and effect.[116]

Further elaborating on the causal link, the Congressman noted the earlier history of mandatory sentencing: "I think that we've learned a lesson as you look back on what we did from the 1950s to the 1970s. . . . as soon as we rescinded the mandatory minimums, drug use went up. Because we lessened our resolve, lessened our commitment [sic]."[117]

Although these tough-sentencing programs seem to serve the common good, they still face serious opposition from the judges. This attitude was expressed in 2005, when a federal judge from the Northern District of New York came out very strongly against a statute that required him to impose a life-without-parole term on a 32-year-old "relatively small-time drug dealer" with an IQ of 72.[118] "The increment of harm in this case bears no rational relationship to the increment of punishment that I must impose," Hurd said at a sentencing proceeding. "This is what occurs when Congress sets [a] mandatory minimum sentence which distorts the entire judicial process. . . . As a result, I am obligated to and will now impose this unfair and, more important, unjust sentence."[119] The judge also said society will suffer nothing "except for the enormous expense" by keeping Powell imprisoned for life. He called the punishment a "black mark on our system of justice."

The principle argument against mandatory minimum sentences is proportionality, which derives from the Eighth Amendment's prohibition of cruel and unusual punishment. The Supreme Court, however, has held that the sentences, even when quite severe, are not in violation of the Eighth Amendment.[120] Nevertheless, state courts have found ways to thwart the intent of the lawmakers and return discretion to the judges.

For instance, in *People v. Superior Court*,[121] the defendant, Jesus Romero, had committed his third felony through the possession of 0.13 grams of cocaine. He faced a punishment of 25-years-to-life due to his prior convictions. The trial court, however, struck Romero's prior felonies for the purposes of sentencing. The California Supreme Court upheld a trial court's right to do that "in the interest of justice." This, of course, dramatically weakened the three strike law by permitting sentencing judges to reject "mandatory" 25-years-to-life sentences.

Many California legislators were outraged. As one assemblyman complained: "This strikes at the heart of the Three Strikes law. . . . It blows a hole in it."[122] While the *Romero* exception is not supposed to be invoked "to accommodate judicial convenience" or if "guided by personal antipathy" for the three strike legislation, judges are smart enough to write opinions that cannot be challenged on these grounds, even when "antipathy" for the law is the primary justification.[123]

Judges have also overturned the mandatory nature of the federal sentencing guidelines. In *United States v. Booker*,[124] the U.S. Supreme Court ruled that the guidelines violate the Sixth Amendment right to trial because they permit judges to impose sentences based on aggravating factors not found by a jury beyond a reasonable doubt. The result of the 124 page opinion (including writings by six justices) is that the guidelines are now merely advisory rather than mandatory. That would be fine, if judges were consistent and firm. Unfortunately, history suggests that problems will recur.[125]

Common people grew weary of reading about judges in criminal cases who impose sentences that are ridiculously light. They responded through the democratic process with required sentences for certain crimes and certain kinds of offenders. Now the judges are poking holes in those laws. No one should fault the judges (or anyone else) for complaining about laws or for trying to amend them through the political process.[126] There are many questions about the effectiveness of these laws.[127] Judges should not, however, take it upon themselves to reform the system and ignore these laws that are specifically designed to rein them in. As Congressman Hutchinson said: "With due respect to the judiciary . . . I think that their primary focus is making sure that due process is followed in the case. If Congress gives specific sentencing directions that should be followed, that's not infringing upon the discretion that a judge might otherwise have."[128]

B. Limitations on the Death Penalty

While there have been occasional shifts in attitude, the American public has supported the death penalty, usually by wide margins, for at least several decades. Indeed, society's right to execute convicted criminals represented "the consensus of Western thought until very recent times."[129] It was also a large part of Christian thought. St. Augustine wrote:

> Surely it is not without purpose that we have the institution of the power of kings, the death penalty of the judge, the barbed hooks of the executioner, the weapons of the soldier, the right of punishment of the overlord, even the severity of the good father. All those things have their methods, their causes, their reasons, their practical benefits. While these are feared, the wicked are kept within bounds and the good live more peacefully among the wicked. . . . It is not without advantage that human recklessness should be confined by fear of the law so that innocence may be safe among evil-doers, and the evil-doers themselves may be cured by calling on God when their freedom of action is held in check by fear of punishment.[130]

Modern American judges, however, often oppose the death penalty.[131] No one should fault any individual for opposing the death penalty; it is a profoundly important and difficult issue. The problem comes when judges refuse to apply the law due to their personal beliefs.

In 2002, U.S. Supreme Court Justice Antonin Scalia addressed the situation of a judge who personally opposes capital punishment but who is called upon to assign or uphold the death penalty. Noting that the Catholic Church had taken a stronger position against the death penalty, he argued that a Catholic judge still could impose the death penalty without violating the teaching of his or her church. This was important because he concluded that if the new Catholic instruction prevented him, as a loyal Catholic, from affirming the death sentence in any case regardless of the facts, he would feel compelled to resign from the Court:

> in my view the choice for the judge who believes the death penalty to be immoral is resignation, rather than simply ignoring duly enacted, constitutional laws and

sabotaging death penalty cases. He has, after all, taken an oath to apply the laws and has been given no power to supplant them with rules of his own.[132]

Fortunately for him, Scalia did not consider the developed Catholic teaching on capital punishment as a proscription on his ability to impose the death penalty (or affirm it on appeal).

Unfortunately, not all judges agree with this logic. In 1994, Supreme Court Justice Harry Blackmun (the author of *Roe v. Wade*) decided that he could no longer uphold capital punishment. He wrote: "From this day forward, I no longer tinker with the machinery of death. . . . I feel morally and intellectually obligated simply to concede that the death penalty experiment has failed."[133] That is a perfectly fine moral and intellectual position for a person to hold, but it is not right for a judge to essentially, as Blackmun did, declare that he will no longer follow the law. Jurors who are unable to impose the death penalty are properly excluded from the sentencing phase of a capital case.[134] In fact, they may even be excluded from the guilt determination phase of the trial.[135] Similarly, jurors who would automatically impose the death penalty in every capital case are also properly excluded from death penalty cases.[136] Judges who have to deal with death penalty cases but are morally prevented from imposing it should resign or recuse themselves. Their job is to apply the law as written, not to find creative ways to avoid that with which they disagree.

The state writes its laws through a democratically elected legislature. Those elected officials are more likely to be in touch with the attitudes of the public than are the comparatively isolated jurists. If judges are unable to follow the law, then—like potential jurors—they should not be put in a position where their duty will come into conflict with their conscience. Unfortunately, rather than resigning or recusing themselves, they often find ways to avoid punishments with which they disagree, thereby thwarting the will of the people and failing to carry out their assigned tasks.

In the 1972 case *Furman v. Georgia*, the Supreme Court ruled that the death penalty, as it was then being applied in every state, was unconstitutional.[137] The death penalty itself is contemplated by the Constitution,[138] so the Court could not find it inherently unconstitutional. Clearly, however, the justices wanted to curtail its usage; they just could not agree how.

Although the Court issued a *per curiam* opinion in *Furman*, all nine justices also wrote separate opinions. The result of the holding was that states could still use capital punishment, if it were "applied regularly and evenhandedly." It was, however, almost impossible to figure out what would meet the Court's standard. Over the next four years, 35 states enacted new capital punishment statutes. Two types of statutes emerged: those requiring mandatory death sentences for certain crimes, and those giving judges and/or juries the discretion to choose between death and some lesser sentence based on various mitigating factors.

In 1976, the Court struck down the mandatory death penalty statutes because they did not provide for jury consideration of mitigating factors such as the circumstances of a crime or the background and character of the defendant.[139] As a result, death penalty laws in 21 states were again invalidated. After states took corrective action to answer this concern, the Court's 1978 *Lockett v. Ohio* decision further refined the "mitigating factor" standard, expressly requiring that *all* aspects of a defendant's character and record be considered before imposition of the death penalty (even though this seemed to be inconsistent with the earlier requirement of "guided discretion").[140]

States kept trying to comply, but the judges kept changing the rules. By the end of 1985, despite a national death row population of 1,642, only 42 involuntary executions had been carried out since 1972.[141] During this same time, courts overturned 1,266 death sentences.[142] In fact, 60 to 79 percent of all death sentences were being reversed as late as the mid-1980s.[143] Clearly, courts and the rest of the population did not seem to be on the same page when it came to capital punishment.

Those different views continue on even today. Particular differences exist with respect to both the type of crime that can justify capital punishment and the type of defendant who should be considered for it.

1. Rape

In *Coker v. Georgia*,[144] the Supreme Court struck down a statute that authorized capital punishment for rape, ruling that the death sentence in itself is not cruel and unusual, but it was disproportionate to the crime of rape of an adult woman. The Court stated that the death penalty in this case was a purposeless and needless imposition of pain and suffering and was grossly out of proportion to the severity of the crime.

The Court's arguments in *Coker* not only go beyond the legitimate realm of judicial decision-making, they also trivialize the suffering of rape victims, who can be left with irreparable psychiatric injury which sometimes leads to suicide. What these victims have lost could therefore arguably merit the most serious punishment that the law has to offer. The retributive limitation of "an eye for an eye" may be valid, but disproportion between rape and capital punishment is by no means self-evident, and the democratic process had authorized it. It was a significant reach by the Court to hold that rape was not serious enough to warrant the maximum penalty, and it angered many citizens.

As the dissent in *Coker* explained, a punishment that is no more severe than the crime does not provide much of a deterrent. After all, most criminals assume that they will avoid apprehension. "For example, hardly any thief would be deterred from stealing if the only punishment upon being caught were return of the money stolen." This was particularly true in the *Coker* case. The defendant was already serving a term of life imprisonment when he escaped and raped a 16-year-old victim (the "adult woman" in question). Coker had previously been convicted of murder, rape, kidnapping, and aggravated assault. Without the death penalty, what else could the state offer to deter or incapacitate his violent behavior?

Georgia citizens thought that the death penalty was appropriate for the crime of rape, but the Supreme Court knew better. Today, other states still provide for capital punishment in the case of the rape of a child. Louisiana, for example permits a jury to sentence a person to death who is convicted of raping a child under the age of 12.[145] At least one such sentence already was imposed.[146] Whether it will be carried out may depend on whether the justices think they know better than the people of Louisiana.

2. The Age of the Perpetrator

Recently, the Supreme Court looked not to the status of the victim to limit the death penalty, but to the age of the perpetrator. In *Roper v. Simmons*,[147] the Court held that it violates the Eighth Amendment's proscription of cruel and unusual punishment to execute people who were younger than eighteen years old when they committed the crime in question. The case involved a seventeen year-old from Missouri who bragged to his buddies that he could get away with murder because he was minor. He then broke into a women's home, put duct tape over her eyes and mouth, wrapped her head in a towel, tied her up with electrical wire, and threw her off a railroad trestle into a river where she drowned.

The Supreme Court ruled that the defendant was too young when he committed the crime to receive the death penalty. Writing for the Court, Justice Kennedy wrote that "any parent knows" and "scientific and sociological studies" show that people under eighteen have a "lack of maturity" and "underdeveloped sense of responsibility" and susceptibility to "negative influences" along with a weak sense of "cost benefit analysis." He cited "evolving standards of decency" and asserted that in recent years a "national consensus" had formed against the death penalty for minors. He also cited "the overwhelming weight on international opinion against juvenile death penalty."

As for what any parent knows, the consensus of opinion is best reflected in the laws of the various states. At that time, the 38 states that had capital punishment, only 18 barred the execution of those who were under age eighteen at the time of the crime. Justice Kennedy did not know better than the voters in Missouri.

As for the citation to laws of other nations, this can hardly be an indication of American attitudes. Robert H. Bork, in his book *Coercing Virtue*, notes the growing tendency of the Supreme Court to cite decisions by foreign court: "That, to put it gently, is flabbergasting. What the decisions of foreign courts have to do with what the framers and ratifiers of the U.S. Constitution understood themselves to be doing is not explained, and cannot be explained."[148] Actually, the recent propensity of judges to cite foreign laws can be explained fairly easily. Those laws support what the justices want to do and give support to the courts' unwarranted assertion of judicial power. That, and that alone, is why the judges cite them.

Roper v Simmons may have reached the appropriate conclusion, but it did it in the wrong way. The arguments offered by the Court, along with their counter-arguments, belong in the legislature, not in the courtroom. It is yet another example of judicial usurpation of the political process.

V. Conclusion

Judges play an important role in our constitutional democracy; they control one branch of government—the judiciary. Of course, they do not reach their decisions in isolation. In every case, there is at least one lawyer urging the judge to make the controversial decision, and behind each lawyer there is a least one client. Nevertheless, the judges make the decisions. They have the authority, and they are the ones who must be held responsible.

The seductive nature of the power given to judges makes it easy for them to forget that their authority is limited. Couple that with the insight that judges feel they have into the criminal process and there is a situation ripe for judicial overreaching. The problem is that this insight does not justify bypassing the democratic process. Exhibits in court must be tested by the rules of evidence, and insights into political solutions to society's problems need to be tested by the democratic process. When political arguments are not subjected to democratic debate, they are quite likely to lead to bad results.

Judges are used to resolving cases and controversies between litigants, not resolving the great political debates of the day.[149] The decisions reached in court are different from those reached through a democratic process. "The adversarial process encourages a winner-take-all attitude and suppresses compromise and accommodation."[150] This can be very counter-productive in the give-and-take world of political decision-making. Moreover, as Supreme Court Justice Antonin Scalia has noted, "judge-moralists," are no better qualified than "Joe Sixpack" to decide society's great moral questions.[151] The public, through elected legislatures—not the courts—should decide the big questions, including those of law and order.

Sometimes, it must be admitted, judicial activism has encouraged the rest of society to move in a positive direction. The federal courts certainly played an important role in bringing segregation to an end and enforcing the civil rights of all citizens, and the judges deserve much credit for that. Too often, however, particularly when it comes to criminal matters, judicial activism has had less admirable results and has created even greater problems for society, primarily by making it harder for society to protect itself against crime.

The powers of the judiciary are carefully balanced against those of the executive and those of the legislature. Judicial activism, however, confuses our constitutional structure of government by, among other things, moving the location of the debate. Rather than hammering out societal issues in the halls of the legislature, judicial activism cases major policy decisions to be resolved in courts that were never designed to address those questions.[152] The clearest example of this relates to the Supreme Court's decision striking down state criminal laws that made abortion illegal.

With *Roe v. Wade*, Supreme Court justices seem to have thought that they were going to resolve one of society's biggest issues once and for all. They were wrong. The abortion debate has continued, and the intensity of the anger has probably been magnified by the poor logic that went into the Court's decision.[153] People on both sides of the debate seem to know that the Court exceeded its authority in that case. Justice Byron White said as much when he dissented in *Doe v. Bolton*, the companion case to *Roe v. Wade*:

> With all due respect, I dissent. I find nothing in the language or history of the Constitution to support the Court's judgment. The upshot is that the people and the legislatures of the 50 States are constitutionally disentitled to weigh the relative importance of the continued existence and development of the fetus, on the

one hand, against a spectrum of possible impacts on the mother, on the other hand. As an *exercise of raw judicial power*, the Court perhaps has authority to do what it does today; but, in my view, its judgment is an improvident and extravagant exercise of the power of judicial review that the Constitution extends to this Court.[154]

Despite these words of caution, the Court made its rulings, pretending that its political resolution of this issue was actually mandated by the Constitution. The Justices did not resolve the issue "once and for all," nor would it appear that they even lessened the tensions.

Judges have great powers in our society, but that does not mean that they are better able than anyone else to understand the important moral and political issues of the day. This is particularly true when it comes to society's decision to express its disapproval and moral outrage through the criminal code. Judges have a defined role to play in our government. When they go beyond that role, they invade the proper province of other branches of the government, they thwart the will of the people, and they may do significant harm to the common good.

ENDNOTES

1. See Michael Pinard, *Limitations on Judicial Activism in Criminal Trials*, 33 Conn. L. Rev. 243, 263 (2000) (complaining about judges helping prosecutors).

2. The principle of subsidiarity teaches that "it is an injustice, a grave evil and a disturbance of right order for a larger and higher organization to arrogate to itself functions which can be performed efficiently by smaller and lower bodies. This is a fundamental aim of social philosophy.... Of its very nature the true aim of all social activity should be to help members of a social body, and never to destroy or absorb them...." Pope Pius XI, *Quadragesimo Anno* (1931); *Catechism of the Catholic Church* §§ 1883–1885 (describing Catholic Church's doctrine of subsidiarity). Assistance should come from the intermediate association *closest to the problem*, with less-involved, more detached associations only used when absolutely necessary. See generally Ronald J. Rychlak & John M. Czarnetzky, *The International Criminal Court and the Question of Subsidiarity*, Third World Legal Studies 2000–2003 at 115.

3. Quoted in *CATO Handbook for Congress*, 105th Congress, part 17, on the Internet at <<http://www.worldnewsstand.net/gov/police_state.htm>>.

4. *Palko v. Connecticut*, 302 U.S. 319 (1937).

5. See *Adamson v. California*, 332 U.S. 46 (1947).

6. See, e.g., *Weeks v. United States*, 232 U.S. 383 (1914).

7. *Palko v. Connecticut*, 302 U.S. 319 (1937).

8. California, for instance, applied the exclusionary rule in state proceedings beginning in 1955, six years before the Supreme Court's decision in *Mapp v. Ohio*.

9. *Robinson v. California*, 370 U.S. 660 (1962).

10. *Gideon v. Wainwright*, 372 U.S. 335, 344 (1963).

11. *Malloy v. Hogan*, 378 U.S. 1 (1966).

12. *Pointer v. Texas*, 380 U.S. 400 (1965).

13. *Massiah v. United States*, 377 U.S. 201 (1964); *Escobedo v. Illinois*, 378 U.S. 478 (1964); *Miranda v. Arizona*, 384 U.S. 486 (1966).

14. *Klopfer v. North Carolina*, 386 U.S. 213 (1967).

15. *Washington v. Texas*, 388 U.S. 14 (1967).

16. *Duncan v. Louisiana*, 391 U.S. 145, 149–50 (1968).

17. *Benton v. Maryland*, 395 U.S. 784 (1969).

18. *Miranda v. Arizona*, 384 U.S. 486 (1966). See Paul G. Cassell and Richard Fowles, *Handcuffing the Cops? A Thirty-Year Perspective on Miranda's Harmful Effects on Law Enforcement*, <<http://www.law.utah.edu/faculty/websites/cassellp/STANFIN.html>>.

19. *Mapp v. Ohio*, 367 U.S. 643 (1961); *Ker v. California*, 374 U.S. 23 (1963).

20. See *Katz v. United States*, 389 U.S. 347 (1967).

21. In 1791, when the Eighth Amendment, which forbids "cruel and unusual punishments," was ratified, the Fifth Amendment, which ordered that no person shall be "deprived of life, liberty, or property, without due process of law," was also ratified. The Fifth Amendment treated "life" exactly the same way it treated "liberty" and "property." In other words, a person could be deprived of life as long as he or she was given due process. In 1791, every state had mandatory death penalty statutes. The list typically included murder, treason, piracy, rape, arson, sodomy, burglary, robbery, and, in some states, counterfeiting, horse-theft, and slave-rebellion.

22. *Furman v. Georgia*, 408 U.S. 238 (1972).

23. A similar situation happened in California when the state supreme court found that the death penalty violated the state constitution. Very quickly the voters approved an initiative changing the state constitution so that the death penalty would be available. See Gerald F. Uelmen, *Review of Death Penalty Judgments by the Supreme Court of California: A Tale of Two Courts*, 23 Loy. L.A. L. Rev. 237, 243–44 (1989).

24. "The number of crimes committed in the US escalated significantly from 1960 to 1971." *Number of Crimes in the U.S.*, The Physics Factbook (Glenn Elert, ed.) <<http://hypertextbook.com/facts/2003/MaryPennisi.shtml>> (suggesting that one cause of the increase in crime may have been "the creation of criminal-friendly rules by the Warren Court.")

25. *Mapp v. Ohio*, 367 U.S. 643 (1961).

26. *Wolf v. Colorado*, 338 U.S. 25 (1949).

27. In *Linkletter v. Walker*, 381 US 618 (1965), the Supreme Court held that the exclusionary rule did not apply to persons who had been convicted in state trials prior to the *Mapp* decision. The Court said: "[Our] purpose [in *Mapp v. Ohio*] was to deter the lawless action of the police and to effectively enforce the Fourth Amendment. That purpose will not at this late date be served by the wholesale release of the guilty victims."

28. Catherine Crier, *The Case Against Lawyers* 95 (2002).

29. *People v. Defore*, 150 N.E. 585 (N.Y.), cert. denied, 270 U.S. 657 (1926).

30. Id.

31. Leon Scully, "Civil Wrongs," *National Review*, May 25, 1992.

32. R. Alexander Acosta, "Clinton's Judicial Flip Flop," *Washington Times*, Oct. 10, 1997, at A20, available at LEXIS, News Library, Wtimes File; Crier, supra note 29 at 96.

33. Jon O. Newman, *The Judge Baer Controversy*, 80 Judicature 156, 156–57 (1997) (reprinting a letter from over 200 congressional members urging President Clinton to call for Judge Baer's resignation).

34. *United States v. Bayless*, 921 F. Supp. 211, 217 (S.D.N.Y. 1996).

35. Crier, supra note 29 at 96.

36. *Massiah v. United States*, 377 U.S. 201 (1964); *Escobedo v. Illinois*, 378 U.S. 478 (1964).

37. See *Malloy v. Hogan*, 378 U.S. 1 (1964).

38. *Miranda v. Arizona*, 384 U.S. 436 (1966).

39. David Simon, *Homicide: A Year on the Killing Streets* (1991).

40. *Berkemer v. McCarthy* 468 U.S. 420 (1984).

41. Crier, supra note 29 at 94.

42. *Id.*

43. See Paul G. Cassell and Richard Fowles, *Handcuffing the Cops? A Thirty-Year Perspective on Miranda's Harmful Effects on Law Enforcement*, <<http://www.law.utah.edu/faculty/websites/cassellp/STANFIN.html>>.

44. *The American Almanac*, Grosset and Dunlap, Inc., (1973); *The Universal Almanac*, John W. Wright, ed., Andrews McMeel Publishing (1996); *Number of Crimes in the U.S.*, The Physics Factbook, Glenn Elert, ed., on the Internet at <<http://hypertextbook.com/facts/2003/MaryPennisi.shtml>>.

45. See Linda Chavez, "False sense of security?", *Jewish World Review*, May 11, 2000 available on the Internet at <<http://www.jewishworldreview.com >>.

46. Crime rates started to fall in the late 1990s, largely because the number of incarcerated criminals increased by about 1.5 million during the 1980s and 1990s. People also turned to more private security in this time, which may also have contributed to the drop. Crier, supra note 29 at 101.

47. "Violent crime in the United States peaked in 1991, when some 758 violent crimes and more than 5,100 serious property crimes were committed per 100,000 population. In 1960, that figure was only 161 violent crimes per 100,000." Chavez, supra note 46.

48. *Regarding Term Limits for Judges, Hearing Before the Subcomm. on the Constitution, Federalism, and Property Rights of the Senate Comm. on the Judiciary*, 105th Cong. (1997) (statement of Sen. Bob Smith), available at 1997 WL 11235410 ("Worst of all, activist

judges have compromised the ability of our criminal justice system to protect our citizens from violent crime. They have created new rules to protect criminal defendants that result in killers, rapists and other violent individuals being turned loose to continue preying on society.")

49. *See, e.g., People v. Stamp*, 2 Cal. App. 3d 203, 82 Cal. Rptr. 598 (1969).

50. There are, however, independent constitutional limitations on the imposition of the death penalty on those guilty of felony murder.

51. Three states (Hawaii, Kentucky, and Michigan) have completely abolished the felony murder rule.

52. *People v. Stamp*, 2 Cal. App. 3d 203, 82 Cal. Rptr. 598 (1969).

53. The American Law Institute's Model Penal Code lists the following crimes for which it is presumed that the defendant acted with a level of intent sufficient to support a murder conviction: robbery, rape or forcible deviant sexual intercourse, arson, burglary, kidnapping, and felonious escape.

54. *People v. Burroughs*, 35 Cal.3d 824, 201 Cal. Rptr. 319, 678 P.2d 894 (1984).

55. Concurring, Chief Justice Rose Bird argued that the court should have done away with second degree felony murder because it did not have a valid deterrent effect. Due largely to a perception that she was out-of-touch with the populace and too easy on criminals, she was voted out of office in November 1986, along with Associate Justices Joseph Grodin and Cruz Reynoso. See Stephen R. Barnett, *The Rose Bird Myth*, Cal. Law., Aug. 1992, at 86; John H. Culver & John T. Wold, *Rose Bird and the Politics of Judicial Accountability in California*, 70 Judicature 81, 86 (1986) (under Chief Justice Bird, the court "steadily extended application of the exclusionary rule, imposed strict standards upon the admissibility of confessions, and broadened its test regarding insanity pleas in a manner favorable to those entering such pleas."). See also Rose E. Bird, *The Instant Society and the Rule of Law*, 31 Cath. U. L. Rev. 159, 169 (1982).

56. The misdemeanor-manslaughter rule is based on a similar theory: if someone dies during the course of a misdemeanor, the perpetrator can be found guilty of manslaughter. Courts, however, are also often reluctant to extend this doctrine as far as the legislature has authorized. See *Todd v. State*, 594 So. 2d 802 (Fla. Ct. App. 1992) (harm was too unforeseen to apply the rule).

58. *People v. Patterson*, 262 Cal.Rptr.195, 197–198, 778 P.2d 549 (Cal., 1989).

59. *People v. Caffero*, 207 Cal. App. 3d 678, 255 Cal. Rptr. 22 (Cal. App.1989).

59. *People v. Washington*, 402 P.2d 130 (Cal. 1965).

60. Under the "agency theory," defendant is only liable for murder "if the defendant or her co-felon actually performed the lethal act." James W. Hilliard, *Felony Murder in Illinois-The "Agency Theory" vs. the AProximate Cause Theory@: The Debate Continues*, 25 S. Ill. U. L.J. 331, 332 (2001). Under the "proximate cause theory," as used in *People v. Stamp*, the defendant is responsible "for any death proximately resulting from the forcible felony or attempted forcible felony." *Id*.

61. See *People v. Hickman*, 12 Ill. App. 3d 412, 297 N.E.2d 582 (1973).

62. *Franks v. State*, 636 P.2d 361 (Okla. Cr.1981).

63. *State v. Harrison*, 90 N.M. 439, 441–42, 564 P.2d 1321, 1323–24 (1977), superseded by rule on other grounds as stated in *Tafoya v. Baca*, 103 N.M. 56, 60, 702 P.2d 1001, 1005 (1985).

64. *State v. Harrison*, 90 N.M. at 442, 564 P.2d at 1324.

65. *Jackson v. State*, 92 N.M. 461, 462, 589 P.2d 1052, 1053 (1979).

66. *State v. Ortega*, 112 N.M. 554, 563, 817 P.2d 1196, 1205 (1991).

67. Rudolph J. Gerber, *The Felony Murder Rule: Conundrum Without Principle*, 31 Ariz. St. L.J. 763, 763 (1999).

68. I have, in the past, had students who went home and checked with their parents. Every student who has reported to me about doing this has confirmed that their parents thought the felony murder rule was fair.

69. Survey data collected at the November 2002 meeting of the American Academy of Matrimonial Lawyers in Chicago looked at the impact of Internet usage on marriages. At this meeting, 62% of the 350 attendees said the Internet had been a significant factor in divorces they had handled during the previous year. They also observed that 68% of the divorce cases involved one party meeting a new love interest over the Internet. And 56% of the divorce cases involved one party having an obsessive interest in pornographic Web sites. *Hearing on Pornography's Impact on Marriage & the Family*, Subcommittee on the Constitution, Civil Rights and Property Rights, Committee on Judiciary, United States Senate, November 10, 2005 (Testimony of Jill C. Manning, M.S.) Available on the Internet at: <<http://new.heritage.org/Research/Family/loader.cfm?url=/commonspot/security/getfile.cfm&PageID=85273>>.

70. The Catechism of the Catholic Church warns against pornography. No. 2354 notes that it not only offends chastity, but also does grave injury by making people the object of base pleasure. Moreover, "It immerses all who are involved in the illusion of a fantasy world."

71. As reported in the New York Times (Jan. 31, 2006), studies have confirmed the longstanding concerns over pornography's corrupting influence. The article reported on the findings published in the journal *Pediatrics* (July 2005), in a study titled *Impact of the Media on Adolescent Sexual Attitudes and Behaviors*.

72. See Victor B. Cline, *Pornography=s Effects on Adults and Children* (2002), on the Internet at: <<http://www.utahcoalition.org/Effects.htm>>.

73. See Catherine MacKinnin, "Only Words: Violent porn promotes violent actions;" *USA Today*, April 22, 1999 (arguing that sexually explicit pornography inspires rape and child abuse).

74. *Barnes v. Glen Theatre Inc.*, 501 U.S. 560 (1991).

75. One ruling involved the owner of a business featuring live sex performances in private rooms. Charles Ciancanelli was convicted of the crime of promoting a live sex show after undercover police paid women to engage in sexual activities while the officers watched in the "performance rooms." The Supreme Court overturned that conviction, but it did uphold Ciancanelli's conviction for promoting prostitution. See *We love Strippers*, Oregon Commentator Online, September 29, 2005 on the Internet at

<<http://www.oregoncommentator.com/archives/2005_09.html>>.

76. *Texas v. Johnson*, 491 U.S. 397 (1989).

77. *United States v. Eichmann*, 496 U.S. 310 (1990).

78. *Ashcroft v. Free Speech Coalition*, 535 U.S. 234 (2002).

79. Larry Magid, *Conflict Over Court Ruling*, PC Answer, April 17, 2002.

80. The FBI interviewed two dozen sex murderers . . . who had killed multiple numbers of times. Some eighty-one percent said their biggest sexual interest was in reading pornography. . . . One killer said that pornography's affect on him was "devastating. . . . I am a homosexual pedophile convicted of murder, and pornography was a determining factor in my downfall." John Dickerson, "Supreme Court's Decision on Computer-Generated Child Pornography Makes No Sense," *Baltimore Chronicle*, May 2, 2002 (quoting, in part, Kirby Anderson's article, "The Pornography Plague.")

81. *Id.*

82. Attorney General John Ashcroft said that the Court had made the prosecution of child pornographers "immeasurably more difficult." Tony Mauro, *High court rejects child-porn law that turns the First Amendment upside down'*, freedomforum.org, April 17, 2002.

83. Wilson Ring (AP), *Vermont's sex offender program brings results*, Boston.com News, March 19, 2006 (The New York Times Company).

84. O'Reilly wrote: "Vermont Judge Edward Cashman must be removed from the bench by the Vermont legislature. And at the same time, the federal government must look into the civil rights situation." Bill O'Reilly, *The Country is Watching the State of Vermont,* Thursday, January 12, 2006 <<http://www.foxnews.com/story/0,2933,181421,00.html>>.

85. The judge was originally quoted as saying: "I am aware that the intensity of some public criticism may shorten my judicial career. To change my decision now, however, simply because of some negative sentiment, would be wrong. I owe it to the judiciary and to my own conscience to maintain a stand that I believe is the best possible option in a very difficult situation." *Vermont Judge Under Fire for Light Sentencing of a Child Rapist*, Foxnews.com, Wednesday, January 11, 2006 on the Internet at <<http://www.foxnews.com/story/0,2933,181320,00.html>>.

86. Republican state Sen. Wendy Wilton plans to introduce a bill based on "Jessica=s law," a nationwide initiative for states that includes barring registered sex offenders from living near schools and parks and requiring them to wear satellite tracking devices. The cornerstone of the measure, Wilton said, is a 25-year minimum mandatory sentence for aggravated sexual assault. *20,000 responses to Vermont judge Messages flood governor's office over '60-day child rapist'*, WorldNetDaily.com, Posted: January 14, 2006, on the Internet at: <<http://www.worldnetdaily.com/news/printer-friendly.asp?ARTICLE_ID=48340>>.

87. *Judge: No prison time for 'gay' rapist teacher: On heels of Vermont outrage, predator gets only probation*, WorldNetDaily.com, Posted: January 18, 2006, on the Internet at <<http://www.worldnetdaily.com/news/article.asp?ARTICLE_ID=48397>>. Delvecchio, the first woman to be appointed chief justice of the Massachusetts Superior Court, was honored in 2000 as the keynote speaker at the Massachusetts Gay and Lesbian Bar Association's

annual dinner. Id.

88. *Again! Homosexual teacher gets no jail for teen assault: Choir instructor at Wisconsin school is 2nd case this week without prison*, WorldNetDaily.com, Posted: January 19, 2006, on the Internet at
<<http://www.worldnetdaily.com/news/article.asp?ARTICLE_ID=48402>>.

89. Thomas Sowell, *Alternatives to reality*, Townhall.com, Mar 21, 2006. Available on the Internet at:
<<http://www.townhall.com/opinion/columns/thomassowell/2006/03/21/190623.html>>.
The author of this chapter debated the need to disclose information about sexual predators on the PBS radio program, Justice Talking, Nov. 18, 2002 (*"Megan's Law Before the High Court"*). Available on the Internet at:
<<http://www.justicetalking.org/viewprogram.asp?progID=235>>.

90. *Planned Parenthood v. Casey*, 505 U.S. 833 (1992).

91. *Bowers v. Hardwick*, 478 U.S. 186 (1986).

92. In fact, in 1791 when the Bill of Rights was ratified, nine of the original thirteen states proscribed the death penalty for sodomy. Even in 1866–68, when the states ratified the Fourteenth Amendment, four states still specified the death penalty for sodomy and eleven others provided for up to life imprisonment.

93. *Lawrence v. Texas*, 539 U.S. 558 (2003)

94. While the court used the European Court of Human Rights to argue in favor of an international consensus on gay rights, it ignored the hostility to sodomy found in China, India, Korea, most African countries, and all Islamic nations.

95. Mark Adams, *Judge Says Anti-Prostitution Pledge for Federal Funds Violates Free Speech*, MichNews.com, May 12, 2006; Samantha Singson, *USAID Sued for Requiring Pledge Against Commercial Sex Work*, Friday Fax, Volume 9, Number 18, April 21, 2006.

96. United States Leadership Against HIV/AIDS, Tuberculosis, and Malaria Act of 2003, Public Law 108–25, 108th Congress (1st Session).

97. See H.R. 972, the "Trafficking Victims Protection Reauthorization Act of 2005," signed into law by President George W. Bush on January 10, 2006.

98. The Romeo and Juliet statute allows for lesser penalties for sexual relations with a 14- or 15-year-old, so long as the partner is under 19, is less than four years older than the victim, and is a member of the opposite sex.

99. The case was brought by Matthew Limon, who was sentenced to 17 years in prison after he was convicted of having sex with a 15-year-old boy a week after his 18th birthday in 2000. If Limon had been convicted of having sex with a 15-year-old girl, he would have received a maximum sentence of 15 months.

100. It seems that the facts underlying *Lawrence v. Texas* were staged to test the Texas anti-sodomy law. George McEvoy, *Was high court gay rights ruling a setup?* Palm Beach Post, August 13, 2005 (reviewing Janice Law, *Sex Appealed: Was the U.S. Supreme Court Fooled?* (2005)).

101. William Jefferson Clinton, *Remarks at Announcement of Victims' Rights Constitutional*

Amendment, June 25, 1996.

102. See *Rights of Crime Victims*, Washington Post, June 29, 1998, at A14.

103. See, e.g., Mississippi Crime Victim's Compensation Act, Miss. Code 99-41-1 *et seq.*

104. See *Idaho Manual on the Rights of Crime Victims*, Office of the Attorney General, 2004 (available on the Internet at <<www.ag.idaho.gov>>).

105. Mark Stevens, *Victim Impact Statements Considered in Sentencing: Constitutional Concerns*, 2 Cal. Crim. L. Rev. 3 (2000).

106. U.S. Senator Dianne Feinstein, on the Internet at <<http://senate.gov/~feinstein/04Releases/vicstories.htm>>

107. The idea behind a VIS is that the judge or jury should consider the impact that the crime has had on the victim when deciding upon the appropriate punishment. It took, however, three trips to the U.S. Supreme Court before even this minor acknowledgment of victims' rights was deemed constitutional in a case that potentially carried the death penalty. See *Booth v. Maryland* 482 U.S. 496 (1987) (VISs violate the 8th Amendment); *South Carolina v. Gathers*, 490 U.S. 805 (1989) (VISs violate the 8th Amendment when used in the sentencing phase of a capital case); *Payne v. Tennessee*, 498 U.S. 1076 (1991) (reversing the earlier decisions).

108. Congressional Victim's Caucus home page, on the Internet at <<http://www.house.gov/poe/vrc/fy07voca-costa.htm>> (statement of Congressman Jim Costa, D-Calif.).

109. See, e.g., *Idaho Manual on the Rights of Crime Victims*, Office of the Attorney General, 2004 (available on the Internet at <<www.ag.idaho.gov>>) (question 18, p. 8, a "violation of the victim's rights does not constitute a mistrial;" and question 17, explaining that there is no provision for a civil suit against the "prosecutor, court, or police" for a violation of the victim's rights).

110. In the 1970s, several states called for mandatory death sentences for certain crimes, but the Supreme Court ruled these statutes unconstitutional. *Gregg v. Georgia*, 428 U.S. 153 (1976); *Woodson v. North Carolina*, 428 U.S. 280 (1976).

111. Peter W. Greenwood et al., *Three Strikes and You're Out: Estimated Benefits and Costs of California's New Sentencing Law* 18 (1994).

112. *Debate: Mandatory Minimums in Drug Sentencing: a Valuable Weapon in the War on Drugs or a Handcuff on Judicial Discretion?*, 36 Am. Crim. L. Rev. 1279, 1281 (1999) (introductory remarks of moderator Cokie Roberts).

113. Id.

114. United States Supreme Court Justice Anthony M. Kennedy speaking to the American Bar Association annual meeting in San Francisco 8/2003 about penal conditions and unjust mandatory minimum sentences, available on the Internet at <<http://mysite.verizon.net/aahpat/pol/kennedy.htm>>.

115. *Id.*

116. *Debate: Mandatory Minimums in Drug Sentencing*, supra note 113 at 1281 (remarks of Congressman Hutchinson).

117. *Id.* Other commentators, however, reject the cause-and-effect relationship between strict sentencing and falling crime rates. See Crier, supra note 29 at 114–15.

118. The law at issue, codified at 21 U.S.C. § 846, was enacted in the mid-1980s to target drug kingpins. Defendants can escape the mandatory minimum sentence only by providing "substantial assistance" to the prosecution.

119. Judge Hurd originally sentenced Powell to 20 years in prison, finding that his two prior crack cocaine possession convictions should be treated as one for sentencing purposes. Following an appeal, the U.S. Second Circuit Court of Appeals remanded the case to Judge Hurd, ruling: "It is...Congress' prerogative to set mandatory minimums, and in this case the mandatory minimum is life imprisonment." See John Caher, *Federal Judge Blasts Mandatory Minimum Sentences: Entire Judicial Process' Distorted By Congressionally Mandated Sentencing, Says Judge*, New York Law Journal, January 20, 2006.

120. See *Harmelin v. Michigan*, 501 U.S. 957 (1991).

121. *People v. Superior Court*, 13 Cal.4th 497 (Cal. 1996).

122. Bill Kisliuk, *The '3 Strikes' Crisis That Didn't Happen*, American Lawyer, January 23, 1997 (noting that many California trial judges are former prosecutors who have not exploited this ruling to the greatest possible extent).

123. Id. ("How much can I jump up and down? . . . Judges are smart enough to cover their bets by saying the right things in order to withstand review. There's nothing we can do.")

124. *United States v. Booker*, 543 U.S. 220 (2005).

125. According to Sentencing Commission statistics, post-*Booker* sentencing has remained fairly consistent with what was happening prior to that decision. The Commission is willing, however, to work with Congress to restore the mandatory nature of the guidelines in a constitutional manner. *Sentencing Commission Feels the Effect of* Booker *and Blakely*, The Third Branch (Newsletter of the Federal Courts) Vol. 37, Number 12, December 2005.

126. In 1994, Congress responded to certain problems with its sentencing scheme, putting a "safety valve" exception in place that would permit a judge to override the guidelines in some cases involving fist time offenders. *Debate: Mandatory Minimums in Drug Sentencing*, supra note 113 at 1281 (remarks of Congressman Hutchinson).

127. See Crier, supra note 29 at 114–21.

128. *Debate: Mandatory Minimums in Drug Sentencing* supra note 113 at 1281 (remarks of Congressman Hutchinson).

129. Antonin Scalia, "God's Justice and Ours," *First Things*, May 2002, available on the Internet at <<http://www.firstthings.com/ftissues/ft0205/articles/scalia.html>>. The Justice explained:

> So it is no accident, I think, that the modern view that the death penalty is immoral is centered in the West. That has little to do with the fact that the West has a Christian tradition, and everything to do with the fact that the West is the home of democracy. Indeed, it seems to me that the more Christian a country is the *less* likely it is to regard the death penalty as immoral. Abolition has taken its firmest hold in post-Christian Europe, and has least support in the church-going United

States. I attribute that to the fact that, for the believing Christian, death is no big deal.

Id. See also Avery Dulles, "Catholicism & Capital Punishment," *First Things*, April 2001 available on the Internet at <<http://www.firstthings.com/ftissues/ft0104/articles/dulles.html>> ("The mounting opposition to the death penalty in Europe since the Enlightenment has gone hand in hand with a decline of faith in eternal life. In the nineteenth century the most consistent supporters of capital punishment were the Christian churches, and its most consistent opponents were groups hostile to the churches.")

130. St. Augustine, *Corpus Scriptorum Ecclesiasticorum Latinorum*, XLIV, 413–414, LXIII, 155.

131. Alan Johnson, *Inmate's Death Wish May Be Closer*, Columbus Dispatch, Dec. 4, 1997, at 1A, available at LEXIS, News Library, Coldis File (describing Ohio's Attorney General's frustration at "'judicial activism' and courts refusing to carry out the wishes of... lawmakers who reinstated the death penalty.")

132. Scalia, *God's Justice and Ours*, supra note 130. Scalia notes that he would be obliged to resign because he does not believe in a "living Constitution." If the death penalty is immoral in the view of a judge who believes in a "living Constitution," then according to Scalia the death penalty "is (hey, presto!) automatically unconstitutional, and he can continue to sit while nullifying a sanction that has been imposed, with no suggestion of its unconstitutionality, since the beginning of the Republic." *Id.*

133. *Callins v. Collins*, 511 U.S. 1141, 1143 (1994) (Blackmun, J., dissenting).

134. *Witherspoon v. Illinois*, 391 U.S. 510 (1968).

135. *Lockhart v. McCree*, 476 U.S. 162 (1986). See James M. Carr, *At Witt's End: The Continuing Quandary of Jury Selection in Capital Cases*, 39 Stan. L. Rev. 427, 457 (1987).

136. *Morgan v. Illinois*, 504 U.S. 719 (1992).

137. *Furman v. Georgia*, 408 U.S. 238 (1972).

138. See supra note 22. Even the 14th Amendment provides that no state shall "deprive any person of life, liberty, or property, without due process of law." By treating "life" exactly the same way it treats "liberty" and "property," it clearly contemplates the possibility of capital punishment. In 1868, all but two states still specified the death penalty for several crimes including murder, rape, and treason.

139. *Gregg v. Georgia*, 428 U.S. 153 (1976); *Woodson v. North Carolina*, 428 U.S. 280 (1976).

137. *Lockett v. Ohio*, 438 U.S. 586 (1978).

141. NAACP Legal Defense and Educational Fund, *Death Row, U.S.A.*, December 20, 1985.

142. *Id.*

143. Victor Streib, *Executions Under the Post-Furman Capital Punishment Statutes*, 15 Rutgers Law J. 444–45 (1984).

144. *Coker v. Georgia*, 433 US 584 (1977).

145. The law, first enacted in 1995, has been found to be constitutional by the Louisiana State Supreme Court, and in 1996, the U.S. Supreme Court declined to hear an appeal on the constitutionality of this law. See David W. Schaaf, *What if the Victim is a Child? Examining the Constitutionality of Louisiana=s Challenge to Coker v. Georgia,* 200 U. Ill. L. Rev. 347 (2000). Oklahoma is also considering enacting such a law. Ron Jenkins, *Bill to execute child molesters in Oklahoma raising skepticism: Constitutionality in question, and some say it could hurt victims,* Associated Press, March 12, 2006.

146. Ariel Hart, "Death Sentence For Rape," *New York Times,* August 28, 2003.

147. *Roper v. Simmons,* 543 U.S. 551 (2005).

148. Robert H. Bork, *Coercing Virtue: The Worldwide Rule of Judges* (2003). See also supra note 95.

150. Gregory Sisk, "The Moral Incompetence of the Judiciary," *First Things* (November 1995) at 34–39.

150. Id.

151. The Associated Press. *Scalia Rails Against the 'Judge-Moralist',* March 15, 2006.

152. That is why American politicians now fight such vicious battles over judicial nominations. See *Id.*

153. See Ronald J. Rychlak, "Abortion, Thinking Americans, and Judicial Politics," 14 *Life and Learning* (Proceedings of the 14th University Faculty for Life Conference, U. of St. Thomas Law School) 77 (2005).

154 *Doe v. Bolton,* 410 U.S. 179, 222 (1973), White, J., dissenting.

Six
The Judicial Assault on Business
By Joseph F. Johnston, Jr.

Introduction

The function of what we call the "rule of law" is to establish and preserve a just, predictable and stable order of human relationships. The rule of law is the line that separates primitive from civilized societies. The Oresteian trilogy of Aeschylus, first produced in Athens in 458 B.C., memorializes this transition from the *lex talionis* (the tribal practice of revenge) to the rule of law. Of the human relationships covered by the rule of law, those we characterize as "commercial" are among the most basic. The protection and fostering of commercial relationships require a legal system that protects property rights and ensures a degree of regularity and predictability. Laws must be intelligible, coherent and relatively constant over time; otherwise people can neither plan for the future nor conform their conduct to the rules.

The United States was founded as a republic based on the rule of law. We are fortunate that the rights of speech and property are better protected in the United States than in many other countries. But, as our founders made clear, we must be constantly vigilant to preserve what we have inherited. Today, we are oppressed by an impenetrable web of constantly changing court decisions, legislation, codes and regulations, requiring an army of lawyers, accountants and bureaucrats to guide the populace through the maze.

In this chapter, we will see how the changes in the American legal system in the twentieth century, together with changes in the legal doctrines applied by the courts, produced a dramatic increase in the frequency and severity of lawsuits, which has been appropriately labeled a "litigation explosion." This explosion has imposed enormous costs on American companies, their shareholders and the economy in general, while it does nothing to encourage economic growth. As a Securities and Exchange Commissioner stated, "Perhaps the number one concern that I hear when I speak to foreign business leaders about their willingness, or un-willingness, to do business in the United States is our culture of litigation. Government officials, political leaders, entrepreneurs and corporate executives see the specter of what they describe to me as a 'lottery system of justice.' This is a disincentive for them to view the United States as an attractive investment destination."[1]

It is instructive to draw a comparison between the American republic today and the late Roman Empire. By the fifth century A.D., the Empire was swamped by a deluge of new laws and regulations; and a swelling volume of time-consuming and expensive litigation was initiated by a growing horde of lawyers. As Edward Gibbon observed, describing the reign of Justinian (emperor and jurisprudent) in the sixth century A.D.:

> "... the civil jurisprudence ... still continued a mysterious science and a profitable trade, and the innate perplexity of the study was involved in tenfold darkness by the private industry of the practitioners. ... the government of Justinian united the evils of liberty and servitude; and the Romans were oppressed at the same time by the multiplicity of their laws and the arbitrary will of their master."[2]

For the Romans of that period, the master and lawgiver was the emperor; for us, increasingly, it is the courts and administrative agencies, as well as a profligate Congress.

The Tort Revolution

Tort law is the branch of the law that deals with accidents and personal injury. Until the mid-twentieth century, tort disputes were governed by a traditional body of rules based on such well-known concepts as intentional harm, negligence and causation. Responsibility for many injuries was governed by contract through sales documents, disclaimers, waivers and the like. Beginning in the 1950s, academic scholars and some judges began to challenge the existing rules because they allegedly gave inadequate compensation, unfairly allocated the costs of accidents to victims and imposed unnecessary "transaction costs." These theorists argued that the solution was to place a greater burden of paying tort costs on the producers of goods. This would act as an incentive to the producers to consider safety more carefully and also to buy more insurance, which the producers could afford while the consumers usually could not.[3] ("Tort costs" are comprised of benefits paid to claimants, legal defense costs and administrative expenses.) Insurance companies could distribute the risk of injury among the public at large as a cost of doing business.[4] The courts were generally responsive to these arguments, and began to impose "liability without fault" (or "strict liability") for harm to persons or property caused by manufacturing defects, design defects and failure to give adequate instructions or warnings.[5] In other words, plaintiff need not show that defendant was negligent if the product is shown to be defective. Moreover, most states replaced the old defense of "contributory negligence" (which was ordinarily a complete defense) with a concept of "comparative fault," under which liability is apportioned in accordance with the degree of fault where the plaintiff was negligent.[6] Disclaimers by product sellers and waivers by purchasers were now generally disregarded by the courts.[7]

Liability without fault represented a radical change in jurisprudential standards, which for centuries had assumed that a defendant should not be held liable unless he had engaged in conduct that was negligent or otherwise wrongful. Further, the new doctrine disregarded the fact that most products have at least some danger associated with them. The acceptance of this new tort rationale by the courts was consistent with the growth of mass democracy and the welfare state, which had similar objectives of redistribution of wealth and transfer of risk. Moreover, these changes were often imposed by courts rather than by legislatures—a sign of judicial overreaching.

Just as these changes were occurring, the courts liberalized procedural rules to favor plaintiffs. The old common-law pleading requirements, which involved specific formalistic language, were discarded and replaced by "notice pleading," under which courts overlooked the form of the pleadings and considered their substance. As a part of the increasing "openness" of the court system, federal and state procedural rules were also amended to encourage the "discovery" process, under which, before trial, plaintiffs and defendants are entitled to obtain access to documents in the possession of the other party and to take deposition testimony from the other party and its agents and officers. Discovery has become a potent weapon used by either party to wear down the other side, to increase its costs and to obtain a better settlement. The discovery process in a major case usually involves numerous motions and the production of large quantities of documents created over decades, a costly and burdensome project. It is not unusual for a defendant in a complex tort or securities case to spend millions of dollars during the discovery phase of the case, before the trial phase is even reached. Once a case goes to trial, there is a tendency for judges to let almost any case go to the jury. This attitude may represent the influence of "nonjudgmentalism" in the legal system. Many judges are reluctant to dismiss even very weak cases, thus leaving in the system many suits that should not be there. And what a jury will do with a complex mass tort case is almost entirely unpredictable, thus impairing one of the key features of the rule of law. The net result of the steep rise in tort costs is to discourage internal investment and increase the price of products and services so that American business is put at a competitive disadvantage

One of the important and unusual features of the American legal system is the "contingent fee." This is an arrangement whereby plaintiff's attorney gets a percentage (normally between 20% and 30%) of the amount awarded to plaintiff if he wins, but nothing if he loses. The large amounts of potential judgments or settlements in mass tort cases provide an enormous incentive to bring cases and can be used as a weapon for extortion against companies that want to settle quickly to avoid the cost and risk of a full lawsuit. In a number of recent, highly-publicized cases, plaintiffs' lawyers have received enormous fees. In the tobacco litigation by states against tobacco companies, for instance, trial lawyers collected several billion dollars. It has been estimated that the legal fees in these cases were equivalent to tens of thousands of dollars per hour.[8] The contingent fee often produces sharp conflicts between the interests of plaintiffs' counsel and those of his clients because, for example, it can be in the lawyer's interest to take a quick settlement, even though the prospects for the lawyer's clients would likely be improved by further litigation.

Another unusual aspect of the U.S. tort system is the practice of awarding "punitive damages" in civil cases as a means of punishing defendants for conduct the jury finds to be highly reprehensible, fraudulent or malicious. For example, in the Merck case, discussed below, the jury awarded a verdict against Merck of $253 million, of which $229 million represented punitive damages. (The amount will probably be reduced under state law.) The Supreme Court has acted to place some restraints on disproportionate punitive damages. In *BMW of North America, Inc. v. Gore*, decided in 1996, Dr. Gore purchased a new BMW and then discovered it had been repainted before delivery. An Alabama jury found BMW liable for $4,000 in compensatory damages, and imposed an additional $4 million in punitive damages to reflect similar repairs to other cars. The Alabama Supreme Court reduced the punitive damage award to $2 million. The U.S. Supreme Court held that the punitive award violated BMW's right to due process of law. The ratio of punitive to compensatory damages (500 to 1) could not be justified.[9] While the Supreme Court has placed some constraints on punitive damages, the outer limits are not clear and courts continue to uphold substantial punitive damage awards. No defendant can be certain that a given punitive award will be thrown out on appeal, so that the threat of punitives will continue to put heavy pressure on defendants to settle. Jury awards of punitive damages are notoriously uncertain and subjective, so that the imposition of such damages resembles a lottery.

The tort revolution has also resulted in a serious adverse impact on the liability insurance markets. As previously noted, the modern theory of tort law assumes the availability of insurance as a mechanism to spread the risk of injury throughout society. As a result of the rapidly accumulating damages spawned by the new tort regime, in the mid-1980s the property/casualty insurance industry suffered the worst underwriting losses in its history.[10] Insurance rates rose dramatically and many businesses and individuals could not buy liability insurance at any price. *Time's* March 24, 1986 cover story was titled "Sorry, America, Your Insurance Has Been Cancelled." While the insurance markets subsequently recovered from the crisis of the 1980s, they have been plagued from time to time by recurring shortages of capacity and underwriting losses, making rates and availability difficult to predict.

Both the number of litigated cases and the related expenses have risen sharply as a result of the tort revolution. Over the last 50 years, the costs of tort litigation in the United States have increased more than a hundredfold. By contrast, the nation's GDP has grown by a factor of 37 and population has grown by a factor of four. U.S. tort costs have increased from $1.8 billion in 1950 (0.62% of GDP) to $245.7 billion in 2003 (2.23% of GDP). The largest contributor to the rise of tort costs in recent years has been the growth in asbestos claims. Other substantial increases were reported in lawsuits against directors and officers of corporations; claims against tobacco companies, pharmaceutical companies and health care organizations; and claims against food establishments for obesity-related injuries. Products that have been targets of mass tort litigation include not just tobacco and asbestos, but also guns, PCBs, various medications and vaccines, heart valves, breast implants, dietary supplements and many others. The increase in commercial tort costs (suits against businesses) has significantly exceeded the increase in personal tort costs (suits against individuals). Less than half of the money recovered in these cases goes to the injured persons: more than 58% of tort costs consist of lawyers' fees and other transaction costs.[11]

The ethical attitudes of the legal profession (like many other social customs) changed rapidly beginning in the 1960s. For centuries, the doctrines of legal ethics in the Anglo-American legal world emphasized that the law was a learned profession and a public service, whose values were higher than those of the ordinary marketplace. The leaders of the bar, for example, held rigorously to the notion that it was unethical for lawyers to advertise for business. This view was consistent with the traditional opposition to "stirring up litigation." During the 1960s, these traditional attitudes began to change. Advertising by lawyers became common, and in 1977, the Supreme Court held that blanket bans on advertising violated the right to free speech.[12] Contingent fees became the standard method of compensating plaintiffs' counsel in mass tort actions. Law firms now concentrate on the "bottom line" as much as commercial businesses do; and from this standpoint the more litigation the better, at least for the lawyers.

These changes in rules and attitudes had the natural consequence of encouraging plaintiffs and their lawyers to file more lawsuits. Claims filed in federal court tripled between 1960 and 1990. "The escalating legal uncertainty and unpredictability," writes Professor Mary Ann Glendon, "'makes U.S. law the subject of endless fascination and horror, especially to foreigners.'"[13]

Let us consider some examples of the risks posed to business by the U.S. tort system.

1. In the 1990s, a number of tort class actions were filed by women alleging injuries from silicone gel breast implants. Even though the plaintiffs' cases on the merits were weak because of the absence of clear scientific evidence of the causal relationship between breast implants and specific injuries, the class actions were settled with defendants contributing a total of approximately $4.2 billion, of which $1billion represented legal fees to plaintiffs' counsel.[14]

2. Perhaps the most highly-publicized example of a legal assault on business is the tobacco litigation. Tobacco, of course, is a lawful product for adults, who have been clearly warned of the dangers of smoking for decades. In a 1998 settlement, tobacco companies agreed to pay $246 billion to 46 state governments seeking to recover the costs of caring for sick smokers. This settlement was followed by an avalanche of private actions. In addition, the federal government has filed a lawsuit against the tobacco companies under the civil racketeering statute claiming $10 billion in damages. (The suit is meritless. Among other things, the government did not lose money on smokers; it has made huge amounts of money over the years from federal excise taxes on tobacco sales. In

addition, smokers tend to die young, so the government saves money it would otherwise have spent caring for them in their old age.) This attempt to extort revenues for the government from the private sector is a good example of regulation through litigation.[15]

3. The asbestos litigation, which has been called "an elephantine mass" that has bogged down American courts for years, is another instructive example of the consequences of mass tort litigation.[16] Millions of American workers have been exposed to asbestos, which can lead to serious illness or even death. The claims allege that asbestos manufacturers failed to take adequate precautions to protect workers from exposure and failed to warn those who were exposed. The most common illnesses attributed to asbestos exposure are mesothelioma, other cancers, asbestos and pleural abnormalities. The diseases arising out of asbestos exposure have very long latency periods—as long as 40 years—making it very difficult to predict the timing and volume of new cases. A study by the RAND Institute for Civil Justice showed that 730,000 people had filed an asbestos claim through 2002, and at least 8,400 entities had been named as defendants. Many of the claimants are not currently ill, but may (or may not) become ill in coming decades. At least 73 companies that had been named as defendants in asbestos claims had filed for bankruptcy through mid-2004. Total spending on asbestos litigation through 2002 was about $70 billion. Claimants' net compensation was $30 billion, about 42% of the total figure. The remainder was eaten up by legal fees, administration and other transaction costs.[17] This is in many ways a shocking statistic; less than half of the money spent on these cases ended up in the hands of the injured persons. Most of the rest was paid to lawyers. Payments to claimants often seem quite arbitrary. "Plaintiffs with the same injuries and economic losses receive widely varying amounts, depending on the skills and incentives of the attorneys representing them, the jurisdiction in which their cases are brought and, perhaps, their own 'attractiveness' as potential trial witnesses."[18] Finally, there are indications of manipulation of the evidence (often called "junk science") produced in the asbestos cases. Plaintiffs' lawyers often use mass-screening techniques to select asbestos workers who may have been exposed. An independent group of experts from Johns Hopkins School of Medicine reviewed hundreds of x-rays used as evidence. The expert witnesses used by plaintiffs' counsel in these cases found evidence of possible asbestos-related abnormalities in 95.9% of the cases, but the independent experts found abnormalities in only 4.5% of the cases. In other words, many claims have been filed by claimants with no asbestos-related impairment. One prominent plaintiffs' lawyer is quoted as saying, "Flooding the courts with asbestos cases filed by people who are not sick against defendants who have not been shown to be at fault is not sound public policy." [19] Congress is considering establishing an asbestos trust fund, but there is no consensus regarding how much should be put into the fund (a Senate version of the bill proposed $140 billion) or who would pay for it. It is predictable that if the trust fund runs out, as seems likely, the taxpayers will be stuck with the bill. It might be more practicable to change the requirements for success in court, for example, by imposing stricter evidentiary controls.

4. In August 2005, a Texas jury awarded to a widow a verdict of $253 million against Merck & Co., finding that the death of her husband was caused by a heart condition (arrhythmia), which in turn was allegedly caused by Merck's popular pain-killer Vioxx (even though Merck's clinical trials had shown no connection between Vioxx and arrhythmia). Of this amount, $229 million was "punitive damages," meant to punish Merck for supposedly concealing the facts about the drug. The verdict will probably be reduced on appeal under state law. Nevertheless, it is likely to stimulate more litigation against Merck and other drug manufacturers.[20] Many corporate defendants will seek quick settlements rather than risk this kind of result. The impact on drug research and bringing new drugs to market is uncertain, but is likely to prove unfavorable. Some companies may be deterred from creating drugs that could be highly beneficial, though not 100% risk free. No one can foresee every possible risk. The case is disturbing because post-trial interviews with jurors indicate that Merck's scientific evidence was simply over the heads of the jury. This is a recognized hazard of complex cases. Juries are notoriously susceptible to populist arguments by eloquent lawyers who ask them to find for the "little guy" against the "big mules," and to "send them a message." Of course, the corporations against which the verdicts are rendered normally pass on the costs to others, so that the real burden falls on ordinary shareholders, employees and consumers of the corporation's products.

5. Health Care Industry. The health care industry has been seriously affected by the litigation explosion. The *Merck* case and the breast-implant cases (see above) are recent examples. It has been reported that the median award in medical malpractice cases has risen from $500,000 in 1997 to $1,200,000 in 2003. The total cost of medical malpractice lawsuits has risen more than 2,000% since 1975, to $26.5 billion.[21] According to a recent Harvard study, about 40% of the medical malpractice cases filed in the United States are groundless. Although a large majority of these cases are dismissed, the volume of meritless cases places a burden on the court system and on physicians.[22] Doctors, hospitals, HMOs and other medical care institutions find it difficult or impossible to get adequate insurance. Some doctors have abandoned their practices altogether.

As we will see, there have been some modest steps toward tort reform, but the dangers of excessive damages, "junk science" evidence and legal uncertainty remain. As economists Eric Helland and Alexander Tabarrok have written, major cases such as the tobacco, breast implant and asbestos cases "have little or no scientific justification and no demonstrable efficiency gains."[23]

Class Actions

The "class action" has created perhaps the most dangerous exposure to liability faced by companies and their directors and officers today. Class actions were originated by the English courts of chancery as a matter of judicial economy and convenience when the courts were unable to join numerous parties in the same case through conventional joinder rules. The objective of convenience and economy of litigation remains a principal purpose of class actions.[24]

The present U.S. federal class action rule (Rule 23 of the Federal Rules of Civil Procedure) was first adopted in 1937 as a restatement of the old rule of equity pleading. Types of claims often brought as class actions include claims involving the purchase or sale of securities, antitrust, consumer fraud, defective products, drug safety, asbestos, tobacco, transportation disasters, environmental pollution, employment discrimination and health care. There are a number of prerequisites for bringing class actions, including a class so numerous that joining all individual members of the class is impracticable, and the existence of questions of law or fact common to the class. Since it eliminates the necessity of trying multiple individual actions, the class action device is popular with judges concerned about their crowded dockets. Many judges are reluctant to dismiss even meritless cases in the belief that it is more prudent to "leave it to the jury." The federal class action rule was amended in 1966 to make it easier to bring class actions. Between 1961 and 1984, federal court tort actions nearly doubled.[25]

One of the peculiarities of the American class action model is that the members of the class, no matter how numerous, are bound by the judgment, whether they wish to litigate or not, unless they affirmatively "opt out" of the class.[26] For most people, the process of opting out is not worth the effort since they will ultimately get their share of any class recovery, although this share is likely to be quite small. While the amounts of judgments or settlements paid by defendants in class actions are often very large, the amount actually distributed per claimant is frequently negligible because of the large number of class members.[27] A common type of class action is the "securities class action" (to be discussed later) in which an action is brought by one or a few shareholders of a corporation on behalf of all shareholders who bought the stock during a certain period. The recent AT&T Corporate Securities Litigation, for example, was settled by a payment of $100 million, less $21,250,000 in attorneys' fees (21%) and $5,465,997 in expenses. The estimated average distribution per share to class members was $0.44 per share before deduction of fees and expenses.[28] It is fair to conclude that, in these kinds of class actions, the only people who benefit are the lawyers. Both plaintiffs' and defendants' lawyers benefit; plaintiffs' lawyers because they are working under a contingent fee arrangement and get a sizeable percentage of the recovery (normally between 20% and 30%), and defense lawyers because they are paid by defendant companies at a healthy hourly rate ($400 or more per hour for senior lawyers). Even when the case is settled with no monetary recovery, according to a recent analysis, legal fees to plaintiffs' counsel averaged $492 an hour.[29]

The growing use of the class action is consistent with other social and political trends in the twentieth century. Instead of the traditional common law process of numerous separate cases occurring over a long period of time, resulting in a "spontaneous order" of legal development, the class action is a form of judicial central planning, in which very large numbers of people are bound by one decision. It thus reflects the twentieth century trends toward (i) collectivist rather than individualist solutions to social problems, and (ii) the redistribution of wealth (in this case from deep-pocket defendants to class members). The proliferation of class actions is part of a general tendency for groups unable to achieve their demands from legislatures to turn to the courts for relief. This practice evidences a growing public expectation that if a social or economic problem exists, and federal and state legislatures are reluctant to deal with it, the federal courts should "solve" the problem. This amounts to a process of regulation through litigation. Other examples of "judicial regulation" include federal court supervision of school districts, prisons and mental health facilities.

In the area of business litigation, with which we are concerned in this chapter, the increasing frequency and severity of damage awards and settlements was based on a growing feeling that anyone who is injured, physically or financially, should be compensated, either by the government or by some other "deep pocket." The courts thus became another instrument of populist politics. Every injury was assumed to be someone else's fault; and you could always find a wealthy malefactor if you looked hard enough. Ancient defenses, such as contributory negligence, assumption of the risk or the common law requirements of pleading and proving fraud, were gradually weakened or eliminated.

As a practical matter, the combination of a large number of claims into one suit puts enormous pressure on a defendant, because the potential damages from hundreds or often thousands of claims would be devastating to a small business, or even to a large one. (Note, for example, the number of substantial companies that have been bankrupted by the asbestos litigation.) Once a class is certified by the court, therefore, defendants will be eager to settle even flimsy cases rather than take the risk (although a small risk) of an astronomical verdict. For example, a 10% risk of a billion dollar verdict is $100 million, enough to ruin a medium-size company. Companies usually have some insurance against most litigation risks, but the amount may be insufficient and all policies contain gaps and exclusions.

Members of the plaintiff class usually have different characteristics that are relevant to defenses that may be asserted against them. To litigate those defenses separately for each class member would make the class unmanageable. To take a well-known example from securities fraud litigation, plaintiffs in traditional fraud litigation were required to prove that they relied on defendants' misrepresentations. To get around this problem in securities cases, courts simply did away with the reliance defense and substituted a requirement known as "fraud-on-the-market," under which plaintiffs need only show that they bought or sold in a market that had been affected by defendants' misrepresentations—a much easier task. A device designed for procedural convenience thus led to a substantive change in the law which should have been left to the legislature.[30]

Securities Class Actions

The lawsuits that are probably of most concern to business corporations and their directors and officers are the securities class actions that arise out of stock market losses. A century ago, such losses were generally regarded as bad luck that inevitably accompanied the risk of investing in stocks. Today, however, whenever a company announces an unexpected negative development and the share price drops, it is likely that class actions will be filed by shareholders arguing that the market loss was attributable to false and misleading statements or other misconduct by the company and its directors and officers, or by third parties such as the company's accountants or bankers. Securities-related suits against underwriters, banks, brokers and law firms have increased in recent years.

Securities class actions are almost always settled because defendants cannot take the risk of an astronomical verdict. Settlements resulting from securities class actions can be very large. NERA Economic Consulting has issued a report on recent securities class actions showing that the top ten settlements from 2003 to 2005 range from $6.1 billion to $300 million.[31] The two largest settlements (WorldCom, $6.1 billion) and Enron (not yet finalized as of this writing, but in the several-billion-dollar range), included major contributions by investment banks and accountants as well as multi-million dollar personal contributions from directors. Even excluding the WorldCom and Enron settlements, the total value of cases settled during 2005 grew to an all-time high of $3.5 billion.[32]

Previously, settlements of securities actions on behalf of directors and officers were almost always funded by directors' and officers' ("D&O") insurance, but in the WorldCom and Enron settlements, the lead plaintiffs (state pension funds) insisted that directors and officers make significant payments, uninsured, out of their personal assets. This was a shock to the corporate community. For decades, it has been recognized that, in order to attract good directors, they must be protected from personal liability by certain standard devices, including indemnification by the corporation, limitation of liability provisions in the corporate charter and D&O insurance. Without these protective devices, few qualified people would want to serve as directors in view of the disparity between the compensation they receive and the enormous liabilities they face.[33] It is noteworthy that the most serious claims in both Enron and WorldCom were based on the federal securities laws, including Sec. 11 of the Securities Act of 1933, which requires defendants to bear the burden of proving that they made a "reasonable investigation" and reasonably believed that the challenged statements in the offering documents were true. This burden is often difficult to meet, especially for independent directors who do not have the time for a detailed, personal investigation. After these cases, as Charles Hansen states, "directors should be prepared for increasing demands that they contribute personally to the settlement of securities litigation, especially when the conduct at issue is highly publicized and egregious."[34]

It remains to be seen whether there will be a serious trend toward requiring personal payments by directors to settle class actions; if so, it is predictable that few independent directors will be willing to expose themselves to this kind of risk. Independent directors, of course, normally have other jobs and do not have unlimited time to investigate financial information provided to them by management. This problem is most acute when, in cases such as WorldCom, Enron and others, management is actively trying to conceal the truth from the directors. As one commentator has pointed out, "it seems unreasonable to hold directors responsible for discovering something that has been deliberately withheld from them."[35] Today, the "corporate governance" movement seeks to require companies to have more truly independent directors at the same time that these directors are loaded down with more and more responsibility, and, it seems, the risk of personal financial catastrophe. The capitalist system, which has produced untold benefits to this nation, operates by encouraging risk-taking. But the present litigation model seems designed to discourage directors from taking risks. This contradiction will have to be sorted out in the future.

As settlements have climbed, so have plaintiffs' attorneys' fees. The average settlement in the first half of 2005 produced an average of over $6 million in fees to plaintiffs' counsel, compared to $3.6 million in 2000.[36] Of course, the company is also required to pay its own counsel for defending the case. Defending class action litigation requires elaborate "discovery" proceedings involving dozens of expensive, time-consuming depositions occupying vast amounts of time on the part of company directors, officers and employees, as well as the review by lawyers of rooms full of documents. Because of the scope and complexity of these cases, defense costs can run into many millions of dollars. When D&O insurance is available, it can be partly or even wholly exhausted by defense costs, leaving the company (that is, the shareholders) and the directors and officers responsible for the rest. The high cost of defending these cases is, in effect, a dead-weight loss for the economy. Nothing here is intended to suggest that corporate wrongdoers should escape liability. The public will always demand that corporations and their managers be regulated somehow. To regulate them through the traditional judicial process is better than direct regulation by government agencies. One would hope that Congress can devise a method to rein in the class action without destroying it. An obvious suggestion is to place some reasonable limitation on contingent fees for counsel. Also, consideration should be given to changing the "opt out" rule to an "opt in" rule, so that classes of plaintiffs will be composed only of those who affirmatively want to litigate. This reform would significantly reduce the size of classes.

Burgeoning class actions are not the only threat facing corporations and their managers. Enforcement actions by the Securities and Exchange Commission (SEC) have become more common. During the year August 2003 through July 2004, the SEC levied a total of $3.5 billion in fines, penalties and disgorgement sanctions. In February 2006, the SEC and the State of New York reached a settlement with insurance giant American International Group (AIG) under which AIG will pay $1.6 billion to settle civil fraud charges arising out of alleged accounting improprieties.[37] Most frightening of all for corporate executives is the possibility of criminal prosecution. We will discuss this in the next section.

Although this discussion has emphasized court decisions, the burden of the regulatory state on business is not imposed solely or even mainly by the courts. The contentious decisions in the securities field, as well as the criminal cases that will be discussed later, were all decided under statutes enacted by Congress or pursuant to regulations promulgated by federal agencies. Similar statutes and regulations have been adopted by state legislatures. Congress, responding to the political pressure to "do something," often adopts ill-considered legislation making the problem worse. An example in the securities field is the Sarbanes-Oxley

Act of 2002 ("SOX"), passed by Congress after the collapse of Enron and WorldCom. As one commentator has noted, "SOX was emergency legislation, enacted under conditions of limited legislative debate, during a media frenzy involving several high-profile corporate fraud and insolvency cases."[38]

Among other things, SOX requires all listed companies to have audit committees composed entirely of independent directors, even though most empirical studies show that independent boards and committees do not improve corporate performance.[39] The statute also prohibits accounting firms from providing specified non-audit services to companies that they audit. Again, most empirical studies find no connection between the provision of non-audit services and audit quality. Professor Roberta Romano has stated that the empirical literature was not even addressed by Congress.[40]

Most controversial of all are the provisions of SOX relating to maintaining internal financial controls and requiring, in connection with the company's periodic reports, a report attested to by the company's external auditor assessing the internal controls. (Section 404) As might have been anticipated, the costs of compliance with Section 404 have been severe, especially for small public companies. It has been estimated that, in 2005, U.S. companies spent more than $6 billion in complying with SOX.[41] Some small companies have said that their auditing fees have trebled or quadrupled because of Section 404. A number of small companies have delisted from the American Stock Exchange and deregistered their securities because of the high costs of trying to comply with SOX. From the standpoint of providing disclosure to investors, this is obviously counterproductive.[42] Reportedly, the SOX requirements have dissuaded a number of foreign companies from listing their shares on U.S. stock exchanges, a result which cannot be in the interest of American investors. It is predictable that the SOX requirements, together with the expansion of personal liability already discussed, will make it more difficult for U.S. companies to attract qualified independent directors. It is hard to disagree with the conclusion of Professor Romano, in her comprehensive analysis of SOX, that the statute was "a public policy blunder."[43] The costs of SOX are measurable and significant, while the benefits, if any, are intangible and remote.[44]

The Sarbanes-Oxley Act is part of a long trend during the twentieth century to undermine the federalist balance between national and state power by having more and more state powers taken over by the federal government. To achieve this result, the courts have stretched the interstate commerce clause to the breaking point. Historically, the key case was *Wickard v. Filburn*,[45] in which the Court held that the defendants' production of grain, which he fed to his own cows, was subject to congress's power to regulate commerce among the several states because it affected the price and quantity of grain sold in interstate commerce. This decision effectively eliminated any significant limits of the power of Congress under the interstate commerce clause.[46]

Loading more cases onto the already-crowded federal court system is undesirable. Former Chief Justice Rehnquist often criticized congress and the President "for their propensity to enact more and more legislation which brings more and more cases into the federal court system."[47] Corporate governance historically has been a matter of state law. The law of Delaware, where many large companies are incorporated, has been particularly effective in developing a flexible and sophisticated system of corporate governance—a system that enforces the fiduciary duties of directors but allows companies wide freedom to manage their own business. There are also federal securities laws that impose obligations of full disclosure on corporate management. This structure has worked well for decades. While there have been serious ethical and legal lapses from time to time, traditional civil and criminal laws are adequate to punish violations. In connection with the recent corporate frauds and failures, dozens of executives have been convicted, imprisoned and subjected to substantial civil penalties. In an era of strong global competition, there is no advantage in federalizing the fiduciary responsibilities of corporate directors and officers, or imposing unnecessary new burdens on corporate America.

White Collar Crime

Until recently, it was quite unusual for corporate executives to be criminally convicted and sent to jail. It was equally rare for a prominent and respected accounting firm to be indicted and convicted. Today, however, corporations, firms and businesspeople "are at greater risk of criminal liability than ever before."[48] As of September 2005, the New York Times reported that 18 high level corporate officers had recently been convicted of or pleaded guilty to accounting fraud, looting the company and other crimes, and sentenced to prison terms ranging from 5 years to 25 years.[49] In one highly publicized case, Tyco International's two former top executives were sentenced to serve 8 1/2 to 25 years in prison for looting the company, in addition to millions of dollars in repayments.[50]

The case of Arthur Andersen provides a poignant example. Andersen was the outside auditor for Enron, which collapsed in 2001 amidst widespread allegations of fraud. Andersen was indicted by the federal government and convicted in June 2002 for obstruction of justice by destroying documents in anticipation of an investigation by the SEC. In June 2005, the United States Supreme Court overturned the criminal conviction of Andersen because of the district court's failure to instruct the jury that Andersen's employees must have "knowingly" and "corruptly" intended to interfere with the federal investigation.[51] By the time the Supreme Court overturned the conviction, however, it was too late for Andersen, which had lost much of its clientele soon after the indictment and collapsed following the conviction. The message is clear: a criminal indictment can be a corporate death sentence. It is hard to see what purpose could have been served by putting Andersen out of business, since the firm had already negotiated a multimillion dollar settlement with Enron's shareholders.

Criminal penalties for individual corporate executives have also increased and are being imposed more frequently. Many businesspeople are not aware of the extraordinary scope of some federal criminal laws. It is a crime, for example, to make false statements to federal investigators or to deceptively conceal material information from officials investigating any matter within the jurisdiction of the federal government, which covers a lot of ground. This statute applies whether or not the individual is under oath.[52] Another broad and dangerous provision is the prohibition against obstruction of justice. The statute forbids "corruptly" altering, destroying or concealing documents or other objects that might be relevant to an investigation by any federal department or agency.[53] This is the charge for which Andersen was convicted. As Professor John Hasnas has said:

> Clearly, false statements and obstruction of justice are offenses designed to aid federal law enforcement efforts. Both offenses make it a separate crime for an individual to do anything that would make it more difficult for the government to convict that individual or anyone else of another substantive crime. . . . One can be guilty of either offense without being guilty of anything else. . . .[54]

An example is the conviction of Martha Stewart. She was charged with and convicted of making false statements and obstruction of justice in connection with an SEC investigation. As Hasnas writes, "Thus, these statutes empower prosecutors to go after not just criminals attempting to avoid detection and punishment, but anyone who interferes with a federal investigation regardless of the reason."[55]

The mail and wire fraud statutes are also potent weapons in the hands of a prosecutor. The mail fraud statute, for example, requires the prosecutor only to establish that the defendant intentionally participated in a scheme or artifice to defraud, even when no one has suffered any harm.[56]

The threat of criminal sanctions against corporate directors and officers is increased by the growing tendency of prosecutors to argue that a corporate defendant should not be permitted to pay legal defense costs of its officers and employees—a standard practice for decades—thus putting heavy pressure on the employees to plead guilty at an early stage and testify against other officers and employees.[57]

In a republic supposedly governed by the rule of law, the open-ended provisions described above are offensive. They do not provide adequate notice of what constitutes a criminal offense. The ancient common law rule that criminal statutes are to be narrowly construed is meaningless for these kinds of enactments. The blame here, of course, rests largely on Congress, not on the courts. These statutes are examples of the irresistible tendency on the part of federal legislators to "do something" to solve any "problem" that has gained a public focus and thus to federalize criminal laws that ought to be left up to the states. The Congressmen then get the credit, if any is due, while the difficulties of interpretation are passed on to the courts.

Another troublesome development during the twentieth century was the enactment of so-called "regulatory offenses" or "public welfare offenses" that do not require any proof of intent ("*mens rea*").[58] The Supreme Court has observed that, in industries or activities that "affect public health, safety or welfare," a violation "impairs the efficiency of controls deemed essential to the social order as presently constituted."[59] Thus, under the "regulatory" criminal statutes, "businesses and individuals can be criminally punished for entirely innocent regulatory violations, at least when the potential penalty is relatively small."[60] What is particularly chilling is the Court's acknowledgement that the *per se* violation of the activities in question (such as the violation of certain health and safety regulations) "impairs the efficiency of [federal] controls deemed essential to the social order as presently constituted." In the Brave New World of today's jurisprudence, regulatory efficiency (perhaps an oxymoron to begin with) may be sufficient justification for criminally convicting people and companies for innocent conduct.[61] The regulatory state becomes its own justification.

State prosecutors have also joined the "white collar witch hunt"[62]—most notably New York Attorney General Eliot Spitzer. State attorneys general have learned that the power to indict, or to threaten indictment, is the power to destroy. As John C. Whitehead, former chairman of Goldman Sachs, has said, discussing Mr. Spitzer's allegations against Hank Greenberg of AIG:

> Something has gone seriously awry when a state attorney general can go on television and charge one of America's best CEOs and most generous philanthropists with fraud before any charges have been brought, before the possible defendant has even had a chance to know what he personally is alleged to have done, and while the investigation is still under way.[63]

To defend an indictment in white collar crime cases often involves hundreds of thousands or even millions of dollars in legal fees, serious injury to one's reputation and the risk of a prison term if the defendant goes to trial and a jury that may not understand the case brings in a guilty verdict. Under these circumstances, there is a powerful incentive for the accused to plead guilty even if he is innocent, to avoid a much longer sentence if he happens to be convicted. "The larger victim," as Stephen Moore has written "is the very integrity and fairness of our criminal justice system itself."[64]

The net result of these developments is that white collar criminal law has been divorced from the moral and historical basis of crime and punishment. Its contemporary purpose seems to be "not the punishment of morally culpable conduct, but the effective enforcement of congressionally-created rules of behavior and regulations" relating to conduct that may or may not be morally blameworthy.[65] The white collar criminal law, at least in regard to the developments discussed here, can be seen as an example of the separation of law and morals that began in the 19th century and continues today.

Traditionally, most people assumed that basic legal principles (in contrast with laws of convenience such as rules of the road) were based on moral principles. These moral principles were embedded in natural law, which can be defined as a system of principles for the guidance of human conduct, derived from the nature of man and ascertainable independently of specific positive law as enacted in any given polity. Legal positivism, in contrast, asserts that law is merely the will of the sovereign and has no intrinsic connection to any moral order. The difference between these two views of law is critical: If there is no natural or higher law, then there is no conceptual basis for arguing that any human law is unjust.[66] In criminal law, the triumph of positivism makes it much easier to punish conduct that the legislators or administrators do not like, whether or not it violates moral norms.

Regulation

In this chapter we have emphasized the role of the courts, but many of the burdens imposed on business stem from the vast body of rules adopted by regulatory agencies. During the New Deal era, politicians were persuaded that government regulation, rather than the free market, was the most efficient way to deal with troublesome aspects of the economy. The Constitution provides that Congress shall make the laws. It does not empower an agency to make laws by regulation. Nevertheless, this practice is now common and has been upheld by the courts, which have given wide deference to the agencies.[67] The statutes authorizing regulatory agencies to enact rules often provide standards that are so broad and general that they provide little or no limitation to what the agency can do. The Securities Exchange Act of 1934, for example, authorizes the SEC to enact regulations in connection with the purchase or sale of a security relating to "any manipulative or deceptive device or contrivance in contravention of such rules and regulation as the Commission may prescribe as necessary or appropriate in the public interest or for the protection of investors."[68] What may or may not be in the "public interest" is left for the agency to decide. The standards for many other agencies are equally vague.

Delegating the law-making function to agencies is politically useful to legislators, since it enables them to take credit with voters for taking action, while later blaming the agency if it suits their interest. "The legislators designed the system so that they could claim maximum credit and take minimum responsibility."[69] Congress created dozens of new agencies—such as the Securities and Exchange Commission, the Federal Communications Commission, the Agricultural Adjustment Administration, the National Labor Relations Board and many others. The theory behind this resort to more federal bureaucracy was that regulatory agencies are more efficient than legislators or courts or states, since they could employ "experts" to manage the economy, and moreover were not bound by the traditional separation of powers, regarded by the New Dealers as a hindrance to efficient management. Many agencies combine executive, legislative and judicial powers all in one entity, and, as previously noted, courts are reluctant to overturn agency action. The doctrine of "deference" leaves interpretation and enforcement of the law up to regulatory agencies run by political appointees who have their own agendas. The delegation of law-making to agencies has led to an enormous increase in the size and scope of federal power, much of it aimed at private business.

In subsequent years, many more federal agencies were created. According to a recent study: "Every year, over 60 federal departments, agencies, and commissions employ a combined staff of roughly 242,000 full-time employees to write and enforce federal regulations. Together, they issue thousands of new rules each year." [70]

The fiscal year 2006 federal budget requests that Congress allocate $41.1 billion for regulatory activities. In addition to the cost to government of writing and enforcing the regulations, the compliance costs for individuals and businesses are very large. According to the Small Business Administration, the cost of federal regulation on American businesses, workers and consumers is close to

$1 trillion per year (more than 8% of U.S. gross domestic product).[71] This is a startling figure, which reflects the scope of regulatory overload.

It may be helpful to examine briefly one prominent agency—the Environmental Protection Agency (EPA)–as an example of the burden that excessive regulation can impose on business. In recent years, more than 400 rules per year have emerged from the EPA.[72] The commands from Congress to the EPA under only one of many statutes the agency enforces (the Clean Air Act) grew from 8 pages in 1965 to 450 pages in 1990. The EPA has issued regulations under the same statute that now run to 7,300 pages. The agency also issues "guidance documents" amounting to thousands of pages to aid in the interpretation of the regulations. State regulations and permit processes then add additional bureaucracy and complexity.[73] "The EPA's regulation 'has grown to the point where it amounts to nothing less than a massive effort at Soviet-style planning of the economy to achieve environmental goals,. . .'"[74] (Needless to say, environmental regulations have also spawned a great deal of litigation in the courts.) The EPA estimated in 1990 that pollution control cost $115 billion per year. Professor David Schoenbrod, a former attorney for the Natural Resources Defense Council, writes that this amount is probably higher now, but EPA has stopped compiling data on the total cost of pollution control.[75] The environmental laws and regulations, like the Internal Revenue Code and regulations, are vast in length and inscrutable in complexity. "This complexity," says Schoenbrod "makes it practically impossible to be in full compliance with environmental laws. . . . And almost every violator is potentially a criminal." [76] Civil penalties can be assessed even though the violation was innocent and did no harm. Schoenbrod recommends that most pollution regulation be left to state and local governments to make it easier for the people most directly affected to play a greater role in the process.

The frequent resort to federal regulation is not just a power grab by self-interested regulators (although that may be part of it). The growth of regulation, like the growth in health, education and other welfare state programs, happens because the American public has been persuaded that every "problem" should be "solved" by government, with the central government (including the federal courts) as the problem-solver[77]. It is not in the interest of public officials to disabuse the populace of this misguided notion, which has made our citizens increasingly dependent on government. The practice of "solving problems" may be valid for a math or chemistry class, but not for government. Government can take action, but it cannot "solve" social and economic problems. As F.A. Hayek argued, this is because government officials cannot possibly know the information and inclinations possessed by 300 million citizens. It is therefore far preferable that these individuals address their own problems or, where regulation is needed, that the problems be addressed wherever possible at the level of government closest to the people affected. The underlying question is: do we want to extend the regulatory state, with its controls and subsidies, or do we want to maintain a society of free and responsible individuals?

Tort Reform

As we have previously seen, the existing system of tort liability is costly and unpredictable, often resulting in "jackpot justice." For many years, as a corrective to the liability explosion, business groups have sought to persuade Congress and state legislatures to enact tort reform. In this political struggle, business has been opposed by politically powerful trial lawyers, labor unions and consumer groups, and over the years the opponents have been able to resist most significant reforms. Recently, however, the business lobbies have had more success. In several states the legislatures have enacted tort reform and voters have elected pro-business judges. Tort reforms at the state level have included one or more of the following measures: limitations on non-economic damages (e.g., pain and suffering) and punitive damages; laws to prevent forum-shopping (e.g., by requiring that venues for lawsuits must be established independently for each plaintiff); replacing joint and several liability with proportionate liability; limitations on pre-judgment interest; allowing certain defenses in product liability cases (e.g., adherence to government standards); providing for immediate appeal of class certification orders; and limits on contingency fees. All of these reforms are useful.[78]

One of the most anti-business jurisdictions was Mississippi. Following recent tort reforms in that state, it is reported that litigation costs have decreased, businesses have returned to the state and insurance is more available. As a Mississippi state senator has written, "tort reform has made the Mississippi legal environment more fair, more predictable and less expensive."[79] It should be noted, however, that the reforms listed above are scattered and often vaguely worded. Most have not been tested in court. In a number of cases, state Supreme Courts have declared certain reforms unconstitutional on the ground that they deprive the plaintiffs of a remedy without due process of law.

While in theory a unified and coherent tort reform could be enacted at the federal level, because of political alignments a major reform of the tort system is unlikely. There are also federalism issues involved. One of the few measures passed by Congress is the Class Action Fairness Act (CAFA), passed by Congress and signed into law in 2005.[80] This law is a modest improvement in that the statute makes it much easier for defendants to remove interstate class actions from state to federal court—for example, when some plaintiffs or class members live in a state different from that of the defendant. CAFA will in many cases enable defendants to escape state courts that tolerate abusive or frivolous suits, but it does nothing to change the *in terrorem* nature of the class action itself. Real class action reform would consist of one or more of the following: (1) Adopt an "opt-in" rather than an "opt-out" procedure (see "Class Actions," above). (2) Prevent certification of a class where the substantive law requires that reliance, causation or damages be proved individually.[81] (3) Place reasonable limits on contingent fees. All of these reforms, of course, would be highly controversial.

It is not the intention of any of these proposed reforms to abolish class actions, which in many cases are the only practical way for small claimants to get their day in court. The point is simply to remedy some of the aspects of class actions that lend themselves to "jackpot justice" and bludgeon defendants into settling a case for more than it is worth because they are afraid they could be wiped out if they go to trial.

Conclusion

The United States has traditionally been praised, or blamed, for its adherence to the principles of a "free market." A successful free market, however, must be based on the rule of law, which in turn requires a degree of certainty and predictability sufficient to enable the citizens to guide their conduct; procedural fairness (an opportunity to be heard in a regularly established tribunal); and a set of principles adequate to protect the individual against invasions of person and property. The laws must be understandable, consistent and coherent. During the twentieth century, there have been many examples of U.S. laws that fail this test, such as the laws and regulations relating to taxation and environmental matters, and, indeed, virtually any set of complex rules enforced by an administrative agency. Political and social forces during the last century have moved the nation in the direction of increased government control of the economy. This has been accomplished by an outpouring of laws, regulations and judicial decisions constituting unmanageable legal overload.

The causes of this "hyperlexis" in American society are complex and varied, but include the following: (1) The prestige of science encouraged the notion that the economy and society could be centrally planned by experts. The "planning," as it turned out, consisted of ever-growing quantities of legislation and administrative regulations, which led inevitably to a dramatic increase in litigation, the number of lawyers and the size of government. (2) The egalitarian democracy predicted by Tocqueville[82] appeared in the twentieth century, stimulated by the popular belief that social and economic equality could be at least partly achieved by government action through taxation, regulation and changes in tort law and legal procedure favoring plaintiffs. This trend was further strengthened by the Populist and Progressive movements in the early part of the twentieth century. (3) There was a shift in political doctrine from classical liberalism to an interpretation of liberalism in terms of socialism rather than individual responsibility. This change was reflected in the collectivist measures of the New Deal, Lyndon Johnson's "Great Society" and the politics of the welfare state. (4) Politicians, judges and voters placed increasing emphasis on rights rather than obligations. This shift was not confined to America, and was carefully delineated by Jose Ortega y Gasset in his masterpiece, *The Revolt of the Masses*, which traced the rise of the demand society and the psychology of the "spoiled child." From this perspective, any personal injury or loss to the individual entitles him to demand relief from someone else in a court of law. The most obvious target was "big business," which was erroneously seen as largely responsible for the economic recessions of the early twentieth century culminating in the Great Depression.

Whatever the causes of the litigation and regulatory explosion may have been, the consequences to business were substantial. The money, time and energy expended by business executives in legal defense and regulatory compliance are heavy costs that detract from the efficiency and productivity of the economy. We may also speculate that the decline of trust, already evident in the society at large, is in part attributable to the proliferation of lawsuits between employers and employees, partners, business associates and ordinary citizens. The constant assertion of individual rights to relief translates into more judges and more lawyers, whose interest is to encourage the assertion of new demands.

The goal of legal reform should be to restrain excessive litigation and to restore the traditional standards of justice. The scope of tort law reform should be broadened "Effective tort reform, . . . must return the system to one based on fault and causation, that holds responsible those who caused the damage, makes the injured whole, and does not impose upon the innocent. This will require careful examination of the current incentives that exist to the filing of lawsuits, especially class action lawsuits."[83] Legal reform should include measures to exclude "expert" testimony based on unsound science.[84] Courts should not be reluctant to dismiss meritless cases. Congress and the courts should place limitations on the power of administrative agencies, many of which operate under standards so general as to be meaningless. The power of Congress to legislate should not be delegated to agencies. The practice of awarding "punitive damages" should be revisited: the civil lawsuit is not a proper forum for punishing people. If punitive damages are permitted they should be carefully restricted by the courts. As noted above, the Supreme Court has already taken some steps in this direction. In white collar criminal cases, the courts should not impose sentences that place businessmen in jail for most or all of their lives, except in truly extraordinary cases; and Congress should reconsider statutes imposing criminal penalties for vague and ill-defined offenses related to government investigations. Finally, Congress and the Supreme Court should restore the commerce clause to its proper place in constitutional adjudication by limiting its reach to encompass only matters directly related to interstate and foreign commerce. We are dealing with trends, however, that have deep roots in the social psychology of modern America and the politics of mass democracy. In the long run, it may be that the most important reform will be the appointment or election of superior judges. In recent years, however, the appointment of judges (especially at the level of the Supreme Court), has become a political issue, making the process even more volatile. The dubious practice of selecting judges by popular election at the state level remains widespread. Finally, serious tort and class action reform is desirable, but this will happen only if there is awareness and strong leadership in the business, legal and political communities.

ENDNOTES

1. Statement of Commissioner Paul S. Atkins at U.S. Chamber Institute for Legal Reform, 02/20/06 p. 2. See also "All These Lawsuits Make 'Bleak House' Look Like a Picnic," *New York Times*, Oct. 16, 2005, Sec. 3, p.2. Companies interviewed report that litigation costs them an average of $8 million per company per year, often accounting for 5% or more of gross revenue.

2. Edward Gibbon, *The Decline and Fall of the Roman Empire*, Vol. IV, p.542 (Bury ed., reprint of 1909, 14th ed., AMS Press, N.Y. 1974).

3. See Peter W. Huber, *Liability: The Legal Revolution and Its Consequences*, pp. 5 *et seq.* (Basic, N.Y., 1988) for a thorough discussion of the history of the tort revolution.

4. See Escola v. Coca-Cola Bottling Company, 150 P.2d 436, 441 (Cal. 1944) (Traynor, J.)

5. See Restatement of the Law Third, *Torts: Products Liability*, Secs. 1 and 2 and Comment, proposed Final Draft (1997).

6. See *id.*, Sec. 17; Louis R. Frumer and Melvin I. Friedman, *Products Liability*, Vol. I, Sec. 8.04[2][a] (Matthew Bender 2005).

7. See Restatement Third, Sec. 18.

8. Eric Helland and Alexander Tabarrok, "Judge and Jury: American Tort Law on Trial," p. 95, note 2, and p. 116 (*The Independent Institute* 2006).

9. *BMW of North America, Inc. v. Gore*, 517 U.S. 559 (1996). See also *State Farm Mutual Automobile Insurance Co. v. Campbell*, 538 U.S. 408 (2003), in which the Court reversed as excessive a punitive verdict of $145 million in a case in which compensatory damages were $1 million. See, generally, George Clemon Freeman, Jr., "Constitutional Constraints on Punitive Damages and Other Monetary Punishments," 57 *Bus. Law.* 587 (2002); and George Clemon Freeman, Jr., and Makram Jaber, "Further Progress in Defining Constitutional Constraints on Punitive Damages," 61 *Bus. Law.* 517 (2006). In the *Gore* and *Campbell* cases, the court instructed courts reviewing punitive damages to consider three guideposts: (1) the degree of reprehensibility of the defendant's misconduct; (2) the disparity between harm suffered by the plaintiff and the punitive damages award; and (3) the difference between the punitive damages awarded by the jury and the civil penalties authorized or imposed in comparable cases, *Campbell*, p. 418, The Court indicated that "few awards exceeding a single-digit ratio between punitive and compensatory damages, to a significant degree, will satisfy due process." *Campbell*, p. 425.

10. See Joseph F. Johnston, Jr., "Causes and Effects of the Liability Insurance Crisis," the Southwestern Legal Foundation, *Private Investors Abroad—Problems and Solutions in International Business,* Chap. 11 (Matthew Bender, N.Y. 1986).

11. U.S. Tort Costs: 2004 Update (Towers-Perrin—Tillinghast 2005) p. 2. www.towersperrin.com/tillinghast/publications/reports/tort 2004; Michael S. Greve, Harm-less Lawsuits? What's Wrong with Consumer Class Actions, p.11, n. 19 (American Enterprise Institute, Washington, D.C. 2005). As Michael Greve has pointed out, following the class-action reforms in 1966 (to be discussed subsequently), "federal and state courts created a novel and remarkably permissive regime for the prosecution and adjudication of mass claims." *Id.* p.8. See also "Trial Lawyers Inc." The Economist, Sep. 27, 2003, p. 67.

12. Bates v. State Bar of Arizona, 433 U.S. 350 (1977).

13. Mary Ann Glendon, *A Nation Under Lawyers: How the Crisis in the Legal Profession is Transforming American Society*, p. 53 (Farrar, Straus & Giroux N.Y., 1994) (quoting L. Gordon Crovitz).

14. John C. Coffee, "Class Wars: The Dilemma of the Mass Tort Class Action," 95 Colum. L. Rev. 1343, 1407 (1995). See Marsha Angell, M.D., *Science on Trial: The Clash of Medical Evidence and the Law in the Breast Implant Cases* (W.W. Norton, N.Y., 1996)

15. See Nanette Byrnes, "The Tobacco Suit That's Going up in Smoke," Business Week, June 27, 2005, p.70.

16. Michelle J. White, "Resolving the Elephantine Mass," Regulation (Summer 2003).

17. Stephen J. Carroll *et al.*, "Asbestos Litigation," pp. xxiv–xxvii (RAND Institute for Civil Justice, 2005) (the "RAND Report").

18. RAND Report, p.127.

19. Mark A. Behrens and Phil S. Goldberg, "Stopping Asbestos Litigation Abuse," Engage, vol. 6, issue 1, p.120–21 (Federalist Society 2005)(quoting Richard Scruggs). There is substantial evidence of fraud. See Roger Parloff, "Diagnosing for Dollars," Fortune, June 13, 2005, p.97; "Screening for Corruption," Wall Street Journal, Dec. 2, 2005, p. A 10; and "The Asbestos Waterloo," Wall Street Journal, June 10, 2006, p. A 12.

20. See John E. Calfee, "What the Texas Jury Did to Patients," American Ent. Inst., September 9, 2005, www.aei.org/publications. See also www. Bloomberg.com/apps/news, Sept. 19, 2005.

21. "Scalpel, scissors, lawyer," The Economist, Dec. 17, 2005, p. 30.

22. See "Study: Four out of 10 malpractice cases are groundless," Advisen FPN, http://fpn.advisen.com/articles/article49465016-1859196561.html (visited 5/15/2006).

23. Helland and Tabarrok, supra, p. 104.

24. Newberg on Class Actions section 1:6 (4th ed. 2002).

25. John C. Coffee, "Class Wars: The Dilemma of the Mass Tort Class Action," 95 Colum. L. Rev. 1343, 1356, n.37 (1995).

26. See Kern v. Siemens Corp., 393F.3d 120 (2d Cir. 2004), cert. den. 125 S.Ct. 2272.

27. Often, plaintiff class members receive in settlement in-kind payments instead of cash, usually in the form of coupons or scrip that class members can apply toward the purchase of the defendant's products in the future. For examples, see Note, "In-Kind Class Action Settlements," 109 Harv. L. Rev. 810 (1996). These kinds of payments are of limited or no value for most class members. The lawyers, of course, are paid in cash.

28. 26 Class Action Reports 327 (2005).

29. Elliott Weiss and Lawrence White, "File Early, Then Free Ride," Corporate Practice Commentator, Vol. 47, No. 2 pp. 379, 413 (2005).

30. See Mark Moller, "Controlling Unconstitutional Class Actions: a Blueprint for Future Lawsuit Reform," Policy Analysis No. 546 (CATO Inst., June 27, 2005). It is arguable that Congress ratified the fraud-on-the-market theory when it passed the Private Securities Reform Act of 1995. But see, Dura Pharmaceuticals, Inc. v. Brundo, 125 S.Ct. 1627 (2005), in which the Court held that Plaintiffs may not rely solely on an inflated purchase price of the shares as the cause of loss to plaintiffs, but must prove that defendants

misrepresentations were the proximate cause of an economic loss to plaintiffs. For examples of courts' elimination of the reliance requirement in fraud cases, see Moller, supra, at p.3.

31. See Elaine Buckberg et al., "Recent Trends in Shareholder Class Action Litigation: Are WorldCom and Enron the New Standard?"p.1 (NERA Economic Consulting, July 2005). Even if WorldCom and Enron are excluded, the average settlement for the first half of 2005 was $26 million, compared to $9 million in 1996. See also Laura E. Simmons and Ellen Ryan, "Post-Reform Act Securities Settlements" (Cornerstone Research 2005). Cornerstone has reported that the number of securities class actions filed decreased in 2005. "Securities Class Action Case Filings-2005," P. 3 (Cornerstone 2006). Cornerstone reported a further drop in the number of securities fraud class actions filed during the first half of 2006. It is too early to tell whether this decrease represents an anomaly or a trend. See also John C. Coffee, Jr., "Reforming the Securities Class Action: An Essay on Deterrence and Its Implementation," Columbia Law School, The Center for Law and Economic Studies, Working Paper No. 293, p. 24 (2006).

32. Simmons and Ryan, supra, p. 1. Note that about 60% of the companies in the Dow Jones industrial index have been sued in securities class actions since 1999. Kenneth M. Lehn, "Private Insecurities," Wall Street Journal, Feb. 15, 2006.

33. See Charles Hansen, "A Seismic Shift in Director Liability Exposure: The WorldCom and Enron Settlements," Corporation, vol. LXXVI, no. 14 (Aspen, July 15, 2005).

34. Id., p.5

35. Peter J. Wallison, "The WorldCom and Enron Settlements: Politics Rears Its Ugly Head," Engage, vol. 6 p.59 (The Journal of the Federalist Society's Practice Groups, Issue 1, 2005). Wallison suggests that the public officials who acted as lead plaintiffs were motivated in part by political considerations.

36. Buckberg, "Recent Trends," supra, p.7.

37. 2004 PricewaterhouseCoopers Securities Litigation Study, p.6 (PricewaterhouseCoopers 2005); "AIG Agrees to $1.6 Billion Settlement," Wall Street Journal, Feb. 9, 2006.

38. Roberta Romano, "The Sarbanes-Oxley Act and the Making of Quack Corporate Governance," 114 Yale L.J. 1521, 1527 (2005). The act is found in 15 U.S.C.A. sec. 7201.

39. Romano, p.1530.

40. Id., p. 1536,1543.

41. "Living with Sarbanes Oxley," Wall Street Journal, Oct. 17, 2005, p.R.1.

42. According to a recent study, compliance costs under SOX average $1.5 million for companies with sales of $100 million to $500 million, and $824,000 for companies with sales under $100 million. For companies listed on the American Stock Exchange, annual compliance costs under SOX are 1.5% of revenues—a serious burden for a small company. Neal L. Wolkoff (Chairman of the American Stock Exchange), "Sarbanes-Oxley is a Curse for Small-Cap Companies," The Wall Street Journal, August 15, 2005, p. A13. The costs are much higher for larger companies.

43. Romano, supra p.1603.

44. See "Special Report: Auditing Sarbanes-Oxley," The Economist, May 21, 2005.

45. 317 U.S. 111 (1942).

46. See Richard A. Epstein, How Progressives Rewrote the Constitution, pp. 67–72 (CATO, Washington, 2006).

47. Quoted in Jennifer S. Schwartz and Laura A. O'Reilley, "Class Actions: Past, Present & Future," 26 Class Action Reports 157 (2005).

48. "Crackdown Puts Corporations, Executives in New Legal Peril," Wall Street Journal, June 20, 2005, p.A1.

49. New York Times, Sec. A P.1, Sept. 20, 2005.

50. "Tyco Figures Will be Jailed at Least 7 Years," Wall Street Journal, Sept. 20, 2005,p.C.I. Seven years is the minimum time the defendants will have to serve.

51. Arthur Andersen v. United States, 125 S. Ct 2129 (2005).

52. 18 U.S.C. A. sec. 1001 (2005).

53. 18 U.S.C. A. secs. 1512, 1519 and 1520 (2005).

54. John Hasnas, "Ethics and the Problem of White Collar Crime," 54 Am. U. L. Rev. 579, 613 (2005).

55. Hasnas, pp. 613–14.

56. Hasnas, pp. 587–88.

57. See "U.S. Pressures Firms Not To Pay Staff Legal Fees," Wall Street Journal, March 28, 2006, p. B. 1.

58. See *Morrissette v. United States*, 342 U.S. 246, 253–56(1952).

59. Id. at 256.

60. Hasnas, supra at 608 (footnote omitted).

61. See United States v. White Fuel Corp., 498 F.2d 619, 621 (1st Cir. 1974). Another interesting aspect of this line of cases is that corporate officers, merely because they have the authority to prevent or correct a violation of law, can be criminally liable for actions of their subordinates. See United States v. Park, 421 U.S. 658, 673–74 (1975).

62. See Stephen Moore, "White Collar Witch Hunt," The American Spectator, Sept. 2005, p. 20.

63. John C. Whitehead, "Mr. Spitzer Has Gone Too Far," Wall Street Journal, April 22, 2005, p. A12.

64. Stephen Moore, supra, p. 25.

65. Hasnas, supra, p.663.

66. Joseph F. Johnston, Jr., "Natural Law and the Fiduciary Duties of Business Managers," Journal of Markets and Morality, Vol 8, No. 2, p. 33.

67. In most cases, an agency's action is subject to reversal by a court only if the agency's action was arbitrary, capricious, an abuse of discretion, or otherwise not in accordance with law. "This is a 'deferential standard' that 'presume[s] the validity of agency action.'" MCI Worldcom Network Services, Inc. v. F.C.C., 274 F.3d 542, 547 (D.C. Cir. 2001). As Justice Scalia has said, in upholding Congress' delegation of power to an agency, the Court has 'almost never felt qualified to second-guess Congress regarding the permissible degree of policy judgment that can be left to those executing or applying the law.'" Whitman v. American Trucking Assn., Inc., 531 U.S. 457, 474 (2001) (quoting Mistretta v. U.S., 488 U.S. 361, 416 (1989) (Scalia, J., dissenting).

68. Section 10(b) of the Securities Exchange Act of 1934, 15 U.S.C.A. Sec. 78 j(b).

69. David Schoenbrod, *Saving Our Environment from Washington*, p. 231 (Yale Univ. Press 2005).

70. Susan E. Dudley, "It's Not Just the Spending," p.1 (Mercatus Center, George Mason University, August 29, 2005).

71. Id., p.2.

72. Clyde Wayne Crews Jr., "Ten Thousand Commandments: An Annual Snapshot of the Federal Regulatory State," p. 22 (CATO Institute 2003).

73. Schoenbrod, supra, pp.60–61.

74. Id., pp. 61–62. (quoting Richard Stewart).

75. Id., p. 187

76. Id., p.211.

77. H.L. Mencken captured the essence of the modern form of popular democracy when he said; "The whole aim of practical politics is to keep the populace alarmed (and hence clamorous to be led to safety) by menacing it with an endless series of hobgoblins, all of them imaginary." www.quotationspage.com/quote/33072.html .

78. The reforms state-by-state are listed by the American Tort Reform Association. See www.atra.org/files.cgi/7927_record7-05pdf.

79. Charlie Ross, "Jackson Action," Wall Street Journal, September 15, 2005, p.A21. See also an article by Senator Ross, "Winning the Tort War," at www.atra.org/files.cgi/7840_winning.tort.war.pdf

80. S.5, 109th Cong., 1st Sess., 119 Stat. 4 (2005).

81. Mark Moller, "Controlling Unconstitutional Class Actions: a Blueprint for Future Lawsuit Reform," Policy Analysis (CATO Institute, June 27, 2005).

82. Alexis de Tocqueville, *Democracy in America*, Vol. II, Bk. II, Chap. 1 (Henry G. Langley, N.Y. 1845).

83. Ronald J. Rychlak, *Trial by Fury: Restoring the Common Good in Tort Litigation*, pp. 77–78 (Acton Institute 2004).

84. The Supreme Court has taken a step in this direction in *Daubert v. Merrell Dow Pharmaceuticals Inc.*, 509 U.S. 579 (1993), mandating stricter rules for expert testimony.

Seven
Judicial Assault on Secondary Education
by Hans L. Eicholz

Not until the middle of the nineteenth century did state courts enter into the area of public education. Prior to that, there was little or no assigned role by state constitutions for the centralized administration of primary and secondary education. Many states did have provisions for some public assistance, often through grants of land, such as that provided in the Land Ordinance of 1785, but decisions about school organization, curriculum, and parental involvement were largely a local and private affair.

This began to change after state governments were pressured by organized interests seeking to control or contain the growing tide of immigrants from Catholic countries in the 1830s. That tide formed one of the primary reasons for early state laws that concentrated power in the hands of "professional" school managers and civil servants, altering what had been a richly variegated system of local and private schools throughout the country.

The "public school" set the stage for the politicization of everything from curriculum choices to attendance requirements. The cause is not mysterious. In a complex modern society, parents possess distinctive goals and values. When they are compelled to utilize the same set of institutions, clashes become inevitable. In the case of public education, the result has been to invite the judiciary, first at the state and then the federal level, to intervene dramatically in the educational future of the country. Over time, that development has removed the locus of decision making from local communities and parents to the ultimate determination of state and federal judges.

As it stands currently, security in the choice of schools, how those schools are to be funded, and what will be taught, is determined by the lottery of judicial occupancy. The failing performance of public schools has brought increased pressure for change, but entrenched interests have fought these proposals every step of the way. The courts have provided the arena in which those interests have often prevailed over the very basic rights of parents to secure the best education for their children.

If the nature of the judicial relationship to education is to change, it will need to begin with state constitutions and those provisions that define the public nature of most state educational systems. Barring such changes, parents will continue to face an uncertain environment with respect to the educational options of their children.

The Early History

Thomas Jefferson is often cited as a leading exponent of public schools, but these sources frequently overlook one major facet of his thinking about public education: the crucial place of parental choice. Never a friend of monopoly, it would be surprising if Jefferson had been an advocate of restricting freedom in schooling. In fact, Jefferson supported a high degree of parental liberty even in the institutional arrangements he thought necessary for cultivating young minds. He asserted this unequivocally to Joseph C. Cabell on February 2, 1816. Having been advised by Cabell that many parents were concerned about being compelled to support public establishments, Jefferson wrote back to express shock that anyone would even consider mandating state wide support of public schools. Let each county, divided into wards, make that decision, and if a particular ward decided that it did not want a public school, then "let them remain without one." He elaborated further:

> If . . . it is intended that the State government shall take this business into its own hands, and provide schools for every county, then by all means strike out this provision of our bill. I would never wish that it should be placed on a worse footing than the rest of the State. But if it is believed that these elementary schools will be better managed by the governor and council, the commissioners of the literary fund, or any other general authority of the government than by the parents within each ward, it is a belief against all experience . . . What has destroyed liberty and the rights of man in every government which has ever existed under the sun? The generalizing and concentrating all cares and powers into one body. . . .[1]

This notion of liberty and the source of its undoing was a commonplace at the time of the American founding and early republic. Nowhere in the U.S. Constitution is there a provision that guarantees a right to an education at public expense. The document, in fact, is silent on the entire subject, and so was the Supreme Court until the early twentieth century. The reasons for this have to do with the nature of the union as a compound federal republic.

The national government was originally conceived as a government of delegated powers for which very specific responsibilities were assigned for securing of national defense, coordinating of foreign policy, and regulating commerce among the states and with other nations. It was not, however, a bill of particulars with respect to the many rights and privileges to be enjoyed by American citizens. Basic rights were to be the domain of the states.

It was at the state level that issues of education were first raised, and initially, few state constitutions called for direct public provision of education. The notable exceptions were in New England where local provision through the townships and churches was required when a settlement reached above fifty families, and in the Old Northwest, where land parcels were set aside for the support of education.[2] New England "common schools" formed a model for the reformers of the 1830s or 40s, but the idea of centralized and uniform political control was far from popular with most Americans at the time. Parents took a powerful interest in seeing to the education of their children, and the earliest attempts at uniform statewide systems of education were strongly resisted. Few were willing to surrender their local control, recognizing what Jefferson saw as the key threat to liberty: centralization of power. Having just fought a revolution for independence, they were not prepared to commit their children's fate to the administration of a central education authority.[3]

Setting the Stage for Conflict

That independence of an earlier republican spirit began to weaken in the 1840s. With the first significant waves of non-Protestant immigrants from Catholic Ireland and southern Germany, reformers played upon the fears of social disorder, urban poverty and ethnic prejudice.[4] It was in this environment that advocates of state control like James G. Carter, Henry Barnard, and Horace Mann, were able to gain political support for the idea of centrally managed public schools run by education "experts." Mann argued that the public schools would work against sectarian divisions and bring about social harmony because "they would teach the whole of religion" by earnestly inculcating "all Christian morals."[5]

Far from separating church and state, these early public school advocates made certain that it would be a "non- sectarian" reading of the *Protestant Bible* that would be taught. Here was to be the place "where the children of all the different denominations are brought together for instruction . . . one place where the children can kneel before a common alter." In Mann's view, public education, "beyond all other devices of human origin" was to be "the great equalizer of the conditions of men—the balance-wheel of the social machinery."[6] His campaign for state government education took firm root in large swaths of the northern and western states from the 1850s and 60s on into the early twentieth century. Both Northern Whigs and many Jacksonian Democrats jumped on the public school band wagon, and increasingly, Antebellum reformers pushed for state level constitutional reforms that guaranteed public provision of primary and secondary education under the ultimate control of the state legislature. Many of these states would adopt nearly identical constitutional language to the effect of mandating that legislatures "provide, by law, for a general and uniform system of Common Schools. . . ."[7] Far from alleviating social divisions, however, such establishments appear to have exacerbated them.

While the liberal Protestant mainstream could tolerate a school system that included Catholics and Jews, so long as everyone was required to read from the same Protestant texts, very often Jews, Catholics, and orthodox Protestants (those who disagreed with the watered down liberal readings of Mann and company) could not. Resistance to particular curriculum prescriptions were, and frequently remain, intense, and the push for some alternative, either public or private, continues to produce considerable friction. Additionally, the question of race, East and West, North and South, both before and after the Civil War, was quite another matter even for many of the most "forward looking" public school reformers. The stage was thus set for a whole series of issues on which the courts would be called into service.[8]

Race and Schools

The first dispute in which a state court ruled in the determination of policy with respect to primary education turned on the question of who would be allowed to attend certain public or common schools of the city of Boston. The conflict developed directly out of the general or public character that schooling took on after 1800. Before the end of the eighteenth century, most schools were predominantly private, funded by parental contributions, although the construction of buildings might receive aid from the township or city, these were more often than not "local and temporary" and there was no official segregation by race.

In Massachusetts, the state constitution simply required that townships provide for a common school after reaching a certain level of population, but provision of public assistance was not required. Usually funding came in the way of private land grants, but after that parents were typically charged a small fee for their children's attendance for each term which would go towards the salary of a teacher and the purchase of materials. On the other hand, parents also had considerable say under such a system in the selection of teachers. These would hardly be considered public schools by any current measure. As Bernard Bailyn noted, "The modern conception of public education, the very idea of a clean line of separation between 'private' and 'public,' was unknown before the end of the eighteenth century."[9] In such an environment, parents would tend to associate with like-minded parents and co-religionists. Sharp disagreements might result in the establishment of different schools, and one very clear example of such "exiting" occurred when black parents, angered by what they considered to be the lack of attention given to their children, chose to establish their own school in 1798. At that time, schools were either private or only partially funded through the city and were not segregated.[10]

Problems of a political nature arose under the supervision of the general school committee and the creation of a city wide publicly supported common school system, itself under the Massachusetts State Board of Education, of which Mann was the state's secretary from 1837 to 1848. By declaring the system to be public, reformers raised the immediate question of who constituted "the public."

Black residents of Boston certainly counted themselves part of the citizenry when they were taxed to support the new system. The education committee of the city, however, acting *parens patriae*, decided otherwise in 1848, and made segregation at public expense mandatory, disregarding issues of convenience or equal protection.[11] The denial of one pupil, Sarah Roberts, to a "common school" precipitated a suit that set the stage for the Massachusetts High Court.

The decision in *Roberts v. City of Boston* was in no way a forgone conclusion. Certain prior Massachusetts decisions had moved strongly in the direction of affirming equality among citizens, one even declaring slavery unconstitutional. Counsel for Sarah Roberts noted that blacks were in fact citizens, fully capable in law to "occupy any office connected with the public schools, from that of governor, or secretary of the board of education, to that of member of a school committee, or teacher in any public school, and as a voter he may vote for members of the school committee."[12] It would be strange indeed to assert that one could be prohibited from attending the very school he might serve, in some capacity, to govern. To affirm such a possibility would be to assert a form of caste, and that is precisely what the courts did, affirming the predominant racial prejudice of the "public."

The court found in favor of the doctrine of separate but equal, citing only the provision of the Massachusetts constitution that made it a duty of the legislature and magistrates "to cherish the interests of literature and the sciences." The empowering provision to erect public schools was read broadly with "no specific direction" as to how schools should be organized, the number of schools that should be built, or who would be admitted to attendance. All this was simply to be determined by the committee "under their power of general superintendence." Far from ameliorating social tensions as education reformers hoped, *Roberts* illustrates powerfully how public institutions invite conflict when segments of *the public* disagree fundamentally about the particulars of that *public* establishment.

From this moment onwards, courts throughout the states and eventually the United States, were asked to rule on the subject of separate but equal public facilities *until* the issue was decided by the U.S. Supreme Court's 1954 decision in *Brown v. Board of Education*. Yet, far from resolving problems with equity in public schools, that decision of the Court invited further litigation on the meaning of equality, due process, and equal protection in the law that would reach to issues of school busing, local control, and disparity in funding.

Nationalizing the Reform Impulse

The urge to reform via the legislative process draws from a deeply felt sense of the imminent possibilities of social progress. The early nineteenth century reformers who made public schooling the agenda for both existing and newly formed state constitutions, had this sense in abundance. It was to serve the goals of social unity, of economic betterment, of social stability, and justice. It rarely mattered that northern Jacksonian Democrats defined these things differently from southern Democrats, or both from Northern or Southern Whigs. They all agreed that a public school system would somehow serve their various and often conflicting objectives.[13] As with any public institution, the real challenge begins with establishment. Once a system is "public" or political, every social group begins to seek political influence rather than merely personal or marketplace influence, to achieve its ends. The reform impulse of necessity begs a judicial response because it quickly becomes apparent that basic values in a modern complex society differ.

By the end of the nineteenth century, the mantle of reform was assumed by those who explicitly saw their efforts as progressive, the implication being that all who stood in their way were "regressive." In his extended essay on the Progressive movement in law, Richard Epstein noted that the earliest traditions of the federal courts affirmed a limited role for national and state government interference with contracts and the freedom to truck and barter. The commerce clause was read, for the most part, restrictively, or in its "dormant" sense, to prevent states from interfering with trade across state lines. To the degree that the power was interpreted positively as a grant of authority to regulate trade among the states and with foreign nations, it was applied sparingly, because it was recognized that the Founders did not intend to take away from individual states the right to regulate their own affairs where there were pressing public concerns of "health, safety, morals or general welfare."[14] Thus Epstein writes, "Our Constitution is a classical liberal document insofar as it recognizes, implicitly, an inherent state police power that allows collective action to enforce the criminal laws against force and fraud, to prevent nuisances, and otherwise to restrain activities that violate the rights of others." That conception was altered by the unremitting pressures after the civil war to nationalize efforts at social reform. When you combine that national effort with massive state involvement in education, you uncover the foundations of our present day predicament. How this came into being is of particular interest and complexity.[15]

As *Roberts v. City of Boston* made plain, there were various understandings of the meaning of equal protection. Different views encouraged a judicial response. That response, in favor of segregation reflected the biases of the majority, and however we might disagree with that decision, the *Roberts* case came to define the position of the states after the Civil War. Thus in *Plessey v. Ferguson*, a case to decide whether a state government could legally segregate railroad passengers, the Federal court accepted the regulations, and cited *Roberts* as precedent.[16]

There is considerable reason to argue that prior to state involvement in either education or transportation, citizens enjoyed the equal right to contract freely in the determination of their children's education or to negotiate with rail lines for transportation. Indeed, as Epstein argued in *Forbidden Grounds: The Case Against Employment Discrimination Laws*, the court might have ruled against the state of Louisiana on the grounds that it interfered with the right of passengers and railroads to freely contract their own seating arrangements. Most of the railroads, it was well known, initially refused to segregate because of the time and expense involved in doing so, and that is in fact why the states passed separate but equal legislation in 1890s. If the rationale of the *Lochner* case, for example, had been applied in this instance, the outcome would have been quite different.[17]

But the Federal Court selected other grounds and set the stage for continuing battles on a *national scale* over conflicting notions of due process and the meaning of equal protection of the laws. The legal environment surrounding education assumed its present state of uncertainty, as opposing state practices in education were complicated by conflicting federal judicial decisions.

Brown v. Board of Education

Considerable historical work has been put forward to reveal the intentions of the Framers of the Fourteenth Amendment and the general consensus since Berger's *Government by Judiciary* appears to be that they had no intention of reaching to the issue of segregated schools. As Berger notes, the intention was to secure equal access to courts of law, to secure rights to the ownership of property, and guarantee the ability of the freedmen to seek remedy for damages.[18] Be that as it may, the practical difficulties in maintaining "separate but equal" facilities were immense. The courts were beset by challenges since *Plessey v. Ferguson* that state governments were not serving all citizens equally.

A number of positions, consistent with time-honored Constitutional modes of interpretation, were available to the courts from the very outset. Some of those have been mentioned with respect to *Roberts*. If citizens could be compelled to support public schools, what construction of equal protection could plausibly deny them access to those very institutions? There was also clear precedent disallowing state practices with respect to all white juries that led to criminal cases being sent back for retrial as inconsistent with the Fourteenth Amendment, and Justice Harlan, in his dissent from *Plessey*, cited these very cases as proof that government could not do otherwise because "this court has further said, 'that the law in the states shall be the same for the black as for the white, that all person's, whether colored or white, shall stand equal before the laws of the states.'"[19] Robert Bork takes another approach.

While the framers of the amendment may not have intended its reaching to segregated public institutions, the very fact that those institutions could not be made equal, but were persistently found to be unequal, would compel the weighing of two competing originalist claims. On the one hand, according to the amendment, citizens were clearly to be equal in their enjoyment of the privileges and immunities afforded by their particular states. Since both blacks and whites were now recognized as enjoying the status of citizens by virtue of their being Americans, that demand had to be honored with respect to all public and governmental bodies. If separate could not be made equal, the courts could not be required to entertain endless litigation over a system that was inherently unworkable. A number of cases involving college admissions had been decided on the grounds that the facilities provided black students were non-existent or substandard. At this point, the framers' goal of equal protection would have had to have been weighed against their lack of intention to undermine segregation. The judge would need to consider which claim was most consistent with a republican form of government and the spirit of both state and federal Constitutions. Under this reading, *Brown v. Board of Education* would have had an originalist basis for the same outcome.[20] But that was not how the court decided the case.

Instead, the Supreme Court dismissed any historical basis, including the history following *Plessy*, and moved rapidly to other grounds—to the damaging psychological and social consequences of segregation.[21] While it thus struck down segregation in law as inherently unequal, it opened a whole new world of interpretation that invited more than just litigation over equal access, but of the harmful subsequent consequences that presumably followed from prior discrimination. Rather than litigating equal access, the courts would now consider the harmful "segregative" effects emanating from past discrimination in law, and all that that might mean for equal protection. Cases would now be brought, not simply for an end to legal segregation, but would also encompass compulsory integration and levels of funding across district lines.

Equally Protecting What?

In what came to be called *Brown* II, the federal court ordered discrimination ended as expeditiously as possible, but left the means for accomplishing the task to the states and federal district courts to determine. The period following was noted for the many attempts to end segregation practices by the compulsory busing of students across school district lines. It was argued that this was especially necessary in areas of the south where the Court's ruling was being ignored.

The more controversial application of busing, however, came with its enforcement in places where legal segregation had either never occurred or had officially ended. In these school districts, white and black students predominated in certain schools simply because of their place of residence. Such forms of segregation were termed *de facto* segregation to distinguish them from legal or *de jure* segregation. While the supreme court only struck down the latter in *Brown* I, it's ruling in *Brown* II left the interpretation of the injurious consequences of past *de jure* segregation open to interpretation. If a school system that had once been segregated by law still showed signs of being segregated in fact, was that a continuation of the evil consequences of the older system? In other words, if *de facto* was simply the legacy of *de jure* segregation, it too might be unconstitutional deprivation of equal protection. The court weighed in on this in *Swann v. Charlotte-Mecklenburg Board of Education* in 1971, and found that this would indeed be a proper application of busing.[22]

But the issue became even more complicated. In *Brown* I, the Court argued that segregation was itself a badge or mark of social stigma, so why shouldn't *de facto* segregation be ended as well, even where it was not the legacy of legally enforced separation of the races? Indeed, the distinction between the two forms of segregation were blurred in *Keys v. School District Number 1* (1973) and *Columbus Board of Education v. Penick* (1979).[23] These cases extended the busing remedy to the North and West, and entailed the transporting of large numbers of children across major metropolitan areas such as Denver and Los Angles.

In an irony that is often overlooked, the purpose of ending discrimination in law was to provide greater educational opportunities to black students by ensuring equal access to state educational facilities. The legally segregated South had been for years dependent on the instrument of busing to maintain separation of the races, and this was one mark of its infringement on the right of parents to participate meaningfully in their children's education. But enforced integration had much the same consequence for parental liberty. It reduced the ability of parents, either black or white, to participate in the affairs of their local schools. School attendance became the business of the courts. As one commentator noted, "Busing has not only destroyed good schools, it has obliterated effective parental involvement. It has placed parents in the ridiculous predicament of having to request a 'special transfer' to have their children sent to a school around the corner!" [24]

By the mid 1990s, these policies became so unpopular that parents filed suit in Boston contending that race based attendance quotas in schools were themselves unconstitutional. School boards were besieged by complaints, and gradually most districts began to abandon the practice. In August of 1999, the Boston School Board announced that in 2000 it would cease using race as criteria for admissions.

Other districts followed, but this happened only gradually as the Supreme Court itself set some bounds to what it considered to be the line between *de jure* and *de facto* segregation, and the degree to which it would tolerate court interference within states over districting. This had its beginning as early as 1974 when the court ruled in *Milliken v. Bradley* that interfering with urban and rural school districts by the courts was only permissible in instances where *segregative effects* could be traced back to official state intent. Thus it held that "before the boundaries of separate and autonomous school districts may be set aside by consolidating the separate units for remedial purposes or by imposing a cross-district remedy, it must first be shown that there has been a constitutional violation within one district that produces a significant segregative effect in another district."[25]

As restrictive as that may sound, the decision left open the interpretation of what constituted a segregative effect. The complexity of these issues has resulted in the difficulty of assessing what the ramifications or consequences of segregation might be. Is the inequality inherent in segregated schools also manifested in differing levels of state funding among districts? When districts possessing a predominance of one race over another reveal greater or lesser affluence in the funding of schools, does that indicate discrimination in law? And does such inequality go beyond black and white? Does it embrace Hispanic, Native American, and other racial groups? And what about economic classes, not necessarily corresponding to any particular racial or ethnic divide?

The court was no closer to answering these questions when it completed the long run of cases in *Missouri v. Jenkins* in the early 90s. In the final case over the district court's order to raise teacher salaries in 1995, the Supreme court found that a District Court could not have unlimited power to reorganize or manage local school districts, but could only order such actions that served "as proper means to the end of restoring the victims of discriminatory conduct to the position they would have occupied absent that conduct."

The case originated in the eighteen year saga of a US District Court's orders respecting the desegregation of the Kansas City, Missouri School District (KCMSD). Over that time, the court had compelled the state to essentially convert the entire school district into a magnet school, because a number of the schools within the district were predominantly black. That had not been the case prior to legal segregation in 1953, so the court assumed that the resulting *de facto* segregation of whites to outlying districts was itself a symptom of the prior *de jure* segregation.

As noted by Justice Kennedy in the 1990 case over court ordered tax raises, that assumption was questioned by the state after expenditures exceeded an annual cost of some 200 million dollars to finance computers, air conditioning, a 2,000 square foot planetarium, Greenhouses and vivariums, a 25 acre farm with an air-conditioned room for 104 people, a model UN wired for language translation, broadcast capable radio and television studios, movie editing and screening rooms, a diesel mechanics shop, animal labs for zoo projects, swimming pools and other facilities.

On average, the state was compelled to allocate some 9,412 dollars per student in the KCMSD, or about four thousand more than neighboring districts. While the state found a sympathetic ear in the majority of the Supreme Court, both in 1990 with respect to taxes and 1995 on salaries, the case can afford little long-term comfort to the proponents of local control and parental liberty. In a series of various concurring and dissenting opinions, one gets a sense of the various judicial opinions in this area, and the tenuousness of each decision.

For Chief Justice Rehnquist the *Jenkins* case regarding salaries hinged on determining whether or not current conditions stemmed from prior legal discrimination and, additionally, if those conditions caused significant segregative effects outside the offending district. Only if this latter condition was met, could the district court order the state to raise the salaries of Kansas City Missouri School District teachers and staff for the purpose of reversing white flight or to attract white residents back to the district from outlying areas. He found the district courts reasoning unconvincing.

For Sandra Day O'Connor, it was a technicality that compelled her to concur with the Chief Justice. The district court apparently had admitted that it could not prove spill-over effects from past discriminatory policies to districts outside of the KCMSD. For the dissent, Justice Souter, speaking for justices Stevens, Breyer, and Ginsburg, contended that there should be wide latitude given to District Courts to correct past injustices so long as a plausible explanation of the facts of current circumstances link those circumstances to past *de jure* segregation.

Only for Justice Thomas was there clear recognition that segregation in law is impermissible, *but* voluntary segregation resulting from demographic change is not. He rejected clearly the sociological bases of past decisions, and argued that such reasoning was itself racist, assuming as it did that black children could not succeed without the presence of white children. Thomas then combined that rejection with a critique of the courts unwarranted and, therefore, unconstitutional application of equity powers. But his was only one voice. Given the opinions of the other members, where the verdict hinged on only the shade of a difference, it is not to be wondered that the district and state courts continue to be beset by endless cases on equal protection.

Any attorney the least bit capable of devising plausible grounds for implying a chain of consequences can have his day in court. The result has been financially devastating for states and ruinous for local parental participation in school districts.

In a bewildering set of cases throughout state and federal district courts these issues are being continually adjudicated. The four Edgewood Cases coming out of Texas give a sense of this complexity and the minutia into which courts are immersed to decide matters of equity in funding.[26] No doubt, the willingness of the courts to enter into such detailed remedies has proven to be a great boon to the exponents of government control and their litigious clientele. There is little that one can do to escape the reach of the courts. As Douglas S. Reed, a leading exponent of equalization along economic lines, has recently argued, courts should pursue the goal of funding equality within states precisely because parents will not be able to escape: "the exit option is less visible and less viable."[27] But he should also have added, less amenable to any final resolution.

While legal segregation was permanently ended, questions of funding equity and what constitutes the "vestiges" of past legal segregation, remain a case-by-case, judge-by-judge issue that feeds on both state and federal constitutional ambiguities. In each case, the outcome of these contests hinge on the uncertainty of multiple perspectives on the Supreme Court that may or may not coincide in any particular instance. One issue is for certain: If government continues in the business of education, any sort of inequality becomes a plausible matter of *de jure* discrimination and therefore actionable. If the court restrains itself today, it is only because it suffers itself to do so.

In *San Antonio School District v. Rodriguez* (1973), the Supreme Court meticulously sifted through financial data and social statistics to find evidence of *invidious discrimination* in funding levels. The decision is often regarded as one of retrenchment and restraint. State legislatures were pronounced to be the proper arena in which decisions about funding were to be decided, but the door was left open to entertain further litigation if such *invidiousness* could be found. The Edgewood cases decided by the Texas Supreme Court proved the point. As a result, the state of Texas was compelled to devise a system of funding that redistributed from wealthier to poorer districts in a complicated system dubbed "Robin Hood."[28] These sorts of cases span the entire country, removing local control over finance to the level of the entire state, or a district court.[29]

As society becomes inured to government institutions, compulsion takes on a more mundane every-day quality. At one time, the right to exit one association and enter into another was simply part of being free. Government changes the nature of association and as a consequence, contention over ends, of what is right or wrong, is inevitable. In a free society, some tolerance for bad and even immoral decisions on the part of individuals must be accepted. Total equalization is simply not a possibility along any conceivable line, but the endless litigation that the idea of equality invites is certainly not compatible with personal freedom and responsibility. The current legal trajectory has placed education and families in an imperiled environment of uncertainly. That uncertainty even reaches to the question of what should be taught.

Values, Content and Conflict

The idea of "incorporation," the judicial doctrine that the rights to be enjoyed by all citizens of the United States are those expressed in the Bill of Rights, took on tremendous force in the twentieth century.

Equal protection as it came to be understood through the adjudication of the Fourteenth Amendment simply means that whatever one's rights are, they should apply to all Americans equally. But the contest over what those rights are created an entirely new realm of litigation. Originally, the Fourteenth Amendment probably meant no more than that those rights enjoyed by Caucasian Americans in their respective states were to be enjoyed by the former slaves, now recognized as fully fledged citizens.[30] But in the early part of the twentieth century, the Supreme Court began to insist that the Bill of Rights itself be applied to the states as well. The Fourteenth Amendment thus reached much farther into the domain of the states than simply adjudication of equity in racial and funding issues. It has fostered an entirely new area not anticipated by the original framers of the Constitution: The twentieth century insistence on the disestablishment of religion *and* the enforcement of free exercise.

Ironically, what began as an attempt to make Catholic children good Protestants, has become a project for the secularization of public education. The federal courts, through an overlaying of judicial interpretation, now declare any mixing of faith and education to be suspect. But more than that, every variance from what someone might regard as strictly secular becomes actionable in the courts. Rather than asserting the values of some community, all values have now become suspect under the scrutiny of the judges. Teachers tread with fear to touch on any religious topic, even though crucial to the historical understanding of so much of American history and American institutions, because offence may be taken and suit brought in court. But the situation is still more complicated.

Any public institution, be it a school or town square, is a *public* place, and the First Amendment also protects freedom of belief and free exercise of religion. The courts struggle with this apparent conflict and the history of how certain basic rights became contradictory, within the same amendment, is the story of how the "public" in public schools became a playground for judicial activism.

The trend of incorporation began with a case unrelated to public education: *Gitlow v. New York* (1925) was based on the due process clause of the Fourteenth. There was little historical evidence to support the interpretation that the Fourteenth demanded the application of the First Amendment to the states, but that reading would be given ever greater impetus in the 1940s. In 1940, Justice Owen J. Roberts simply asserted in the decision in *Cantwell v. Connecticut*, that "The First Amendment declares that Congress shall make no law respecting an establishment of religion or prohibiting the free exercise thereof. The Fourteenth Amendment has rendered the legislatures of the states as incompetent as Congress to enact such laws."[31] With respect to church and state issues, this has remained the position of the federal courts.

Almost from the start, the assertion of incorporation has resulted in endless disputes about the extent to which schools may include religious themes in their classrooms, require the pledge of allegiance, have clergy to their official functions, or decide how far students may go in the expression of their religious beliefs.

Among the first cases concerned the question of free exercise. Jehovah's Witnesses complained early that the requirement of a pledge of allegiance violated their belief in the Biblical injunction against the taking of oaths. Initially the court found that a free society required "the binding tie of cohesive sentiment." Under such circumstance, Justice Frankfurter chose to respect the state legislature's powers to enact such law in *Minersville School District v. Gobitis* (1940). That changed just three years later when a new majority on the court contended that the constitutional liberty of the individual was to prevail. In *West Virginia State Board of Education v. Barnette* (1943) the Court argued that "We think the action of the local authorities in compelling the flag salute and pledge transcends constitutional limitations on their power and invades the sphere of intellect and spirit which it is the purpose of the First Amendment to our Constitution to reserve from all official control."[32] This sort of back and forth is not unusual. By the very nature of legal disputation, it is characteristic of judicial history in this area. Differences in rulings hinge on the nuances of each case.

Thus in 1947, in *Everson v. Board of Education*, the Supreme Court decided that reimbursement of transportation to parents for the cost of sending their children to Catholic schools by a New Jersey school board constituted a violation of the establishment clause. Only a complete separation of church and state seemed acceptable. This appeared to be confirmed in 1948 in *McCollum v. Board of Education* (1948), when the Court found that religious instruction cannot be provided in public schools, even if it is voluntary, with parental permission, *unfunded* by the public, and during a period of "released time." Almost the same situation, however, was deemed constitutional so long as the religious instruction occurred off the school premises in *Zorach v. Clauson* (1952).[33] By far the most controversial cases concerning establishment have been those involving school prayer.

Beginning with *Engel v. Vitale* (1962), the Court emphatically rejected the sponsoring of prayers in public schools. In 1985, it extended this ban to include state laws authorizing moments of silence for "meditation or voluntary prayer," and then further still to prohibit prayers by clergy at public high school graduation ceremonies in 1992. In each case, local communities supported these activities, many of which had been time honored practices. It was this growing trend to see establishment in the merest reflections of faith in public schools that led Congress to intervene with the Equal Access Act (1984). Two cases specifically in the early eighties—two federal appellate court decisions—had ruled that student groups with a religious purpose could not use public school facilities for their gatherings and remain in compliance with the Establishment Clause.[34]

In opposition to these decisions, the Equal Access Act required all public schools that allow student organizations, of whatever sort, to use their facilities during off hours, had to grant the same privilege to *all* student groups—regardless of their religious, political, or philosophical orientation. The Act was found constitutional by the Court, but the very fact that it was a result of Court actions in the first place, indicates the degree of popular discord with past rulings. Free exercise has come into tension with non-establishment. As Justice Thurgood Marshal noted in his concurring opinion in *Board of Education v. Mergens* (1990),

> This case involves the intersection of two First Amendment guarantees—the Free Speech Clause and the Establishment Clause. We have long regarded free and open debate over matters of controversy as necessary to the functioning of our constitutional system. That the Constitution requires toleration of speech over its suppression is not less true in our Nation's schools.
>
> But the Constitution also demands that the State not take action that has the primary effect of advancing religion. The introduction of religious speech in the public schools reveals the tension between these two constitutional commitments.[35]

The framers of the US Constitution and those who later ratified the Bill of Rights did not foresee such a tension. Liberty was not the source of conflict in a government of delegated powers where the First Amendment was clearly applied only to Congress, and where primary and secondary education was largely a local and private affair. Each state had its own constitution and each state was to manage education in its own way. Only now, with the conjoining of two political trends, centralized public administration at the state level, and incorporation doctrine at the level of the national judiciary, do we see two aspects of American liberty set against each other.

The non-establishment of religion was meant to prevent the domination of any faith or philosophy over all others. It was aimed at the sort of Church establishments common in Europe and was seen as a bulwark in the defense of the free exercise of religion by individuals in their personal and private spheres of civil association. That original conception has been gravely weakened in the present day.

By centralizing school administration and making nearly all of education public for the vast majority of individuals, the states created a battleground among citizens over fundamental values. We saw this development from the very start of the common school movement in New England. By incorporation of the First Amendment, the Courts nationalized this battlefield, and have forced a distant and even more removed authority on our schools, taking the administration of them even further out of the hands of parents. Where the problem began is where the focus of change must begin as well.

School Choice and the States

Ironies abound in the field of American primary and secondary education. Liberty collides with itself. The structure of the American Constitutional order, a structure originally conceived to defend basic liberties, necessarily mangles and complicates all attempts at nationalizing and centralizing. The U.S. Constitution is not the only legal text informing political action. It must share that role with the state constitutions.

When the idea of separate jurisdictions was more clearly understood, when the national government was one of delegated powers, the states retained what was not granted, and confusion over the rules applying to education was minimal. It was even less confused when the states themselves had little involvement with education directly, but maintained constitutions that were limited to basic rules and the protection of basic rights.

As the various governments of these many states began to expand their roles along with the federal government, contradictions abounded and conflict, demanding mediation, became the common stock of both state and federal courts. The state constitutions, in this brave new world of governments, are as much to blame as any particular organ of our political order.

Today, suits are brought not simply on the grounds of equal protection afforded by the national constitution, but by the states themselves. Each state, while similar in overall structure, has different language pertaining to the provision of equality before the law, and each has somewhat different language with respect to what is offered in the way of public schools. That in itself is not a bad thing. Choice among states is one of the leading protections afforded to freedom. Bad laws can be avoided by simply leaving one state for another. Unfortunately, most states have opted for greater centralization and management of their schools, and while some now explore the options for parental choice, such as vouchers, school tuition tax credits or deductions, and charter schools, they are meeting stiff opposition from interests dependent on government. From its very first inception, choice in the form of charter schools was challenged by teachers unions in Milwaukee, Wisconsin, and nearly every other form of program affirming parental liberty has been taken to court.[36]

School choice is the idea that parents ought to be free to choose the schools their children attend. This can take the form of a voucher program, with each voucher representing a portion of what the state takes in by way of taxes for the support of schools. Parents may utilize their voucher towards a school of their choosing. Tuition Tax Credit programs work much the same way, but allow parents to write the expense off their state taxes. The money thus stays with parents rather than filtering through the state. Charter schools provide for choice by bringing the element of local independent school management, characteristic of private schools, into the public sector. Each of these is designed to increase the liberty element once so central to American education.[37]

Among the regions currently employing vouchers in some limited fashion are Florida, Milwaukee in Wisconsin, Cleveland in Ohio, Utah, and Washington D.C. Most are limited to families in financial need. Those employing tuition tax credits tend to reach a broader swath of the population, and are currently being utilized in Arizona, Florida, and Pennsylvania. By far the most widely embraced program is that of charter schools, existing in some 40 states as of 2005 and Washington, D.C. Complications, however, arose early in all of these programs because many private schools are religious in orientation, and their acceptance of vouchers was quickly challenged on establishment grounds.[38]

In a landmark decision, the Supreme Court ruled in *Zelman v. Simmons-Harris* (2002) that so long as the parent's choice is truly voluntary, and no preference is given to any particular school by the state, religious or otherwise, the First Amendment is satisfied. It also reversed itself in other areas to permit direct assistance to students attending private institutions of a religious nature. But each of these instances depends on the current composition of the courts.[39]

Judicial tenure is a thin reed upon which to rest so important a freedom as choice in schools, and the opponents of parental liberty are far from giving up. Indeed, they are turning to the very source of the original problem: the states themselves and the state courts.

The Arena of the States

Suits continue to be adjudicated throughout the country on the whole range of issues with respect to funding. These will not go away until parents gain greater control over the purse strings of their respective states. Here particular school districts will face challenges for increased expenditures and courts will persist in micro managing these decisions.

One need only look at *Abbott v. Burke*, a case running from 1981 to 2003(!) in New Jersey to see this sort of technical, detailed intervention at work: A top-down managed school system, centralized by the state's constitutional obligation to provide public education, is asserted to produce inequities that can only be addressed by a judge. The story is often accepted as a matter of course. Many of the issues involved, however, could have been effectively addressed by introducing some form of parental choice in schools. The idea is not so complicated but tragically many continue to think along top-heavy centralized lines of reasoning, and apparently the New Jersey Education Association is determined they continue to do just that, asserting that a debate on choice would only "waste time." The increased funding promised by the Courts in *Abbott,* will supposedly obviate the need for parental freedom. Already outlying districts feel otherwise, and the battle over funding will rage on.[40]

Far more ominous is the very recent decision in Florida, *Bush v. Holmes* (2006). The court found Florida's voucher program to be in violation of the state's constitutional provision demanding that the state provide "by law for a uniform, efficient, safe secure, and high quality system of free public schools. . ."[41] Since vouchers could be used to purchase education at many different institutions with differing approaches to child education, the court found the system to be anything "but 'uniform' when compared with each other or the public system." In other words, the Supreme Court of Florida has interpreted the uniformity clause to say that one size must fit all. There can be no variation among schools in the mode or delivery of education. What is ominous is the legal grounding given to the opponents of school choice because large numbers of states have very similar language from Indiana to Arizona. According to a Heartland Institute assessment of the Florida decision, some thirteen states currently have uniformity language similar to that of Florida.

Uniformity provisions were originally crafted as early as 1851 when Indiana rewrote its state constitution. It was the product of the same middle nineteenth century reform movements that brought into being the public school systems generally. Originally "uniformity" was meant to ensure that there would be *a system* of education provided *throughout* the territory of each state. It was *not* a prescription for how or what to teach, but an attempt to assure that some form of education would be available. More amazing is the fact that the Florida case was not even brought on uniformity grounds, but on a First Amendment establishment basis. Apparently realizing that such a case would no longer hold with the current Supreme Court in light of *Zelman*, the Florida court, on its own, chose to invoke the uniformity clause of the State's constitution. In effect, the judges opted to reformulate the case against vouchers on behalf of the plaintiffs! Such an act of judicial fiat points to the difficulty of placing too much faith in the rule of men, even if they happen to be judges.

In a recent response to the Florida ruling, Professor Epstein noted that the case "illustrates the danger of adopting hortatory constitutional provisions that promise particular levels of state services as opposed to the allocation of powers and responsibilities that are the traditional fare of most constitutions."[42] Clearly the Supreme Court of Florida was not required to read the state's constitution in the manner that it did, but that makes the essential argument of this paper: Judicial occupancy should not be the guarantee upon which we base the security of our freedoms. The more language regarding education in a constitution, the more there is to interpret, and the greater the likelihood a judge will exercise personal discretion in the determination of the law.

Conclusion: Free Our Children

If the ability to take back a fundamental freedom is hobbled by the very instruments intended to protect that freedom, the focus of discussion should be on correcting the instruments.

The peoples of the various states in the federal union need to examine their constitutional provisions carefully and determine if educational choice is worth protecting. This can be done by explicitly declaring parental liberty as guaranteed, or perhaps by simply replacing current provisions that "promise particular levels of service," with more general language assuring simply that the state will *assist* in primary and secondary education. To adapt what Jefferson wrote to J.C. Cabell to the education clauses of our current constitutions seems particularly apt: "by all means strike out this provision. . ." Barring that, the current state of education can be expected to persist, subject to judicial intervention and prompted by endless disputes respecting fundamentally different values in society.

Not all parents want their children to pray. Not all parents want their children to be prohibited from prayer. Some parents wish their children to be taught the values of particular faiths, but not those of other faiths, and some wish to be spared the teachings of any faith at all. These are not easily negotiated differences, but once a system is public, each difference becomes actionable and the decision will then be made, not by those involved in the education of their children, but by a judge. There will be losers and winners, and the social rifts will not lesson, but become more divisive with each contest.

In the area of equal protection and funding, choice in schools makes particular sense. If the state simply divides the receipts of taxes, or gives tuition tax credits to those who pay taxes with assistance to those who cannot, every one stands to gain. The funds collected will go to each student in equal shares to be expended in a real educational market. Flexibility, and the assurance that only markets can provide respecting the quality of every other good and service available in the economy, will assure that the needs of families are met. No complicated adjudication of state budgets would be necessary and the power to determine local school policies would remain where it belongs: the parents and the schools themselves.

ENDNOTES

1. Jefferson to J.C. Cabell, February 2, 1816, in Merrill Peterson, ed., *Jefferson, Writings*, (New York, The Library of America; 1984), pp. 1379–1380.

2. James Mulhern, *A History of Education*, (New York, The Ronald Press; 1946), pp. 279, 468–473.

3. Andrew J. Coulson, *Market Education* (New Brunswick, Transaction Publishers; 1999), 78–82; Richard D. Brown, *The Strength of A People, The Idea of an Informed Citizenry in America, 1650–1870* (Chapel Hill, University of North Carolina Press; 1996), pp. 139; Ronald G. Walters, *American Reformers 1815–1860* (New York, Hill and Wang; 1978), pp. 207–208.

4. Myron Lieberman, *Public Education: An Autopsy* (Cambridge, Massachusetts, Harvard University Press; 1993), p.14–16; Coulsen, p. 80.

5. Horace Mann, "Report of the Massachusetts Board of Education," in Daniel J. Boorstin, ed., *An American Primer* (New York, Meridian; 1966), p. 371.

6. *Ibid.*, p. 372.

7. Indiana State Constitution, Article VIII, section 1 at http://www.in.gov/legislative/ic/code/const/art8.html. For Indiana state constitutional history see William P. McLauchlan, *The Indiana State Constitution: A Reference Guide* (Westport, Connecticut, Greenwood Publishing Group; 1996), pp. 1–14, 15–16; 127–132.

8. For an excellent discussion of the conflict over Mann's program see Coulsen, *Market Education*, pp. 81–85. For a good discussion of the prevailing attitudes towards race and education at the time, see Brown, *The Strength of A People*, pp. 170–183.

9. Bernard Bailyn, *Education in the Forming of American Society* (New York, WW Norton & Co.; 1960), p. 11.

10. See http://brownvboard.org/research/handbook/prelude/prelude.htm#roberts. See also, Coulsen, pp. 75–78.

11. *Ibid.*

12. *Sarah C. Roberts v. The City of Boston*, 59 Mass. 198, 5 Cush. 198 (November Term, 1848) at 203.

13. On the contest of Whigs and Democrats see McLauchlan, pp. 7–10. See also Emma Lou Thornbrough, *Indiana in the Civil War Era 1850–1880* (Indianapolis, Indiana Historical Society; 1965), pp. 461–534.

14. Richard A. Epstein, *How the Progressives Rewrote the Constitution* (Washington DC, CATO Institute; 2006), pp. 19–35

15. *Ibid.*, 16.

16. *Plessey v. Ferguson*, 163 US 537 (1896); Taunya Lovvell Banks, "Plessy v. Ferguson," in Joseph R. Marbach, Ellis Katz, Troy E. Smith, ed., *Federalism in America: An Encyclopedia*, vol. 2 (Westport, Connecticut, Greenwood Press; 2006), p. 479–481.

17. Richard A. Epstein, *Forbidden Grounds: The Case Against Employment Discrimination Laws* (Cambridge, Massachusetts, Harvard University Press; 1992), pp. 103–108.

18. Raoul Berger, *Government By Judiciary: The Transformation of the Fourteenth Amendment* (Indianapolis, Liberty Fund, Inc.; 1997), pp. 201–207.

19. Justice Harlan's dissent in *Plessey v. Ferguson*, 163 US 537 (1896) at http://www.bgsu.edu/departments/acs/1890s/plessy/dissent.html

20. Robert H. Bork, *The Tempting of America: The Political Seduction of the Law* (New York, The Free Press; 1990), pp. 82–83.

21. Norman Redlich, John Attanasio, Joel K. Goldstein, *Understanding Constitutional Law*, 3rd ed., (Newark, New Jersey, Lexus Nexus; 2004), pp. 365.

22. Kenneth L. Karst, "School Busing," in Philip Weinberg, ed., *The Supreme Court: Selections from the Four Volume Encyclopedia of the American Constitution and Supplement* (New York, Macmillan Library Reference USA; 1999), 687–689.

23. *Ibid.*, p. 688.

24. See Genevieve Mitchell, "The Busing Nightmare Continues," *Issues and Views* (Spring 1996) at http://www.issues-views.com/index.php/sect/1003/article/1046.

25. See *Milliken v. Bradley*, 418 U.S. 717 at http://www.law.cornell.edu/supct/html/historics/USSC_CR_0418_0717_ZS.html.

26. For a review of the four Edgewood cases see, Sharon Hope Weintraub, "School Days and Legal Maze: Constitutional Challenges to Public School Finances in Texas;" Senate Research Center, September 2003 online at Http://www.senate.state.tx.us/SRC/pdf/School_Days2.pdf

27. Douglas S. Reed, *On Equal Terms: The Constitutional Politics of Equal Opportunity* (Princeton; Princeton University Press, 2001), 45.

28. See http://www.texasinsider.org/election_watch/Opinion_Bill_Keffer_12_12_2005_School_Ruling.htm.

29. See for example *Montoy v. State of Kansas;* http://www.kscourts.org/kscases/supct/2005/20050103/92032.htm; or Kenneth Karst, "California Serrano v Priest's Inputs and Outputs," *Law and Contemporary Problems*, Vol. 38, No. 3, *Future Directions for School Finance Reform (Winter-Spring, 1974), pp 333–349;* or *Idaho School for Equal Opportunity v. Evans.* At http://www2.state.id.us/fourthjudicial/Districe%20Judge%20Docs/iseeo%20permissive.pdf

30. Berger, *Government by Judiciary*, p. 65.

31. Terry Eastland, ed., *Religious Liberty in the Supreme Court: The Cases That Define the Debate over Church and State* (Washington DC, Ethics and Policy Center; 1993), p. 17

32. *Ibid.*, pp. 25–26; 39–47

33. Norman Redlich, John Attanasio, Joel K. Goldstein, *Understanding Constitutional Law*, 3rd ed., (Newark, New Jersey, Lexus Nexus; 2004), pp. 690–694.

34. Eastland, *Religious Liberty*, pp. 125–136; 333–364; 439–465.

35. *Ibid.*, p. 430

36. See http://www.ij.org/schoolchoice/milwaukee/index.html

37. Among the best discussions of the various possible reforms to restore parental choice is Coulsen, *Market Education*, pp. 293–321; 323–365.

38. For a general overview of school choice programs currently operating see: http://www.allianceforschoolchoice.org/. For the challenge on establishment grounds see, http://www.ij.org/schoolchoice/florida/index.html.

39. *Zelmann v. Simmons Harris*, 536 U.S. 639 (2002) 234 F.3d 945, reversed. For a review of *Zelman* see http://www.ij.org/schoolchoice/ohio_ussc/index.html.

40. Edith A. Fulton, "A Voucher Battle Will Only Waste Time," *Star Ledger*, November 8, 2003. See also New Jersey Education Association website at, http://www.njea.org/PressRoom/oped_110803.asp. See also The Editorial, "Hold the Abbots Accountable," *The Times*, New Jersey, April 18, 2006.

41. *Bush v. Holmes*, Supreme Court of Florida, No. SCO4-2323 (2006). For complete opinion see: http://www.ij.org/schoolchoice/florida/index.html.

42. http://hispanicpundit.com/2006/01/24/richard-epstein-on-florida-vouchers-ruling/.

Eight
The Judicial Assault on Higher Education
by Dane Starbuck

Introduction

Higher education in the United States, much like business, has experienced a tremendous explosion of governmental regulatory control in the past several decades and the courts have been willing accomplices to this fact. What is interesting is that higher education's formative years were not significantly influenced by central government authority. Many of our nation's founders, including Presidents Washington, Adams, Jefferson, and Madison, proposed that a *national university* be established, but the idea never caught on, presumably out of fear that the graduates of such an institution would dominate civic values and affairs.[1]

Alexis de Tocqueville, the great French social commentator on early American life, observed that centralization of government was not a factor of the new nation. He wrote in *Democracy in America*:

> In the American republics the central government has never as yet busied itself except with a small number of objects sufficiently prominent to attract its attention. It has not tried to regulate the secondary affairs of society. There is no sign that it has even conceived the desire to do so. . . .[2]

With specific regard to public education, de Tocqueville observed:

> . . . [A]ny one is free to found a public school and to direct it as he pleases. It's an industry like other industries, the *consumers* being the judges and the state taking no hand whatever. . . . You ask me if this unlimited liberty produces bad results. I believe it produces only good.[3]

Contrary to de Tocqueville's appraisal, the role of *colonial* and *state* government in the early history of higher education in the United States is a mixed bag. On the one hand, colleges and universities established in the original 13 colonies, almost all private, enjoyed special privileges of taxpayer support and a virtual monopoly by virtue of the colonies' willingness to grant limited corporate charters.[4] Later, after the formation of the nation, 21 new states were admitted to the union before the Civil War, almost all of which were recipients of land grants by Congress to establish state universities. In total, the amount of land granted by Congress, in addition to the 17,430,000 acres given to the states under the Morrill Act of 1862, resulted in the contribution of approximately 30,000 square miles of federal lands (about the size of South Carolina) for the establishment of public institutions of higher education.[5] Thus, in the formation of our nation's early colleges and universities, government played an extremely important if narrow role.

But on the other hand, de Tocqueville was correct. Hundreds of schools and colleges, many with but a handful of students and a single teacher or professor, were established throughout the young nation with little government involvement. Prior to the Revolutionary War, 12 colleges existed in the United States; by the time of the Civil War, 262 had been formed and 182 of these survived into the twentieth century. Many, if not most, of these institutions had a religious denominational affiliation or were supported by civic minded benefactors who wanted their towns to prosper and who saw the establishment of a college to be one means of achieving community prestige and economic growth.[6]

But if the role of the federal government in higher education was extremely limited in the first 150 years of our nation's existence, it has exploded in the past 80 years. It has done so in a circuitous way that perhaps no one could have anticipated and a way in which the courts have played a critical, if little recognized, part. In 1935, there were 1,450 institutions of higher education in the United States. Fifty years later, in 1985, there were 3,301 institutions of higher education. In 1935 universities did about 20 percent of all research in the United States; in 1985, universities performed 33 percent of all research in the country.[7]

But the true telling part about the federal government's growing influence in higher education is what follows: In 1935 private foundation support for research in universities was 1.5 times greater than federal governmental support. By 1985, a complete reversal had taken place with the federal government funding of academic research dwarfing that of private foundations by a ratio of 9 to 1. Further striking is where federal research funding was going: 90% to the physical sciences; 5% to the social sciences; and 5% to the humanities.[8] In addition, federal government support in the form of student aid has grown at a perilous rate: in 1958, Congress passed the National Defense Student Loan (NDSL) program, which appropriated $31 million to 24,831 students with loans averaging $383. By 1990, student aid had grown 32,097 percent, to $9.95 billion providing grants to more than 9.0 million students.[9] One study concluded that in 2002 university students at American schools received more than $40 billion worth of grants from federal and state governments and universities in addition to government backed loans.[10] Another study found that the total taxpayer support of higher education in 2002 was approximately $66 billion.[11]

What is striking about the tremendous increase in federal financial support of higher education through research grants and student aid funding is the inevitable and corresponding governmental control. This control has taken the form of legislation and regulations, government action that the courts have been all too willing to sanction. It is an intriguing situation that deserves closer scrutiny.[12]

Growing Federal Control and the Role of the Courts

In recent decades, educational establishments have been far from alone as the targets of the tremendous onslaught of federal regulations and oversight. Nearly every aspect of American life and culture in post World War II times has experienced the exponential growth and cost of federal bureaucracies. But colleges and universities are especially ripe for regulation due to the nature of their enterprise. Nearly 30 years ago then Secretary of the U.S. Department of Health and Human Services, Joseph A. Califano, Jr., spoke out about the "domination of education by the federal government." Ironically, it was at the very time the Administration he served under (the Carter Administration) was creating a new and separate Department of Education. Eighteen months into his position, Secretary Califano proclaimed,

> If I have seen anything made plain in the last year and a half, it is that when programs and dollars multiply, bureaucracies and regulations multiply also; paperwork and reporting requirements multiply; the temptation to interfere, however well meaning, grows. And thus the danger grows that the job we are trying to do with our programs will, ironically, be made even more difficult by the unwieldy requirements and burdensome procedures that these programs bring.[13]

Other commentators have been quick to point out just how vulnerable colleges and universities are to federal government influence by the nature of their constituencies and dependency upon financial support. Paul Seabury, former Professor of Political Science at the University of California at Berkeley, noted this in 1979:

> Federal administrators appear to regard the university as one sector on the battle line of a federal war against every conceivable social problem. As Clark Kerr (former Chancellor and President of the University of California at Berkeley) has said, the American university is now a public utility. It also has become a national social laboratory.[14]

But just 30 years before, in 1949, former president of Harvard University, James Bryant Conant, dismissed concern about federal influence of higher education by virtue of federal subsidies. Conant adamantly disagreed with those who opposed federal aid because it would lead to increased federal control. This attitude, he wrote,

> ... fails to appreciate the real need [for federal assistance], and on the other is too defeatist about the nature of our democracy. Granted a sufficient number of wide-awake citizens with a national interest in public education to act as watch dogs on Congress, we need not be too apprehensive about educational bureaucracies or centralized control.[15]

The federal government's efforts in the 1960s to expand the notion of equality among the races far exceeded its support of the Civil Rights movement. In the area of education, the Higher Education Act of 1965 was passed and at least one of its primary goals was to promote its drafters' views of social justice through access to education. U.S. Senator Daniel Patrick Moynihan, who had played an important role in crafting educational policy at this time, wrote in reference to the Higher Education Act of 1965:

> Once again higher education policy was deployed by the national government to serve external political needs, in this case to press further to fill out a central theme of the Kennedy and Johnson administration[s]—that of equality. Higher education was a means of obtaining goals elsewhere in the political system.[16]

This staggering trend begs the question as to what role the courts—the least analyzed branch with regard to influencing education policies—have played in supporting the expansion of governmental intrusion into higher education on the one hand and in projecting their own policy views on higher education on the other. An analysis of the courts' role in the arena of higher education is fraught with challenges given that there is such a wide diversity of thought about the role of higher education itself in society and who should have input into shaping that role. Colleges and universities, just as in business, government, and labor, have many factions wrangling for influence and control. From time to time interest groups such as students, alumni, trustees, donors, faculty, administrators, regulatory and accrediting bodies, taxpayers, state legislatures, and Congress all play a part in shaping matters dealing with higher education policy. Not least of these groups have been state and federal courts. Their growing involvement is quite evident since the landmark decision handed down in *Brown v. Board of Education* in 1956.[17]

Furthermore, in the past fifty years the roles that higher education have assumed have grown substantially, expanding into areas that have little to do with the traditional student classroom learning experience. For many colleges and universities, the attention and support of high profile and often lucrative athletic programs, collective bargaining agreements with faculty, real estate and economic development initiatives, social and entertainment engagements, study abroad programs, and basic and applied research have become as much as a priority, or more so, than the training of students' minds. No doubt the courts have and will continue to find themselves confronted with challenging issues in these areas. One such example that has already caught the courts' attention is the constitutionality of Title IX, giving women equal access to college athletic opportunities through scholarships in NCAA Division I schools.[18]

Admissions to Higher Education and the Courts

The landmark Supreme Court decision of *Gratz and Hamacher v. Bollinger*[19] is a very recent example of the Court's willingness to intervene in matters of higher education policy. The admission of students to highly competitive colleges and universities has long been a process shielded from outside scrutiny. For the freshman class entering Harvard College in the fall of 2006, more than 23,000 high school students vied for 1,650 openings. Nearly as strong of competition exists for hundreds of top private and public colleges and universities throughout the United States. How precisely students are selected is not always disclosed, but a multitude of factors are likely. Unlike Japan or most European countries where admissions to select schools is based solely on school or national test scores, in the United States most institutions of higher education take a much broader approach. In addition to standardize test scores such as the Scholastic Aptitude Test (SAT), admissions officials often take into account a student's grades, the competitiveness of the student's high school, extracurricular activities, possible writing samples, geography, whether the applicant is a relative of an alumnus, and outstanding leadership or personal talents or skills. Indeed, one of the benefits of the *Gratz* decision was a fuller disclosure of this process.[20]

An area that the courts have all been too willing to intervene is admission decisions where race or ethnicity is an issue. In *Gratz*, Jennifer Gratz and Patrick Hamacher were residents of the State of Michigan, Caucasian, and both had applied for admission to the University of Michigan's College of Literature, Science, and the Arts in 1995 and 1997, respectively. Both were denied admission although they were within the qualified range of applicants. The university had instituted a policy of automatically awarding 20 points to applicants from underrepresented racial or ethnic minority groups such as African-American, Hispanics, and native American Indians. The maximum number of points that a student could receive was 150 and generally those who received 100 or more were admitted. Up to five points could be awarded to a student that displayed extraordinary talent.

Gratz and Hamacher sought, among other things, declaratory relief finding that the University had violated their rights to nondiscriminatory treatment and injunctive relief enjoining the university from continuing to use its race-conscious freshmen admissions policy. The petitioners filed the class action alleging that the University of Michigan's use of racial preferences violated the Equal Protection Clause of the Fourteenth Amendment, Title VI of the Civil Rights Act of 1964 and 42 USC Sec. 1981.

The case of *Gratz* was a lightning rod. More than 100 colleges and universities filed *amicus curiae* briefs, mostly in support of allowing colleges and universities to use race as part of their admissions policy. As the argument went, centuries of discrimination against certain minority groups had resulted in members of these groups failing to have an opportunity to participate in mainstream society. Admission to colleges and universities was one such way to try and correct the age-old practice. Furthermore, advocates of race-based admission policies argued that having a diverse student population was good both for majority and minority student populations. Michigan attempted to use this latter argument to fulfill the holding in *Regents of the University of California v. Bakke*[21]. As the President of the University of Michigan wrote in a law review article shortly after he left his position, the *Bakke* decision didn't sufficiently address the problem:

> The difficulty this posed [justifying the consideration of race solely on the basis of creating a diverse student body] for higher education was essentially that no one really believed that the past could or should be ignored or that the present society is by any means free of discrimination. Race and ethnicity in American life, past and present, were and continue to be defining forces of who we are and what we need to do, including how we compose the student populations at our leading educational institutions.[22]

In *Gratz* the Court found that the University's use of race was not sufficiently narrow to achieve its asserted interest and goal in diversity. In its finding, it held that the University's policy of automatically awarding each underrepresented minority applicant 20 points did not fulfill the holding in *Bakke* because it did not take into account individual characteristics in awarding the points, merely the race or ethnicity of applicants per se. The Court further found fault with this assessment when it considered that a student exhibiting "extraordinary talent" received only five points towards the total needed for admissions.[23]

Much of the Court's holding in *Gratz* was based upon the decision in *Bakke*, a landmark case that had been decided 25 years before and which is still the reference point for admission cases involving race in higher education. In *Bakke*, the facts are important. In 1968 the University of California at Davis opened its medical school and admitted 50 students to its first class. In the first year, only three Asian students enrolled and no African-American, Hispanic, or native American Indian students were admitted. In the next year, a special admissions program was devised to accept disadvantaged or minority students and eight slots were reserved for members of these populations. In 1971, the class size was enlarged to 100 students and the faculty voted to double the number of slots for selected minorities. In 1973, the Davis Medical School received 2,464 applications for the 100 entering positions. In 1974, the medical school received 3,737 applications. Allan Bakke, a Caucasian California resident applied in both 1973 and 1974 but was denied admission in each year. In both years applicants to the special admissions program were admitted with grade point averages, MCAT scores, and benchmark scores significantly lower than Bakke's. Bakke brought an action against the University of California alleging discrimination on the basis that the special admissions program violated the Equal Protection Clause of the Fourteenth Amendment and Sec. 601 of Title VI of the Civil Rights Act of 1964.

Justice Powell wrote the majority opinion for the Court. In brief, the majority opinion held that the special admissions program amounted to a quota system and violated Bakke's equal protection rights. The Court held that while the medical school could consider race as a factor for the purposes of creating a diverse class, it could not reserve a specific number of slots for members of minority or disadvantaged populations. The University of California had shown a disregard for individual rights as guaranteed by the Fourteenth Amendment and failed to demonstrate that the special admissions program furthered a substantial state interest.[24]

Justice Thurgood Marshall wrote in a separate dissenting opinion. He argued that rectifying centuries of discrimination against African-Americans and attempting to bring them into the mainstream of American life should be of the highest state interest. Further, he argued that neither the history of the Fourteenth Amendment nor past Supreme Court decisions precluded a university from working to remedy past discrimination by increasing the number of African-American doctors. Thus, he found that the special admissions program should not be held unconstitutional.[25]

The rulings in *Bakke* and *Gratz* are examples of where the Court has intervened using the concept of equal protection to formulate higher education policy. It has justified its encroachments by reading the Fourteenth Amendment so broadly that it begs the question as to what degree the Court is willing to adopt to impose its views on how a college or university may benefit a particular class or group. It held that since the University of California and the University of Michigan accept federal assistance, the equal protection clause applies.

By analogy, if General Electric (GE) adopts a policy to reserve a certain percentage of new hires for a designated race (e.g., African-American or Hispanic), will the Court strike it down because GE may have received a federal government contract at some point? Would the Court only accept the policy if it furthered diversity within the workforce, not if GE chose to do it out of some sense of social justice to try and lift the living standards and opportunities for underrepresented, minority populations and even if this was disclosed to share holders and approved? That is the reading one finds when reviewing the Court's broad interpretation of the equal protection amendment and Section 601 of Title VI regarding race based admissions cases. There are very few colleges or universities that do not receive federal assistance of some kind.[26] As Justice Marshall wrote in *Bakke*, the Court had long ago, in interpreting the post Civil War amendments, found that "in any fair and just construction of any section or phrase of these [Civil War] amendments, it is necessary to look to the purpose which we have said was the pervading spirit of them all, the evil which they were designed to remed...." (citing *Slaughter-House Cases*, 16 Wall., 72).

Justice Marshall went onto to write:

> It is plain that the Fourteenth Amendment was not intended to prohibit measures designed to remedy the effects of the Nation's past treatment of Negroes. The Congress that passed the Fourteenth Amendment is the same Congress that passed the 1866 Freedmen's Bureau Act, an Act that provided many of its benefits only to Negroes.[27]
>
> ... [I]t is inconceivable that the Fourteen Amendment was intended to prohibit all race conscious relief measures. It "would be a distortion of the policy manifested in that amendment which was adopted to prevent state legislation designed to perpetuate discrimination on the basis of race or color" (omit-

ting cite), to hold that it barred state action to remedy the effects of that discrimination. Such a result would pervert the intent of the Framers by substituting abstract equality for the genuine equality the Amendment was intended to achieve."[28]

In a dissenting opinion, Justice Harry Blackmun wrote in *Bakke* that programs "of admissions to institutions of higher learning are basically a responsibility for academicians and for administrators and the specialists they employ. The judiciary, in contrast, is ill-equipped and poorly train for this."[29] He found it ironic that colleges and universities discriminate all the time by awarding admission to children of alumni or whose parents may be able to bestow huge gifts to the institution or those having "connections with celebrities, the famous, and the powerful;" yet the University of California at Davis couldn't be open about trying to assist certain minorities to become doctors.[30]

In a dissenting opinion in *Gratz*, Justice Ruth Bader Ginsberg's reasoning for sanctioning the affirmative action admissions policy at the University of Michigan was quite similar to that of Justice Blackmun's in *Bakke*.

> ... Without recourse to such plans, institutions of higher education may resort to camouflage. For example, schools may encourage applicants to write of their cultural traditions in the essays they submit, or to indicate whether English is their second language. ... If honesty is the best policy, surely Michigan's accurately described, fully disclosed College affirmative action program is preferable to achieving similar numbers through winks, nods, and disguises.[31]

The Court's rulings in *Bakke* and *Gratz* are two extremely well known cases, but there are many others in which the Court has insisted in foisting its own policy preferences in the area of higher education.[32] What the Justices have done in these rulings is substituted their own views and, as Justice Blackmun wrote in *Bakke*, denied the policy making decisions by academicians, administrators, and specialists, all of whom are answerable to the university's governing body and would have a better understanding of their respective institution's missions and goals.

The fact is the controversy in *Gratz* is an excellent case in point of how the democratic process can play out. As the named defendant in the case, Michigan President Lee Bollinger took the opportunity to explain in a very public way why the University decided to adopt the race based admission policy. Even 50 years after the *Brown v. Board of Education* decision, educational integration in Michigan (and also true to a lesser or greater degree nationwide) had failed. As Bollinger wrote:

> Few people might know that the majority of students who come to many of our nation's schools, such as Michigan, come from high schools that are virtually all white or all black. ... That metropolitan Detroit is more segregated today [in 2003] than in 1960 is not a pleasant reality to face, and many of us don't.[33]

Bollinger made dozens of visits to editorial boards of newspapers; he solicited and received the support of well known figures such as former President Gerald

Ford and Harry Pearce, Vice Chair of General Motors. President Ford wrote a powerful Op-Ed column in the *New York Times* and Pearce got General Motors to file an *amicus* brief in support of the University's admission policy. Other corporate leaders came to the aid of the University in discussing the need for higher-education policies that took race and diversity into account. The combined efforts showed how the democratic process can play out if those who are the rightful decision-makers are allowed to operate without the intrusion of the courts.[34]

In the case of the *United States v. Commonwealth of Virginia*,[35] the United States Attorney's Office brought suit against Virginia on grounds that it was illegally denying women an opportunity to receive a military education. This was because, argued the federal government, Virginia Military Institute (VMI) was the only tertiary military college in Virginia and it only admitted men. The United States claimed in this action that the only remedy which complied with the requirements of the equal protection clause was for women to be admitted to VMI under the same conditions as men. But the Fourth Circuit allowed VMI to remain an all male institution so long as Virginia established a comparable school for women.

Notwithstanding the U.S. Government's claim, the Fourth Circuit allowed "separate but equal" institutions for men and women so long as Virginia could demonstrate that it had formulated, adopted, and implemented a plan that conformed to the principles of equal protection. Even though the court allowed VMI to remain single-sex, it required an extraordinary detailed plan by Virginia to show how it would comply with the Court's order. As a result, a lower district court was given ongoing jurisdiction and control in reviewing, approving, and monitoring nearly every aspect of the creation and operation of the new "Virginia Women's Institute for Leadership" at Mary Baldwin College (MBI).

The case is an excellent example of how the courts have justified making policy decisions by using the doctrine of equal protection.[36] Furthermore, it is an instance of the courts intervening in an area that was not necessary. If it was true that there was a large number of women who wanted to have the experience of being trained as a "civilian soldier" similar to what men experienced at VMI, then it is highly likely that such a program could have been created at Mary Baldwin College or at another female or coed college through market or political pressures. The playing out of market and/or political forces would have eliminated the need for the Court's intervention and most certainly would not have required the detailed plan mandated by the Fourth Circuit. There is no evidence that this was attempted. The federal district court and court of appeals were only too willing to assume the power of approving and monitoring with incredible detail how a female student military education experience would work.

"Academic Freedom," "Tenure" and Intervention by the Courts

The discussion of the role of education in society goes at least as far back as the ancient Greek philosophers. In Plato's *The Republic*, he states it is the goal of education to train the young by conveying to them the right stories as decided by those who are knowledgeable in society.[37] The modern courts have usurped the prerogative of local control about what is to be taught through many decisions. It has done this blatantly in decisions expanding the notion of "academic freedom."

The concept of "academic freedom" can be traced back to nineteenth century ideals contained in German thought and adopted in the United States as early as 1915 by the American Association of University Professors (AAUP). According to a Declaration of Principles adopted by the AAUP in that year, "freedom of inquiry and research; freedom of teaching within the university or college; and freedom of extramural utterance and action" required that university professors have broad discretion in disseminating research and opinions. It concluded that these ideals could not be furthered if the actions of professors were left to the review and direction of untrained and self-interested boards of trustees.[38]

> . . . For that reason, the Declaration provided for a norm of self-governance achieved by peer review and a norm of insulation for professors provided by a system of tenure. It characterized faculty members as "appointees" rather than "hired hands" and painted the relationship between the boards and the faculty as analogous to the relationship between the executive branch and appointed federal judges. According to the Declaration, if a university wished to be designated as a "true" university deserving of public support, it must have vowed to protect faculty freedom in this way and to maintain a stance of institutional neutrality.[39]

One of the most widely cited definitions of academic freedom is contained in the 1930 edition of the *Encyclopedia of Social Sciences* attributed to philosopher Arthur Lovejoy:

> Academic freedom is the freedom of the teacher or research worker in higher institutions of learning to investigate and discuss problems of his science and to express his conclusions whether through publication or in the instruction of students, without interference from political or ecclesiastical authority, or from the administrative officials of the institution in which he is employed, unless his methods are found by *qualified bodies of his own profession* to be clearly incompetent or contrary to professional ethics. (emphasis added)[40]

Thus, the original notion of academic freedom was not grounded in any constitutional or natural rights theory, but originated from a code or declaration birthed by the very group that benefits most from its adoption—university professors. But over time, the U.S. Supreme Court and lower courts have been only too willing to embrace the concept. The early adopters regarded academic freedom as an established right and later based the notion on First Amendment freedom of expression. One of the first to do this was Justice William O. Douglas, who, in a dissenting opinion in *Adler v. Board of Education of City of New York*[41], wrote, "What happens under this law is typical of what happens in a police state. . . . A pall is cast over the classrooms. There can be no real academic freedom in that environment. . . . The Framers knew the danger of dogmatism. . . We forget these teachings of the First Amendment when we sustain this law."[42]

In *Adler* the majority of the Supreme Court upheld the Feinberg Law, which allowed the City of New York to dismiss a teacher who belonged to a communist organization; nonetheless, Justice Douglas's dissenting opinion opened the door for the protection of academic freedom under the First Amendment. In *Wieman v. Updegraff*[43] the majority of the court invalidated a statute that required public employees to undertake loyalty oaths. Justice Felix Frankfurter noted that by applying the law to teachers, it went against the First and Fourteenth Amendments because a loyalty oath would "chill that free play of the spirit [of unfettered speech] which all teachers ought especially to cultivate and practice."[44]

This decision and several that followed clearly brought the concept of academic freedom under the protection of the First Amendment. Those decisions included *Barenblatt v. United States*,[45] *Shelton v. Tucker*,[46] *Sweezy v. New Hamshire*[47] and *Keyishian v. Board of Regents of University of State of New*.[48] In *Keyishian*, Justice William Brennan wrote for the majority:

> Our Nation is deeply committed to safeguarding academic freedom, which is of transcendent value to all of us and not merely to the teachers concerned. That freedom is therefore a special concern of the First Amendment, which does not tolerate laws that cast a pall of orthodoxy over the classroom.[49]

But the Court's insistence that academic freedom is protected speech, grounded in the First Amendment, has ramifications that have not been fully appreciated. It has elevated the notion of academic freedom and the protections of tenure to such lofty positions that it has substantially compromised and hand-strung the decision making authority of trustees and other entities such as administrators who are answerable to a broader constituency. In this sense, unfettered academic freedom is in a curious way "anti-democratic." It allows the professor and his peers to be the ultimate decision-making authorities as to what the professor can and can't say or instruct. This is only too evident when one examines the forced resignation by Harvard President Lawrence Summers. Confronted with a no-confidence vote by Harvard's faculty, Summers chose to resign out of true "peer pressure." It wasn't the university's trustees, alumni, students, or upper administration that demanded Summers to step down, but the university's own faculty who turned against him; ironically, at least one reason for the no confidence vote was as a result of Summers suggesting at a faculty-only seminar on "Women and the Sciences" that men and women might have marginal cognitive differences. This seminar was supposedly run under the concept of the "free exchange of ideas."

A major source of confusion about the concept of "academic freedom" and the willing intrusion by the courts to enforce it is the assumption that the professor exists to promote the free exchange of ideas. The fact that a professor has been given such wide latitude under this justification often conflicts with a governing power's responsibility to respond to legitimate public or private concerns. Furthermore, because it has been assumed that such a "right" exists under the

First Amendment, courts have simply applied various functionality tests to determine whether the speech in question falls into the category.

One example is *Hardy v. Jefferson Community College*.[50] In *Hardy*, a professor's contract was not renewed after the administration received complaints from an African American student about the professor's use of racial slurs in a communications class. The professor's explanation for using the words was to demonstrate how "language is used to marginalize minorities and other oppressed groups in society." The Sixth Circuit Court of Appeals reversed the college's decision and stated that Hardy's speech was in furtherance of the "free exchange of ideas" and was therefore protected.[51]

On the other hand, in *Dambrot v. Central Michigan University*,[52] Dambrot was the head coach of the university's men's basketball program. During a locker-room session with his players, he used the offensive word "nigger" in an attempt to inspire them to be "fearless, mentally strong and tough" both at school and on the basketball floor. The Sixth Circuit refused to categorize Dambrot's speech as protected under the notion of "academic freedom" because, unlike the classroom teacher, it was not said within the context of the "free exchange of ideas." The court held that the university's goal for the coach was to win games, not to sensitize his players about how the use of language marginalizes certain racial and ethnic groups.[53]

The courts in each of these instances justified their decisions on the basis of the nature of the speech in relation to whether it was carrying out the school's goal. But the courts' erroneous assumption is that universities, and the professors who teach at them, have *one* goal that is paramount to all others and that is deserving of special protection. That goal is the "free exchange of ideas" and it has been determined that academic freedom is synonymous with this phrase. Likewise, if speech is used within a context that does not fall within the "free exchange of ideas" it is not protected (thus, use of the racial slur is protected by the speech teacher in *Hardy* but not by the basketball coach in *Dambrot*).

As a result, when academics get fired or demoted for something said or an action taken, they argue that they had "the right" to do so because their speech or act is protected under "academic freedom," speech that the courts have protected under the First Amendment. The protections afforded those who claim academic freedom rights have become as strong *de facto* as those classes singled out for special protection by the Constitution or Congress such as "race, creed, national origin, and age." But a more primary and prescient question is "should academic speech ever have been protected under the First Amendment to begin with?"

One of the criticisms that has plagued higher education for decades from non-academics is the lack of transparency in what is being taught on campus. Despite the incredible proliferation of public relations efforts to recruit students, donors, and enhance an institution's prestige, colleges and universities seldom discuss the philosophical, political, or economic beliefs of its faculty. As the late University of Chicago professor George Stigler, Nobel Prize laureate, once recounted,

Most college administrations have found it desirable. . .not to emphasize the fact that on their campuses the students will be confronted by faculties far more liberal or left-wing than the prevailing point of few among parents, trustees, taxpayers, and donors. In how many college catalogs do you find prospective students and their parents given any information on the social philosophies to which the student is exposed on that campus? Do they say, "Send your son to College X and he will be taught by 5 Marxist, burn-down-the-buildings activists, 15 non-Marxist, just-seize-the-buildings activists, 100 left-of-center modern liberals, 10 Ripon Society Republicans, and 2 eccentric conservatives just reaching retirement?" . . . [T]he typical university catalogue would never stop Diogenes in his search for an honest man."[54]

The Problem of Academic Freedom & How the Courts Have Created It

There are more than 3,300 colleges and universities in the United States that confer at least a bachelor's degree. In addition, there are thousands of professional, community, and trade schools for those who seek professional or vocational training and certification. There are literally billions of dollars spent annually in scholarships, grants in aid, and college savings plans to assist those who want to pursue educational opportunities at a tertiary institution. Never before has a person—young or old, rich or poor, majority or minority race—had as much opportunity to pursue higher education than in the past few decades.

Yet the underlying philosophy—at least in the social sciences—of what is taught within this large number of institutions is remarkably monolithic and often contrary to mainstream societies views.[55] How this has developed is through the concepts of "academic freedom," "peer review," and "tenure" and the courts have played an instrumental role in upholding and strengthening these notions. Because tenured faculty members are insulated from most external pressures such as non-academic forces (e.g. the opinions of trustees, administration, alumni), they do, indeed, have incredible freedom to teach, write, and espouse almost any views they wish within the academy in which they are employed. But because tenure, at least at most prestigious research universities, is dependent upon publication, there is incredible pressure to write and reach conclusions that conform to the *academic community's* underlying philosophical beliefs. Those professors whose views or research do not conform to such beliefs have a much less chance of obtaining publication in prestigious journals or of receiving lucrative and often well publicized lecture invitations. As a result, they run the risk of not being published and of not receiving tenure. As a highly successful Indiana businessman once wrote,

> To impose on the individual entering the relationship of teaching through being hired by any given college, restrictions and responsibilities, including the right to dismiss him, is an entirely different matter from restrictions on individual liberty apart from such employment. . . .
> This confusion between individual freedom and academic freedom—the success with which teachers and their power-seeking organization have confused the human liberty of the individual to seek truth and exercise free will—

especially freedom from the state—has been the cloak behind which individuals have indulged in irresponsibility, undeveloped reason, insufficient education, irrational activity, the arrogance of infallibility, and personal and collective power.[56]

Thus, the existence of "academic freedom" which has been essentially deemed "a right" under the First and Fourteenth Amendments by the courts has had the effect of severely limiting property and contractual rights by institutions of higher education. Academic freedom has given educators protection that no other profession enjoys. *See McAuliffe v. Mayor of New Bedford,* ("The petitioner may have a constitutional right to talk politics, but he has no constitutional right to be a policeman.");[57] *Pickering v. Board of Education of Township High School* (high school teacher could not be fired for expressing views contrary to those of governing body about issues of public importance).[58]

Academic Control, Funding, and the Courts

The courts have been invited to step into many occasions where control of an institution of higher learning is at issue. These often revolve around attempts by state legislatures to influence academic content by withholding funds. One of the first decisions was in 1819 in the case of *Trustees of Dartmouth College v. Woodward.*[59] In the Dartmouth College case, the Supreme Court ruled that Dartmouth, a private college, was free of legislative interference even though its charter was issued by the New Hampshire legislature and it sought state financial support. Indeed, state support was essential to the establishment of the earliest institutions of higher education, almost all of which were private in nature. From the late 1700s up to and including 1926, state legislatures provided support for private colleges. Examples of such support are as follows: Columbia University (formerly King's College) received $140,000 and the University of Pennsylvania received $287,000 from their respective states in the late 1700s; Harvard was granted $10,000 per year from 1814 to 1823; Dartmouth received public lands in which to sell to provide operational support and $200,000 from 1893 to 1921 and Princeton was given the right to conduct lotteries in New Jersey, Pennsylvania and Connecticut to support itself.[60]

In the case of *Sterling v. Regents of University of Michigan,*[61] the state legislature in 1896 attempted to compel the University of Michigan to close a college of homeopathic medicine in Ann Arbor and relocate the college in Detroit. The board of regents of the University resisted, stating that the state legislature did not have the authority to govern the University. The Supreme Court of Michigan supported the board of regents, finding that the state constitution of 1850 gave control to the governing body of the University (the regents) and the state legislature could not alter that control by simple legislation. In very plain and succinct language, the separation of powers was acknowledged:

> The board of regents and the legislature derive their power from the same supreme authority, namely the [Michigan] Constitution. In so far as the powers of each are defined by that instrument, limitations are imposed, and a direct power conferred upon one necessarily excludes its existence in the other, in the ab-

sence of language showing the contrary intent. . . . They are separate and distinct constitutional bodies, with the powers of the regents defined. By no rule of construction can it be held that either can encroach upon or exercise the powers conferred upon the other.[62]

The State of Michigan was host in 2003 to another controversy regarding control of content and curriculum in higher education. That year State Representative Jack Hoogendyk introduced a constitutional amendment, not simply legislation that would give the legislature authority to determine how public universities spend taxpayer appropriated money. Hoogendyk's action was taken largely as a result of curricular offerings at the University of Michigan, including a course entitled "How to be Gay: Male Homosexuality and Initiation." While the constitutional amendment did not pass and was not brought before the Michigan courts, a spate of decisions exist that show that courts have refused to allow state legislation to interfere with curricular choices at taxpayer funded schools.[63]

However, in *Urofsky v. Gilmore*, the U.S. Court of Appeals for the Fourth Circuit reversed a lower court on the issue of whether professors at the University of Virginia had protected (First Amendment) speech rights to access sexually explicit material over the internet for work-related research.[64] In *Urofsky*, the state legislature passed a law restricting state employees from accessing sexually explicit material on computers that were owned or leased by the state without obtaining prior approval from a university committee. A group of professors challenged the legislation and a federal district court granted them summary judgment, finding that their First Amendment rights had been violated.[65] The University of Virginia appealed and the Fourth Circuit reversed, finding that the professors did not have First Amendment protection. The irony of this decision, when compared with the ones dealing with "academic freedom," is that a professor apparently has full First Amendment protection to *teach* students at taxpayer expense about pornography (under the guise of academic freedom) but not to *research* it.

The fact remains that the courts have given professors almost unfettered discretion to be the judges in their own behalf. It has done this through invalidating legislation, denying standing to taxpayers to bring actions, and other means.[66] If there is any limitation to professors' action, it would appear to have to reside with the institution in which they teach.[67] But because a large majority of the faculties at institutions of higher learning have a particular ideology that sanctions almost any type of conduct or academic course or research as legitimate, this provides almost no control at all.

The Supreme Court has recognized that educational decisions are better left to educational experts when it suits the court's notion of what those decisions are about. If they are about curricular and research choices, then such discretion is almost completely unfettered.[68] If it is about admissions, the courts have been too willing to intervene to support their own ideas about equality.

Conclusion

The courts have played a significant if little recognized role in advancing the social agenda of federal governmental policies dating back to at least the 1950s. In addition, judges have often taken it upon themselves to make policy decisions that are better made by the legislative or executive branches, or, in the most ideal world, by college trustees and administrators themselves. The result is intrusiveness and leveling in higher education that has helped destroy diversity, especially diversity of thought, on the campuses of thousands of colleges and universities. This fact appears especially self-contradictory given that the academy holds itself out as the epitome of the "market-place of ideas." Professor Paul Seabury makes this point in his essay on the effect of bureaucracy on education:

> ... [A]s federal directives governing university policies multiply in meticulous detail, they apply equally to all affected institutions. Clearly, considering the federal government's desire to evenhandedly pursue its social goals through institutions of higher learning, one effect of this is to gradually or even spasmodically obliterate the dynamic diversity of higher education in the United States. . . . To be sure, a few Don Quixotes can be found on the landscape of American higher education—private institutions like Hillsdale College in Michigan—which staunchly resist receiving a single cent from the federal government, thus to escape its regulatory clutches. But it would be fanciful to assume that the example can be widely imitated.[69]

The notion of "academic freedom" has been elevated to a preeminence and given protections that were never envisioned by the Founders but which the courts have only been too willing to embrace. It has been transformed from something that has, or could have, desirous and beneficial attributes (viz. the promotion of open discussion), to an obligatory right that precludes other goals that institutions of higher education may wish to pursue. The courts have only been too willing to impress upon colleges and universities this viewpoint and to adopt its own social agenda regarding the operations of higher education.

In 1957, Justice Felix Frankfurter, a former Harvard Law School professor himself, reached the following conclusion in the case of (find case):

> These pages need not be burdened with proof, based on the testimony of a cloud of witnesses, of the dependence of a free society on free universities. *This means the exclusion of governmental intervention in the intellectual life of the university.* (emphasis added)[70]

What is so ironic is that Frankfurter didn't consider the courts' decisions rendered in higher education cases as either "governmental" or "interventionalist" when, in fact, they are both. Our failure to object to the courts' complicity in shaping higher education policy has resulted in a corresponding loss of freedom for both the University and society. It is a failure that we cannot continue to tolerate.

ENDNOTES

1. *See Bureaucrats and Brainpower: Government Regulation of Universities*, ed. Paul Seabury, Institute for Contemporary Studies, (San Francisco, 1979). The exception to the creation of a national university was the establishment of the U.S. Military Academy at West Point in 1802.

2. *See The Tocqueville Reader: A Life in Letters and Politics*, ed., Olivier Zunz and Alan S. Kahan, Blackwell Publishing (2002), p. 110 (summarizing Chapter 8 of vol. one of *Democracy in America, 1835*)

3. In de Tocqueville's diary (1831) entitled "Public Instruction" (Pierson 1959: 293–94).

4. Roger E. Meiners, "The Evolution of American Higher Education," contained in *The Academy in Crisis: The Political Economy of Higher Education*, ed., John W. Sommer (Transaction Publishers, New Brunswick, Conn.), 1995, pp. 22–23.

5. *Ibid.*, pp. 29–31.

6. Joel H. Spring, "In Service to the State: The Political Context of Higher Education in the United States," contained in *The Academy in Crisis, Ibid*, p. 47.

7. John W. Sommer, "American Higher Education: State of the Art or Art of the State?" *The Academy in Crisis, Ibid.*, p. 8.

8. *Ibid.*, p. 9.

9. C. Ronald Kimberling, "Federal Student Aid: A History and Critical Analysis," *The Academy in Crisis, Ibid.*, pp. 69–70.

10. *See* Neal McCluskey, "Taxation U," *National Review*, Nov. 4, 2003 (stating that only 18.5% of public university revenue comes from tuition and other student fees and that taxpayers also provide 16.4% (or $12 billion) of support in 2002 to private colleges).

11. *See* John Buntin, "Setting Colleges Free," *Governing,* Sept. 2003, at 18, 19 (describing how state and federal legislators are frustrated because they do not know what public university students are learning).

12. By 1979, at least 34 congressional committees and 74 sub-committees had jurisdiction over some aspect of higher education funding or policy. From 1965 to 1977, the number of pages of federal laws regarding higher education increased from 90 to 360 pages and the number of pages in the *Federal Register* had grown from 92 to more than a 1,000. *See* Robert S. Hatfield "Regulating the University: A Businessman's Perspective, *Bureaucrats and Brainpower, Ibid.* p. 4.

13. *Ibid.* p. 7.

14. Paul Seabury, "The Advent of Academic Bureaucrats," *Bureaucrats and Brainpower, Ibid*, p. 21.

15. *Id.*, p. 10.

16. *See* William V. Mayville, *Federal Influence on Higher Education Curricula*, (Washington, D.C.: American Association of Higher Education, 1980), pp. p. 16.

17. 347 U.S. 483 (1954) (litigating for the right to integrate schools to have equal educational opportunities).

18. Title IX was included in the educational reauthorization act of 1972. It provides that colleges and universities are in essential compliance if the number of women participating in sports is proportional to the percentage of women at a particular college or university. The National Collegiate Athletic Association (NCAA) fought the legislation, arguing that its members shouldn't have to comply because federal funds were not going to fund athletic scholarships. In a round of cases, the NCAA lost. The result is that whereas in 1972 approximately 32,000 women participated in intercollegiate sports on athletic scholarships, in 2005 the number had increased to more than 150,000.

19. 539 U.S. 244 (2003)

20. *See* "College Admissions: Is Gate Open or Closed?" *The Wall Street Journal.*, March 25, 2006, p. A7, c 1.

21. 438 U.S. 265 (1978)

22. Lee C. Bollinger, "Examining 'Diversity' in Education: A Comment on Grutter and Gratz v. Bollinger," 103 Colum. L. Rev. 1589 at 1591.

23. *Gratz* at 282.

24. 438 U.S. at 320.

25. 438 U.S. at 396.

26. "No person in the United States shall, on the ground of race, color, or national origin, be excluded from participation in, be denied the benefits of, or be subjected to discrimination under any program or activity receiving Federal financial assistance."

27. *Id.*, at 396–397.

28. *Id.*, at 398.

29. *Id.*, at 404.

30. *Id.* See also, "How Lowering the Bar Helps Colleges Prosper," *The Wall Street Journal.* Sept. 9, 2006, c.4.

31. *Gratz* , 539 U.S. at 304.

32. *See Gong Lum et al. v. Rice et al.*, 275 U.S. 78 (1927) (Supreme Court ruled that the operation of a dual school system—one for whites and one for blacks—did not violate the Equal Protection Clause of the Fourteenth Amendment)

33. *See* Bollinger, 103 Colum. L. Rev. at 1594

34. *Id..* (Bollinger summarizes the public relations efforts that he and several went to explain the need for affirmative action programs in both education and business.)

35. 976 F.2d 890, 892 (1992), case remanded to district court for determination of remedy. *See* 852 F. Supp. 471 (1994).

36. Virginia had to provide a very detailed "remedial plan" to the district court to show that the program offered to women at VWIL was so similar to the one offered by VMI that there was little difference between the two. *See* 852 F.Supp. at 491–502.

37. Penguin Classics, p. 5.

38. Am. Ass's of Univ. Professor, 1915 Declaration of Principles, reprinted in Academic Freedom and Tenure, app. A at 157-76 (Louis Joughin ed., 1969).

39. Rebecca Gose Lynch, 91 Calif. L. Rev. July 2003, 1061 at 1067 (citing 1940 AAUP Statement of Principles on Academic Freedom and Tenure, AAUP Pol'y Documents & Rep. 3 (1984).

40. 1 Encyc. Soc. Sci. 383 (Edwin Seligman & Alvin Johnson, eds., 1930).

41. 342 U.S 485at 492 (1952).

42. *Id.* at 510–511.

43. 344 U.S. 183 (1952).

44. *Id.* at 195 (Frankfurter, J., concurring); *see also*, Lynch, *ibid* at 1069.

45. 360 U.S. 109 (1959) (teacher had been held in contempt of Congress for refusing to testify on knowledge of communist activities in classroom and the Court upheld the right of refusal).

46. 364 U.S. 479 (1960) (Court upheld teacher's refusal to list all organizations that she had belonged to in past five years as was required by school system as a prerequisite to employment).

47. 353 U.S. 234 (1957)

48. 385 U.S. 589 (1967)

49. 385 U.S. at 603.

50. 260 F.3d 671 (6th Cir. 2001).

51. *Id.*, at 677.

52. 55 F.3d 1177 (6th Cir. 1995).

53. *Id.*, at 1186.

54. "The Intellectual and the Market Place," *Selected Paper*, No. 3, Graduate School of Business, University of Chicago, February 1967, p. 7.

55. *See* Jonah Goldberg, "Big sham on campus," *The Indianapolis Star*, May 15, 2006, p. A8.

56. Pierre F. Goodrich, *Education Memorandum*, (privately published by Liberty Fund, Inc.) (1949), pp. 32–33.

57. 155 Mass. 216, 220, 29 N.E. 517, 517–18 (1892).

58. 391 U.S. 563 (1968).

59. 17 U.S. 518 (1819).

60. *See The Academy in Crisis*, ed., John W. Sommer (Transaction Publishers, New Brunswick), 1995, p. 24.

61. 110 Mich. 369 (1896).

62. *Id.*, at 382.

63. *See* Laura A. Jeltema, "Legislators in the Classroom: Why State Legislatures Cannot Decide Higher Education Curricula," 54 Am. U.S. Rev. 215 (October 2004), pp. 215.

64. 216 F.3d 401 (2000), deciding the constitutionality of Va. Code Ann 2.1-804 to -806.

65. *See Urofsky v. Allen*, 995 F. Supp. 634 (E.D. Va. 1998)

66. In the case of *Doremus v. Board of Education*, 342 U.S. 429 (1952), the Supreme Court held that taxpayers do not have standing to complain about curricula they do not agree with. The Court found that "the grievance which it is sought to litigate here is not a direct dollars-and-cents injury but is a religious difference" and therefore the requisite injury was lacking. *Id.* at 434–35.

67. *See* J. Peter Byrne, "Academic Freedom: A 'Special Concern of the First Amendment," 99 Yale L.J. 251 (November 1989), p. 252. (Professor Byrne claims that the First Amendment protection of "academic freedom" resides with the institution, not with a particular professor. Therefore, college and university decisions' should be immune from outside forces such as legislatures, Congress, the executive branch, etc.).

68. *See Regents of the University of Michigan v. Ewing*, 474 U.S. 214, 226 (1985) (quoting *Board of Curators of the University of Missouri v. Horowitz*, 435 U.S. 78, 90 (1978) (emphasizing that decisions about curriculum require "an expert evaluation of cumulative information and [are] not readily adapted to the procedural tools of judicial or administrative decision-making").

69. "Advent of the Academic Bureaucrat,"*Ibid.*, pp. 23–24.

70. 77 S. Ct. 1203, at 1217–18.

Nine
The Judicial Assault on Public Philosophy
by E. Robert Statham

> *The least dangerous branch of the American Government is the most extraordinarily powerful court of law the world has ever known. The power which distinguishes the Supreme Court of the United States is that of constitutional review of the actions of the other branches of government, federal and state. Curiously enough, this power of judicial review, as it is called, does not derive from any explicit constitutional command. The authority to determine the meaning and application of a written constitution is nowhere defined or even mentioned in the document itself.*
>
> Alexander M. Bickel[1]
The Least Dangerous Branch:
The Supreme Court at the Bar of Politics

The United States Supreme Court has become the most powerful branch of the Federal Government, and this, in violation of the Constitution and its animating principles. Paradoxically, the reason for the Judiciary's disproportionate power is the result, not of the Constitution, but of the judicial misinterpretation of it. Contrary to popular opinion, the three branches of Government, while separate in accordance with the principle of the separation of powers, were not intended to be co-equal.[2] The Judiciary was expected to be the least powerful of the three branches precisely because it was not granted either legislative or executive power, but only the power of judgment.[3] However, the Judiciary has become the most powerful and dangerous branch of government by usurping legislative and executive functions through the abuse of judicial review.

Alexander Hamilton defended the Judiciary against its Anti-Federalist critics in *Federalist #78*.[4] He pointed out that the "judiciary, from the nature of its functions, will always be the least dangerous to the political rights of the constitution" because it would be "least in a capacity to annoy or injure them."[5] But

Hamilton qualified this contention in admitting that the judicial power would need to "remain truly distinct from both the legislative and the executive functions."[6] Otherwise, the Judiciary would presumably be the *greatest* threat to the political rights of the Constitution. And this is exactly what it has become. The Supreme Court has progressively rendered decisions that have served to divide the American public and undermine the Constitution.[7]

Much controversy now surrounds the Judiciary. In his book *Men in Black: How the Supreme Court is Destroying America*, Mark Levin levels the following serious charge:

> America has turned from the most representative form of government to a de facto judicial tyranny. From same-sex marriage, illegal immigration and economic socialism to partial-birth abortion, political speech, and terrorists' 'rights,' judges have abused their constitutional mandate by imposing their personal prejudices and beliefs on the rest of society.[8]

And Levin is not alone. Grave questions have recently been raised concerning judicial tyranny and the ultimate legitimacy of the American political order.[9] Some have wondered openly if "we have reached or are reaching the point where conscientious citizens can no longer give moral assent to the existing regime." Judge Robert Bork has gone so far as to state that the only solution to abuses of judicial power is "a change in our institutional arrangements" where democratic majorities could effectively override judicial decisions. But he takes a further step in suggesting that "courts might be deprived of the power of constitutional review."[10] The "judicial usurpation of power" has called into question the legitimacy of the Judiciary.[11] And, to no small extent, to question the legitimacy of the Judiciary is to call into question the Constitution itself.[12] Indeed, George W. Carey has considered that "the document crafted by our Founding Fathers in Philadelphia over the course of the summer of 1788 is a dead letter."[13]

I

The question arises as to whether the fundamental problem with the judicial power under the Constitution is primarily structural and institutional or substantive and philosophical. I wish to argue that the problem is, at the core, the latter. I have elsewhere, and at length, maintained that the power of judicial review was not only intended by the Framers of the Constitution, but that it is implicit in the very concept of constitutionalism.[14] At issue is, in my estimation, not the power of judicial review, but the *substantive* exercise of it.

The exercise of judicial power entails the philosophical analysis and explication of what the Constitution is and what it means. And what the Constitution means has gradually become controversial as "there is no longer a consensus, an understanding, or agreement among the people concerning fundamental constitutional questions."[15] The controversy surrounding the Judiciary is symptomatic of a crisis of public philosophy.[16] This crisis of public philosophy is the result of a profound loss of the following understanding: The Constitution, the fundamental law of the American political order, has a higher or natural law foundation.[17]

The American political order is *not* a democracy. Neither was it intended to be so.[18] Democracy is, by definition, majority rule that is a form of tyranny (majoritarian). The Constitution limits and qualifies democracy through the institutional mechanisms of the separation of powers, checks and balances, federalism and republican representation while maintaining popular rule. In this way, legal structures serve to regulate the deleterious, passionate, self-interested aspects of human nature that endanger and often destroy liberty.[19] The structural-institutional portion of the Constitution is one half of the dialectic of a constitutional order.[20] The institutions of the Constitution are designed to prevent tyranny and anarchy.

The substantive-philosophical element of the Constitution relates to its meaning and purpose and forms the other half of the dialectic of constitutionalism.. But the *substance* of the Constitution is not, and could not be explicitly stated in the document. As Justice John Marshall pointed out in his decision in *McCulloch v. Maryland*, "a Constitution, to contain an accurate detail of all the subdivisions of which its great powers will admit," would "partake of the prolixity of a legal code," could "scarcely be embraced by the human mind," and "would probably never be understood by the public."[21] The meaning or substance of the Constitution is found in the transcendental standard that informs it: higher or natural law. Edward S. Corwin, in his classic essay "The 'higher law' Background of American Constitutional Law," provides a particularly important explanation of the substantive-philosophical element of the Constitution. Corwin observes that:

> There are . . . certain principles of right and justice which are entitled to prevail of their own intrinsic excellence. . . . Such principles were made by no human hands; indeed, if they did not antedate deity itself, they still so express its nature as to bind and control it. They are external to all will as such and interpenetrate all reason as such. They are eternal and immutable.[22]

Corwin is referring to principles of transcendental justice which form the intellectual and moral context of the Constitution. He understands that the "*legality* of the Constitution, its *supremacy*, and is claim to be worshipped" are grounded in the "belief in a law superior to the will of human governors."[23]

The higher or natural law must be differentiated from statutory law. Statutory law is law made by legislatures. The higher law is not made, it is *discovered*. It provides the intellectual and moral foundation for all law and government.[24] The Constitution, as fundamental law, is intended to embody the principles of higher law. Inherent in the very concept of a Constitution is the understanding that human beings are basically flawed and that this leads governmentally to tyranny (the rule of will). The rule of law is intended to prevent tyranny (and anarchy or chaos). However, and this is a point of critical importance, the Constitution, as fundamental law, must be interpreted. And the branch of government intended to interpret the Constitution is the Judiciary.

Hamilton, in *Federalist #78*, observes that the "courts must declare the sense of the law," and they were "designed to be an intermediate body between the people and the legislature" so as to assure that "the representatives of the people" could not "substitute their *will* to that of their constituents."[25] The *will* of the people's representatives is expressed in statutory law. The *will* of the people is expressed explicitly (in structure and form) and implicitly (in substance) in the Constitution, which is, as Hamilton noted, "and must be regarded by the judges as a fundamental law."[26] The courts are the "bulwarks of a limited constitution against legislative encroachments," and "the interpretation of the laws is the proper and *peculiar* province of the courts (emphasis added)."[27]

The *peculiar* province of the courts derives from the nature of the Judiciary. The role of the Judiciary is the exercise of "judgement."[28] The need to exercise judgement occurs when the ordinary acts of the people's representatives (usually and primarily via statutory legislation) come into conflict with the Constitution explicitly (in word), and/or implicitly (in sense or meaning). This is why Hamilton maintains that judges are supposed to:

> Guard the constitution and the rights of individuals from the effects of those ill humours which the arts of designing men, or the influence of particular conjunctures, sometimes disseminate among the people themselves, and which, though they speedily give place to better information and more deliberate reflection, have a tendency, in the mean time, to occasion dangerous innovations in the government, and serious oppressions of the minor party in the community.[29]

Intriguingly, Hamilton does not provide an explication of the standard by which judges would engage the power of the interpretation of the laws and, for this reason, his philosophical explication of the Judiciary is "incomplete in a very real sense."[30] He provides an argument for the need for a Judiciary without addressing the *substance* of judicial review.[31]

Roscoe Pound traces the distinction between law which is by nature (eternal and immutable) and law that is by convention (law made by human hands) to the Greeks.[32] The "natural law was that which expressed perfectly the idea of law" whereas "legislation and edict . . . were but imperfect and ephemeral copies of this jural reality."[33] This distinction led to the differentiation of law making by convention (legislation) and law making by judges (interpretation) so that "jurist-made and judge-made law have been molded consciously or unconsciously by ideas as to what law is for; by theories as to the end of law."[34] The role of the Judiciary in the American constitutional order is the interpretation of legislation (statutes) over against the substantive meaning and purpose (end) of the Constitution which is found in higher or natural law. Judicial interpretation is the making of constitutional law. This, Hamilton does not state, but it is implicit in his argument for the need and power of judicial review.

II

The higher or natural law is the public philosophy. As Walter Lippmann points out, the public philosophy "is the premise of the institutions of the Western society," in what Ernest Barker referred to as the "traditions of civility."[35] These traditions:

Were expounded in the treatises of philosophers, were developed in the tracts of the publicists, were absorbed by the lawyers and applied in the courts. At times of great stress some of the endangered traditions were committed to writing, as in the Magna Carta and the Declaration of Independence. For the guidance of judges and lawyers, large portions were described—as in Lord Coke's examination of the common law. The public philosophy was in part expounded in the Bill of Rights of 1689. It was re-enacted in the first ten amendments of the Constitution of the United States. The largest part of the public philosophy was never explicitly stated. Being the wisdom of a great society over the generations, it can never be stated in any single document. But the traditions of civility permeated the peoples of the West and provided a standard of public and private action which promoted, facilitated and protected the institutions of freedom and the growth of democracy.[36]

This higher or natural law, the public philosophy, provides the background of American constitutional law that Corwin refers to. J. Rufus Fears observes that the very conception of liberty derives from a heritage in which natural law is of central importance. He derives assistance from Cicero in understanding that "true law is right reason in agreement with nature, universal, consistent, everlasting, whose nature is to advocate duty by prescription and to deter wrongdoing by prohibition."[37]

Corwin draws the connection between higher law and judicial review in pointing out that there is "discoverable in the permanent elements of human nature" a "durable justice which transcends expediency," and "the positive law must embody this if it is to claim allegiance of the human conscience." When "that which wears the form of law is at variance with true (higher) law," the solution is, as suggested by Cicero, "something strikingly like judicial review" (emphasis added).[38] The *substantive* role of the Judiciary (judicial review) in the American political order is the interpretation of the laws in reference to the public philosophy.

The nature and difficulty of the task is precisely why Hamilton makes an extensive argument in *Federalist #78* for judicial independence. He understands that "there can be but few men in society, who will have sufficient skill in the laws to qualify them for the stations of judges," as understanding the law requires "long and laborious study." He further observes that there are even fewer individuals who can "unite the requisite integrity (character) with the requisite knowledge" (emphasis added).[39] The knowledge that Hamilton is referring to is the understanding of the common law which entails the study of legal cases and precedents. The character he is referring to he does *not* expound upon. The character that he does not expound upon is that of a judge.

Judges must have the knowledge of a lawyer and the character of a political philosopher. In a judge, knowledge must be combined with the virtue of "right reason in agreement with nature."[40] Judges must combine knowledge of the laws with knowledge and fidelity to the public philosophy. They are the guardians of the Constitution precisely because their loyalty must be to it, and not to any particular constituency or interest. They must be impartial to partial interests and partial to the general (higher law) interest of the Constitution. Their *peculiar* role requires independence in the form of life tenure because they must have the interest of the Constitution as their own. And in having the Constitution as their own interest, judges guard the *fundamental* interests and rights of the people.

We now arrive at the crux of the problem. Over time, the public philosophy has been progressively neglected, discarded and "relegated to the attic" as it were.[41] As Walter Lippmann pointed out over half a century ago, the "institutions built upon the foundations of the public philosophy still stand," but "they are being used by a public who are not being taught, and no longer adhere to it."[42] The American people are "alienated from the inner principles of their institutions.[43] In the estimation of George W. Carey "our dilemma today. . .is almost totally attributable to the public's ignorance of the principles and morality" of the "constitutional cosmos" of natural or higher law, of the "traditions of civility."[44]

The crisis of public philosophy appears to be without parallel. The institutions created within the context of the public philosophy are no longer guided by it. And the Judiciary is one of those institutions, probably the most important of them insofar as its primary role is the explication of the meaning and purpose of the Constitution. The meaning and purpose of the Constitution cannot be stated independently of the public philosophy. To do so would be to pervert the Constitution. And, this perversion in terms of judicial decision making has increasingly occurred. In Carey's view, the Judiciary has "usurped power in the name of democracy."[45]

Aristotle provides an analysis of the different political orders in *The Politics*. He divides the orders quantitatively into the rule of one, the few and the many, and then proceeds to demonstrate that each of these has a qualitatively just and perverted form.[46] Constitutional government provides a just form of the rule of the many while democracy is the perverted form. Inherent in each just form of rule is the potentiality for its perversion. The perversion of constitutionalism is *democratization*. The democratization of the American political order is the source of the crisis of public philosophy.

The neglect of the public philosophy in the name of democracy has challenged the basic meaning and purpose of the American political order. Democratization places overemphasis on the values of individualism and equality at the expense of liberty and law.[47] Furthermore, democratization results in a perverted intellectual and moral framework. Mass public opinion is the highest value in a democracy so that truth is grounded in what is popular. In this way, truth, especially the truths found in the public philosophy (higher or natural law) is depreciated by democratic sophistry. Indeed, the democratic intellectual and moral outlook tends toward relativism. The two absolutes of the public philosophy and of Western civilization, God (Judeo-Christianity) and Reason (political philosophy), are relativized democratically.[48] The neglect of the public philosophy is the result of the processes of democratization.

The Judiciary has succumbed to the processes of democratization (in addition to the American citizenry). Judges tend to be trained as lawyers in law schools. Thus, according to Ed McLean:

> From whence do lawyers derive their ideas about the nature of the constitution? The answer is, unfortunately, from their law professors, who, in large measure,

obtain their ideas in turn from the writings of other law professors, whose understanding of the Constitution, is, to say the least, inadequate and incomplete.[49]

Indeed, George Anastaplo has commented that the "best law school faculties are the most apt to be swept along by fashionable opinions," so that the kinds of ideas generated in law schools are democratically sophisticated.[50] Indeed, it is safe to say that few judges have been well trained in the public philosophy for a few generations, and perhaps more.

III

Judicial decision making has increasingly reflected the democratization which has brought about the crisis of public philosophy. Lippmann observed that "for several generations it has been exceptional and indeed eccentric" for philosophers, scholars and popular educators to use the language of the public philosophy.[51] Thus, the language of judicial decisions has become increasing democratic and devoid of the terms, principles, themes and concepts of higher or natural law. Higher or natural law thinking about the Constitution, which is essential for understanding it, is probably the least accepted approach to the study of constitutional law contemporaneously. The impact of this development has been devastating.

In *Regents of the University of California v. Bakke* (1978), the Supreme Court issued a decision that perverted the Constitution's principles of equality of opportunity and nondiscrimination, thereby creating policies of affirmative action and reverse discrimination that have divided the country and raised (not lowered) racial tension and consciousness. *Bakke*, a white male, had applied for admission to the University of California, Davis Medical School. The school had devised a policy of creating two pools of candidates, a general pool for all candidates, and a special pool for minorities. The median science grade point average of those admitted to the general pool was 3.51 with MCAT scores of the 76th percentile and 83rd percentile. Special admittees had corresponding scores of 2.62, 24th percentile and 35th percentile. *Bakke* had scores of 3.44, 94th and 97th percentiles. He was not admitted.[52] The California Supreme Court held that "taking race into account in admissions decisions violated the equal protection clause of the 14th Amendment" of the United States Constitution and ordered *Bakke* be admitted.[53] The United States Supreme Court overturned the California Supreme Court decision.

The Supreme Court held that the UC Davis Medical School's desire to attain a more diverse student body is "clearly a constitutionally permissible goal for an institution of higher education." The Court found that a University has the freedom to "make its own judgements as to education" which "includes the selection of its student body," and that "the atmosphere of 'speculation, experiment and creation' so essential to the quality of higher education—is widely believed to be promoted by a diverse student body."[54] And while the Court admitted that the "use of an explicit racial classification" in admissions policies disregarded "individual rights guaranteed by the Fourteenth Amendment," it concluded:

> In enjoining petitioner from ever considering the race of an applicant, however, the courts below failed to recognize that the State has a substantial interest that legitimately may be served by a properly devised admissions program involving the competitive consideration of race and ethnic origin. For this reason, so much of the California court's judgment as enjoins petitioner from any consideration of the race of any applicant must be reversed.[55]

The *Bakke* decision opened the door for universities and colleges to use race as one criteria of several in admissions policies in order to create more diverse student bodies. While this objective appears reasonable on the surface, in actuality it is grounded in democratic sophistry.

The *Bakke* decision did not address the constitutional issue of racial discrimination.[56] That was indeed the issue before the court; whether Bakke had been discriminated against. The UC Davis Medical School had grouped students together in two applicant pools, a general majority pool and a special minority pool. The academic standards and requirements for the general pool were substantially more stringent than for the minority pool. At the core of the school's admissions policy was the creating of distinctions between majorities and minorities. Bakke was disallowed consideration for the special minority pool because he was considered to be part of a majority: He was white and male. He was denied admission, even though his grade point average and MCAT scores were higher than a substantial number of other applicants in the special minority pool who were admitted.

Now if academic standards were the measure of the admission policy, then the relevant distinction between the majority pool and the special minority pool would be that the qualifications of the general pool applicants were much better (quantitatively) than the qualifications of the special minority pool. Justice Powell, the author of the decision, disregarded merit in favor of a policy of grouping applicants in terms of characteristics other than those most pertinent to the very purpose of the school itself. The UC Davis Medical School is a school of *medicine*. Medical schools teach medical science and practice. The qualifications for studying and practicing medicine are, and most certainly must be, grounded in the capacity to engage in the study and practice of the science involved. Grade point averages and MCAT scores are of considerable importance in determining the capacity of applicants to study and practice medicine. Whether applicants are tall or short, Eastern or Western, white or black, democratic or republican, or prefer ketchup to salsa, are presumably considerations of little to no importance with respect to the study and practice of medicine. Neither is it clear that the "robust exchange of ideas" is of particular importance in medical school as compared to graduate programs in the social sciences and humanities. The *Bakke* decision emphasized the application of *democratic* criteria instead of the appropriate *merit-based* criteria of grade point averages and MCAT scores. This raises an interesting question. When an individual has heart disease, or has contracted cancer, or some similar serious medical condition, would they prefer to be treated by a medical doctor who fits a particular minority status unrelated to the crafts and skills of the practice of medicine in order to support the objective of democratic diversity, or would they prefer a physician with outstanding qualifications based upon past performance in the field, irrespective of race, ethnicity or gender?

Justice Powell's decision in *Bakke* disregarded Bakke's rights under the Fourteenth Amendment of the U.S. Constitution and then created proportional representation based judicial legislation regarding admissions policies for colleges and universities. There is nothing in the Constitution that stipulates proportional representation by law. On the contrary, James Madison, in *Federalist #10*, makes it clear that:

> The diversity in the faculties of men, from which the rights of property originate, is not less an insuperable obstacle to a uniformity of interests. The protection of these faculties is the first object of government. From the protection of different and unequal faculties of acquiring property, the possession of different and degrees and kinds of property immediately results.[57]

From this observation by Madison, we note that Bakke's relevant faculties were his demonstrated aptitudes for studying medical science based upon his MCAT scores and his undergraduate grade point average.

The UC Davis Medical School Admissions policy discriminated against *Bakke* because he was part of an overrepresented group on the basis of characteristics that had nothing to do with his individual faculties (race, ethnicity, gender), and discriminated in favor of applicants deemed to be underrepresented on account of those same non-meritorious characteristics even although their merit-based qualifications were comparatively deficient. In writing *Bakke* in support of such a policy, Powell inserted language and meaning into the Constitution that is not there, and was not intended. The result has been the general and progressive lowering of standards of excellence, reverse discrimination, and heightened racial, ethnic, and gender tension and resentment throughout the nation.[58]

IV

The courts are now engaged in the reconstruction of socio-political institutions and relations in terms of democratization. It is only a matter of time before, for example, a case regarding "same-sex" marriage will reach the Supreme Court on appeal from one of the various states. In Vermont, the case *Baker v. State* (1999) dealt with this very issue. The Vermont Supreme Court addressed the question of whether the State could "exclude same-sex couples from the benefits and protections that its laws provide to opposite-sex couples."[59] Consistent with the democratic values of radical individualism and radical egalitarianism, the Court held that the "State is constitutionally required" to extend the same benefits and protections of its laws as are extended to opposite-sex married couples to same-sex couples in accordance with the "Common Benefits Clause of the Vermont Constitution (ch. 1, art 7)."[60]

The Court, in rendering its decision, legislated from the bench. The laws of Vermont do not extend the same benefits and protections of its laws to same-sex couples as are extended to opposite-sex married couples. Thus, the Court had to stipulate that the extension of benefits and protections would have to be engineered:

> Whether this ultimately takes the for of inclusion within the marriage laws themselves or a parallel 'domestic partnership' system or some equivalent statutory alternative, rests with the Legislature. Whatever system is chosen, however, must conform with the constitutional imperative to afford all Vermonters the common benefit, protection, and security of the law.[61]

The Vermont Legislature is in this way mandated by the Vermont Supreme Court to pass legislation that it has not passed. The Court did not exercise the power of judicial review in striking down legislation that was deemed to be unconstitutional. It did not strike down existing marriage laws that extend benefits and protections to opposite-sex married couples. It held that same-sex couples were entitled to the benefits and protections of civil marriage licenses and that the only remaining issue was the determination of the "appropriate means and scope of relief compelled by this constitutional mandate."[62]

It should be noted, as the Court points out in the decision, that "in 1996, the Vermont General Assembly enacted, and the Governor signed, a law removing all prior legal barriers to the adoption of children by same-sex couples."[63] This legislation weakened the arguments of the State in asserting that it has an interest in "promoting the link between procreation and child rearing."[64] The State's desire to promote the link between procreation and child rearing is consistent with higher or natural law. It is congruent with the public philosophy. The legislation to remove all barriers to the adoption of children by same-sex couples is supported by the values of democracy, as opposed to the rule of law. The Court interpreted the Vermont Constitution democratically in holding that the Common Benefits Clause applies to all Vermonters (in this instance with respect to same-sex couples), and emphasized that "Vermont's first charter was the 'most democratic constitution produced by any of the American states.'"[65] In this way, the Court could show contradictions between Vermont's marriage laws and its 1996 legislation demonstrating that Vermont's progressive disregard of the public philosophy is not entirely judicial.

The general argument of the State, however, was rooted in the public philosophy. The State maintained that marriage statutes apply expressly to opposite-sex couples who wish to marry and "exclude anyone who wishes to marry someone of the same sex."[66] The State held that it had a "strong interest . . . in promoting a permanent commitment between couples who have children to ensure that their offspring are considered legitimate and receive ongoing parental support," all within the context a the larger goal of "furthering the link between procreation and child rearing."[67] The State's interests hinge upon the very definition and purpose of politics.

In *The Politics*, Aristotle addresses the question of the political by stating that every polity or state is a community of some kind, and every community is established with a view of justice. Aristotle's standard for understanding politics is *nature* as it is disclosed by *reason*. He proceeds to define the political by breaking it down into its constituent parts. Thus, he begins by analyzing the structure of the household, the smallest and most basic part of a polity as a whole. He sees that in nature "there must be a union of those who cannot exist without each other, for example, of male and female, that the race may continue," and "this is a union which is formed not of a deliberate purpose, but because, in common with other animals and plants, mankind have a natural desire to leave behind them an image of themselves."[68] The first union of a polity is between male and female so that they may support and complete themselves, perpetuate the species, and leave behind a posterity.

What is the relevance and status of "same-sex" marriage politically? Two individuals of the same sex are unable to reproduce, by nature. The old Biblical adage "be fruitful and multiply and fill the earth" is not possible between those of the "same-sex."[69] The *political* aspects of marriage are, as has been noted, grounded in the understanding that the bond between a man and a woman that completes each and then perpetuates the human race is the foundation of civil society. And, of course, within the *political* unit of marriage, is an *economic* element; the two go together. Marriages create natural bonds between spouses and children that are necessary for not merely the perpetuation of a polity, but for its justice. "Same-sex" linkages cannot do this. They are, as Allan Carlson points out, "sterile," and "cultural dead-ends."[70] Indeed, in some respects, "same-sex" coupling is politically irrelevant. It might very well be that one of the most important issues of our time is not "same-sex" marriage (and the economic benefits that the State can provide to homosexual pairings) at all, but divorce between married heterosexual couples and the profound negative impact it is having on them, their children, and society politically, economically, psychologically and emotionally. The Vermont Supreme Court failed to see this precisely because it did not interpret the case before it in light of the public philosophy.

V

The public policy issue that is most prominent in debates and controversy surrounding the judiciary is abortion. The American citizenry are very divided between "pro-life" and "pro-choice" ideological stances as a result of the Supreme Court's decision in *Roe v. Wade* (1973). When the judicial process does not render decisions arrived at by reason in accordance with the transcendental standard of the public philosophy, then the policy issues under scrutiny remain unresolved. This is what has occurred with the issue of abortion.

Roe is a fictitious name for a pregnant single woman who challenged a Texas abortion statute. At issue was whether there is a right under the Constitution to an abortion that the state of Texas prohibited. The Court found that there is such a right and that it is justified on grounds of privacy:

> The right of privacy, whether it be founded in the Fourteenth Amendment's concept of personal liberty and restrictions upon State action, as we feel it is, or

as the District Court determined, in the Ninth Amendment's reservation of rights to the people, *is broad enough to encompass a woman's decision whether or not to terminate her pregnancy* (emphasis added).[71]

The Court appropriately noted that pregnancy may in some instances cause "specific and direct harm" that are medically diagnosable.[72] Intriguingly, the Court did not address the instance of pregnancy as a result of force or rape. However, the most important aspects of the *Roe* decision devolve around its emphasis of individualism over against natural or higher law.

Justice Blackmun delivered the opinion of the Court in terms of individual choice (pro-choice). He held that the State would "impose detriment" on a woman by denying her the choice of whether or not to have an abortion. Note that Blackmun defines pregnancy individualistically and possessively in the sense that each individual pregnancy belongs to each pregnant woman exclusively. He then proceeds to outline numerous possible instances and circumstances in which a woman might wish to terminate a pregnancy:

> Maternity, or additional offspring, may force upon the woman a distressful life and future. Psychological harm may be imminent. Mental and physical health may be taxed by child care. There is also the distress, for all concerned, associated with the unwanted child, and there is the problem of bringing a child into a family already unable, psychologically and otherwise, to care for it. In other cases, as in this one, the additional difficulties and continuing stigma of unwed motherhood may be involved. All these factors the woman and her responsible physician necessarily will consider in consultation.[73]

Blackmun's opinion is rendered in terms of democratic individualism to the exclusion of the public philosophy. This is derivative of his placing emphasis on privacy instead of the facts of the case before him. He states that while "the Constitution does not explicitly mention any right of privacy" the "Court has recognized that a right of personal privacy, or a guarantee of certain areas or zones of privacy, does exist" under the Constitution. This raises an important question. Is abortion a private matter or a political one? If it is a private matter, then it must have no political significance or importance. If, however, abortion has some significance beyond the individual, then it must be a political matter.

The issue in *Roe* is not abortion. It is pregnancy. Blackmun misses this important point because his reference points for making his determinations exclude the context of higher or natural law and defy reason. His placement of emphasis on individual privacy and choice result in his inability to make a definitional distinction between *abortion* (the termination of a pregnancy) and *contraception* (the prevention of a pregnancy). Most importantly, Blackmun emphasizes individual freedom or "rights that can be deemed 'fundamental,' without recognizing concomitant responsibility.[74] This is why he offers up numerous instances in which a woman might wish to have an abortion.

Pregnancy is the result of successful conception. And conception takes place as a result of the sexual union of a man and a woman. There is no other way, by nature (as opposed to technological artifice), for pregnancy to occur. Blackmun's opinion starts with an already pregnant woman. There is no mention of the man who impregnated the woman, the father. Women do not impregnate themselves—they must be impregnated. For this reason, pregnancy is the *responsibility* of the mother *and* father who freely created it. Blackmun's focus on abortion derives from his discarding of the nature of political society. Individual members of political society can be no more free than they are responsible. And the responsibility for pregnancy rests on the two parties that create it.

So does an individual pregnant woman have a right under the Constitution to have an abortion (absent instance of rape or medically diagnosable harm)? No, the woman and man who create a pregnancy are responsible for it and for all that follows from it. That is why the public philosophy has traditionally placed emphasis on the institution of marriage. This is why Edward Westermarck points out that "among the lowest savages, as well as the most civilized races of men, we find the family consisting of parents and children."[75] Not only does abortion counter the life process that is naturally started by conception and pregnancy, it disregards marriage, the family, community and the political. The *Roe* decision is yet another example of the extent to which the Judiciary has engaged in an assault on the traditions and institutions that are essential for political life and the pursuit of happiness and justice.

VI

The judicial assault on the Constitution is largely a symbolic symptom of a crisis of public philosophy. That crisis consists in a disregard of the wisdom, of the customs and traditions of the ages. In particular, it is the result of a process of democratization that is guided by mass public opinion. Even judges, individuals who are at least presumably supposed to have the ability to exercise reason in correspondence to the transcendental standard of nature, increasingly express opinions of a mass, vulgar and deficient variety. As Walter Lippmann pointed out in 1955, "there has developed a functional derangement of the relationship between the mass of the people and the government" where "the people have acquired power, which they are incapable of exercising" because "a mass cannot govern."[76] Lippmann understood that:

> Where mass opinion dominates the government, there is a morbid derangement of the true functions of power. The derangement brings about the enfeeblement, verging on paralysis, of the capacity to govern. This breakdown in the constitutional order is the cause of the precipitate and catastrophic decline of Western society. It may, if it cannot be arrested and reversed, bring about the fall of the West.[77]

With respect to the judiciary, the crisis of public philosophy has brought many to see little to no difference between judges and the masses.[78] The opinions of judges have come to reflect and represent mass democratic opinion, albeit with more *sophistication*. When judges no longer engage judgement in terms of the utilization of reason as it reflects the fundamental law, then the exercise of judicial power is a most dangerous expression of opinion (as opposed to knowledge or wisdom) that in actuality contradicts the very purpose of limited, free government.

There is a problem of rule that even very good and sincere scholars often fail to fully comprehend. Ultimately, there is a need for rule, for the allocation of power, in order for a polity to function. Put differently, the power to make laws, execute laws, and interpret laws must be granted to certain individuals in some way, shape or form. In a constitutional order, the principle of the separation of powers divides these three exercises of power into three distinct branches so as to prevent a consolidation of power, which is the very definition of tyranny.[79] But the separation of power does not address the *substantive* exercise of power. The substantive exercise of power requires the use of reason (as opposed to sophistry) in varying degrees and ways. The substantive exercise of judicial power is the most intricate and difficult precisely because it entails the articulation of the meaning of the fundamental law proper: it requires political philosophy.

The difficulty lies in that judgement requires, demands, reason and wisdom. But reason and wisdom are rare qualities in human beings. This results in a paradox. There is a need for a judiciary, a branch of government consisting of individuals who have training in the laws and a requisite character to interpret them wisely and in a limited way.[80] For this reason, Hamilton prescribed judicial independence or life tenure for judges so as to enable them to render decisions without outside interference. And yet, when judges are tenured and they are either poorly trained, or lack sufficient character, or both, then they are institutionally protected to engage in constitutional sophistry of a kind that severely damages the core principles of the regime, of the American political order. This problem is, it would appear, without parallel (although expressions of it are certainly visible in the academy).

The judicial assault on the Constitution is a substantive problem derivative of the apparent inability to procure good judges, judges who are well-trained in the law, but who also *understand* the Constitution. There is nothing intrinsically flawed with having an independent judiciary, unless that is, if the possibility of judgement is negligible, humanly speaking. Indeed, on what grounds could an independent judiciary be justified if good judgement could not emanate from it? It would appear that the failure of the judicial process is a symptom of the altered and alienated condition of the contemporary American political order. The entire "constitutional cosmos" of higher or natural law that informs American political processes and institutions has been neglected and distorted.[81]

James Madison poignantly stated in the heart of the *Federalist* that "justice is the end of government," that "it is the end of civil society," and that "it ever has been, and ever will be, pursued, until it be obtained, or until liberty be lost in the pursuit."[82]82 Certainly the "courts of justice" must play a pivotal and central, if not limited role to this end. However, when the judiciary fails in its obligations and exercise of power, the essential, principled core of the Constitution is perverted and liberty is indeed threatened. Can there be a constitutional order without a branch that exercises independent judgement in the interest of justice? And yet, what is to be done when that branch uses its independence to advance the cause of sophistry to the extent that it destroys the very foundations of the political order? The judicial assault on the Constitution is reflective of a crisis of public philosophy.

ENDNOTES

1. Alexander M. Bickel, *The Least Dangerous Branch: The Supreme Court at the Bar of Politics* (New Haven: Yale University Press, 1986), p. 1.

2. Jonathan Turley, "Unpacking the Court: The Case for the Expansion of the United States Supreme Court in the Twenty-first Century," *Perspectives on Political Science*, Vol. 33, No. 3 (Summer 2004), p. 155

3. Alexander Hamilton, John Jay, James Madison, *The Federalist*, #78, Gideon Edition, George W. Carey & James McClellan, eds., (Indianapolis: Liberty Fund, 2001), p. 402.

4. Ibid.; See also the essays of Brutus in the *Anti-Federalist* regarding the judiciary in Herbert J. Storing, ed., *The Complete Anti-Federalist* (Chicago: University of Chicago Press, 1981), pp. 417–428.

5. Ibid.

6. Ibid.

7. See case examples in Robert H. Bork, *Coercing Virtue: The Worldwide Rule of Judges* (Washington, D.C.: American Enterprise Institute, 2003), pp. 52–84.

8. Mark R. Levin, *Men in Black: How the Supreme Court is Destroying America* (Washington, D.C.: Regnery Publishing, Inc., 2005), p. 10; See also, for a classic critique and analysis of the judiciary, Charles S. Hyneman, *The Supreme Court on Trial* (Westport, CT: Greenwood Press, 1963).

9. See, for example, Richard John Neuhaus, ed., *The End of Democracy?: The Judicial Usurpation of Politics* (Dallas: Spence Publishing Company, 1997).

10. Robert H. Bork, "Our Judicial Oligarchy," in Richard J. Neuhaus, ed., *The End of Democracy?: The Judicial Usurpation of Politics* (Dallas: Spence Publishing Company, 1997), p. 17.

11. George W. Carey, "The Philadelphia Constitution: Dead or Alive?," in Mitchell S. Muncy, ed., *The End of Democracy? II: A Crisis of Legitimacy* (Dallas: Spence Publishing Company, 1999), p. 237.

12. Edward B. McLean, "Introduction," in Edward B. McLean, *Derailing the Constitution: The Undermining of American Federalism* (Bryn Mawr: Intercollegiate Studies Institute, 1995), pp. 7–15.

13. George W. Carey, "Who or What Killed The Philadelphia Constitution?," *Tulsa Law Journal*, Volume 36, Number 3 (Spring 2001), p. 621.

14. See E. Robert Statham, Jr., Of Judges and Philosopher Kings: The Supreme Court, Judicial Review, and the American Political Order (forthcoming).

15. George W. Carey, "The Philadelphia Constitution: Dead or Alive?" in Mitchell S. Muncy, ed., *The End of Democracy? II* (Dallas: Spence Publishing Company, 1999), p. 237.

16. See Walter Lippmann, The Public Philosophy (New York: Mentor Books, 1955); See also E. Robert Statham, Jr., The Constitution of Public Philosophy: Toward a Synthesis of Freedom and Responsibility in Postmodern America (Lanham: University Press of America, 1998).

17. Edward S. Corwin, "The 'Higher Law' Background of American Constitutional Law," *Harvard Law Review*, Vol. XLII, No. 2 (December, 1928), pp. 149–85.

18. A careful reading of the *Federalist* demonstrates that the Constitution was intended, in no small fashion, to limit and qualify democratic rule.

19. Alexander Hamilton, John Jay, James Madison, *The Federalist*, Gideon Edition, George W. Carey & James McClellan, eds., (Indianapolis: Liberty Fund, 2001), pp. 43–4, 268–69.

20. E. Robert Statham, Jr., *The Constitution of Public Philosophy* (Lanham, MD: University Press of America, 1998), pp. 3–6.

21. *McCulloch v. Maryland*, 4 Wheat. 316 (1819), in Martin Shapiro & Rocco J. Tresolini, eds., *American Constitutional Law* (New York: Macmillan Publishing Co., Inc., 1983), p. 128.

22. Edward S. Corwin, "The 'Higher Law' Background of American Constitutional Law," *Harvard Law Review*, Vol. XLII, No. 2 (December, 1928), p. 152.

23. Ibid., p. 153.

24. James Stoner, "Constitutionalism and Judging in *The Federalist*," in Charles R. Kesler, ed., *Saving the Revolution: The Federalist Papers and the American Founding* (New York: The Free Press, 1987), p. 212.

25. Alexander Hamilton, John Jay, James Madison, *The Federalist*, Gideon Edition, George W. Carey & James McClellan, eds., (Indianapolis: Liberty Fund, 2001), pp. 404–05.

26. Ibid., p. 404.

27. Ibid., p. 405.

28. Ibid.

29. Ibid.

30. James Stoner, "Constitutionalism and Judging in *The Federalist*," in Charles R. Kesler, ed., *Saving the Revolution: The Federalist Papers and the American Founding* (New York: The Free Press, 1987), p. 218.

31. Intriguingly, a substantive discussion of judicial review is offered by Brutus in the *Anti-Federalist*. See Herbert J. Storing, ed., *The Complete Anti-Federalist* (Chicago: University of Chicago Press, 1981), pp. 417–428.

32. Roscoe Pound, *An Introduction to the Philosophy of Law* (New Haven: Yale University Press, 1982), pp. 4–10.

33. Ibid., p. 10.

34. Ibid., p. 12.

35. Walter Lippmann, *The Public Philosophy* (New York: Mentor Books, 1955), pp. 77–9.

36. Ibid., pp. 77–8.

37. J. Rufus Fears, "Natural Law: The Legacy of Greece and Rome," in Edward B. McLean, ed., *Common Truths: New Perspectives on Natural Law* (Wilmington: ISI Books, 2000), pp. 19–20.

38. Edward S. Corwin, "The 'Higher Law" Background of American Constitutional Law," *Harvard Law Review*, Vol. XLII, No. 2 (December, 1928), p. 159.

39. Alexander Hamilton, John Jay, James Madison, *The Federalist*, Gideon Edition, George W. Carey & James McClellan, eds., (Indianapolis: Liberty Fund, 2001), p. 407.

40. J. Rufus Fears, "Natural Law: The Legacy of Greece and Rome," in Edward B. McLean, ed., *Common Truths: New Perspectives in Natural* Law (Wilmington: ISI Books, 2000), p. 20.

41. Walter Lippmann, *The Public Philosophy* (New York: Mentor Books, 1955), p. 81.

42. Ibid., p. 80.

43. Ibid.

44. George W. Carey, "The Philadelphia Constitution: Dead or Alive?" in Mitchell S. Muncy, ed., *The End of Democracy? II* (Dallas: Spence Publishing Company, 1999), pp. 246; 250.

45. George W. Carey, *In Defense of the Constitution* (Indianapolis: Liberty Fund, 1995), p. 138.

46. Robert Brown, ed., *Classical Political Theories: From Plato to Marx* (New York: Macmillan Publishing Co., 1990), pp. 117–26.

47. See Alexis de Tocqueville, *Democracy in America, Vol. II* (New York: Vintage Books, 1990).

48. See Leo Strauss, "Progress or Return?," in Thomas L. Pangle, *The Rebirth of Classical Political Rationalism* (Chicago: University of Chicago Press, 1989), pp. 227–270.

49. Edward B. McLean, "Introduction," in Edward B. McLean, *Derailing the Constitution* (Bryn Mawr: Intercollegiate Studies Institute, 1995), p. 14.

50. George Anastaplo, "Law & Politics," *The Political Science Reviewer*, Vol. XXV (1996), p. 157.

51. Walter Lippmann, *The Public Philosophy* (New York: Mentor Books, 1955), p. 81.

52. *Regents of the University of California v. Bakke* 438 U.S. 265; 98 S.Ct. 2733; 57 L. Ed. 2nd 750 (1978), in Martin Shapiro & Rocco J. Tresolini, eds., *American Constitutional Law* (New York: Macmillan Publishing Co., 1983), pp. 604–05.

53. Ibid.

54. Ibid., p. 609.

55. Ibid., p. 611.

56. Terry Eastland, *Ending Affirmative Action: The Case for Colorblind Justice* (New York: Basic Books, 1997), p. 79.

57. Alexander Hamilton, John Jay, James Madison, *The Federalist*, Gideon Edition, George W. Carey & James McClellan, eds., (Indianapolis: Liberty Fund, 2001), p. 43.

58. Terry Eastland, *Ending Affirmative Action*, p. 84.

59. *Baker v. State* (98-032), December 20, 1999, Supreme Court of Vermont.

60. Ibid.

61. Ibid.

62. Ibid., p. 6.

63. Ibid.

64. Ibid., p. 2

65. Ibid., p. 3.

66. Ibid.

67. Ibid.

68. Robert Brown, ed., *Classical Political Theories* (New York: Macmillan Publishing Co., 1990), p. 99.

69. See for reference Genesis 1:27–28; 2:24.

70. Allan Carlson, "Two Becoming One Flesh: Marriage as a sexual and Economic Union," *The Intercollegiate Review: A Journal of Scholarship & Opinion*, Vol. 40, No. 1 (Fall/Winter 2004), p. 21.

71. *Roe v. Wade* 410 U.S. 113; 93 Sup. Ct. 705; 35 L. Ed. 2d 147 (1973), in Martin Shapiro & Rocco J. Tresolini, eds., *American Constitutional Law* (New York: Macmillan Publishing Co., 1983), p. 744.

72. Ibid.

73. Ibid.

74. Ibid., p. 743; See also E. Robert Statham, Jr., *The Constitution of Public Philosophy* (Lanham, MD: University Press of America, 1998), pp. 139–154.

75. Edward Westermarck, *The History of Human Marriage, 5th Edition* (London: Macmillan, 1925), pp. 26–37, 69–72.

76. Walter Lippmann, *The Public Philosophy* (New York: Mentor Books, 1955), p. 19.

77. Ibid.

78. See Mark R. Levin, *Men in Black: How the Supreme Court is Destroying America* (Washington, D.C.: Regnery Publishing, Inc., 2005); See also Robert H. Bork, *The Tempting of America: The Political Seduction of the Law* (New York: Simon & Schuster, 1990).

79. Alexander Hamilton, John Jay, James Madison, *The Federalist*, Gideon Edition, George W. Carey & James McClellan, eds., (Indianapolis: Liberty Fund, 2001), pp. 267–72.

80. Ibid., #78, p. 407.

81. George W. Carey, "The Philadelphia Constitution: Dead or Alive?," in Mitchell S. Muncy, ed., *The End of Democracy? II* (Dallas: Spence Publishing Company, 1999), p. 246.

82. Alexander Hamilton, John Jay, James Madison, *The Federalist*, Gideon Edition, George W. Carey & James McClellan, eds., (Indianapolis: Liberty Fund, 2001), p. 271.

Biography

Joseph F. Johnston, Jr., is a retired partner in the firm of Drinker Biddle & Reath. A graduate of Princeton University and Harvard law School, Mr. Johnston specialized in corporate law and has taught a course in the liability of corporate directors and officers at the University of Virginia Law School. He is the author of *The Limits of Government* (Regnery 1984) and has written numerous articles on legal and historical topics.

Allan W. Carlson is President of The Howard Center for Family, Religion & Society in Rockford, Illinois. His books include *Conjugal America: On the Public Purposes of Marriage*, and *The American Way: Family and Community in the Shaping of the American Identity*.

Ronald J. Rychlak is Mississippi Defense Lawyers Association Professor of Law and Associate Dean for Academic Affairs at the University of Mississippi, School of Law. He learned his BA (*cum laude*) from Wabash College and his JD from Vanderbilt University School of Law. His areas of research include Evidence, Criminal Law and Procedure, and International Relations. Professor Rychlak is a member of the committee appointed to revise the Mississippi Criminal Code, on the editorial board of *The Gaming Law Review*, and an advisor to the Holy See's delegation to the United Nations. He is author or co-author of six books and numerous articles and book chapters.

Jack Wade Nowlin is Associate Professor of law and Jessie D. Puckette, Jr., Lecturer in Law at the University of Mississippi School of Law. He received his A.B. from Angelo State University, his J.D. from the University of Texas and his M.A. and Ph.D. in Politics from Princeton University. Nowlin teaches in the areas of constitutional law and jurisprudence. His book chapters have appeared in *The Eminent Tribunal: Judicial Supremacy and the Constitution*, and *Liberalism at the Crossroads: An Introduction to Contemporary Liberal Political Theory and Its Critics*. His articles have appeared in The Illinois Law Review, The Notre Dame Law Review, The Kentucky Law Journal, and Vera Lex.

Dane Starbuck is a native of Winchester, Indiana, and a practicing attorney in Carmel, Indiana. He holds law degrees from Oxford University and Georgetown University Law Center. He has also earned degrees in English from Huntington College, Indiana University, and Melbourne, Australia. He is author of *The Goodriches: An American Family*, and a novel, *To Love and African Violet*.

E. Robert Statham, Jr. is a Fellow at Liberty Fund, Inc. He was formerly Professor of Political Science and Chair of Social Sciences at the University of Guam, USA. He holds a Master's Degree from the California State University and a Ph.D. from the University of Nevada. He is author of a number of books including *Political Science and Public Philosophy, Colonial Constitutionalism: The Tyranny of United States' Offshore Territorial Policy*, and his forthcoming book *Of Judges and Philosopher Kings: The Supreme Court, Judicial Review, and the American Political Order*.

George W. Carey is Professor Government at Georgetown University. He received his AB degree from Northwestern University, and his Ph.D. from Indiana University, Bloomington, Indiana. He is author and editor of several works including *The Federalist: Design for a Constitutional Republic, In Defense of the Constitution*. He is also author of numerous articles, and editor of *The Political Science Reviewer*, an annual review of leading works in political science and related disciplines.

Hans L. Eicholz is a Senior Fellow at Liberty fund, Inc., an educational foundation based in Indianapolis, Indiana. He received his doctoral degree in American history from UCLA and has taught courses in both American and World history for the California State University at Los Angeles and the UCLA. He is the author of *Harmonizing Sentiments: The Declaration of Independence and the Jeffersonian Idea of Self-Government*.

Edward B. McLean is Professor Emeritus in Political Science at Wabash College Crawfordsville, Indiana. His A.B., M.A., and Ph.D. degrees are from Indiana University, Bloomington, Indiana and his J.D. degree from Indiana University at Indianapolis, Indiana. He served nineteen years as Deputy Prosecutor in Montgomery County Indiana. He is the author of two books and editor of four.

Charles E. Rice is Professor Emeritus of Law at the University of Notre Dame Law School. He received the B.A. degree from the College of the Holy Cross, a J.D. from Boston College Law School and an LL.M. and J.S.D. from New York University. He served in the Marine Corps and is a Lt. Col. in the U.S. Marine Corps Reserve (Ret.). He practiced law in New York City and taught at New York University Law School and Fordham Law School before joining the faculty of law at Notre Dame in 1969. He is an editor of the American Journal of Jurisprudence. He has published among many other books and articles: *Where Did I Come From? Where Am I Going? How Do I Get There? The Winning Side: Questions on Living the Culture of Life Fifty Questions on the Natural Law: What it Is and Why We Need It The Supreme Court and Public Prayer: No Exception, A Pro-Life Imperative Beyond Abortion*